BECOMING YOUR BEST SELF

To

From

I wish for you a life of wealth, health, and happiness; a life in which you give to yourself the gift of patience, the virtue of reason, the value of knowledge, and the influence of faith in your own ability to dream about and to achieve worthy rewards.

— **Jim Rohn**

BECOMING YOUR BEST SELF

Receive Special Bonuses When Buying the *Becoming Your Best Self* Book

To access bonus gifts and to send us your testimonials and comments,
please send an email to

gifts@yourbestselfbook.com

Published by
Kyle Wilson International
KyleWilson.com

Distributed by
Kyle Wilson International
info@kylewilson.com

© Copyright by Kyle Wilson International 2025

All rights reserved worldwide. No part of this book may be reproduced or transmitted in any form or by any means, electronic or mechanical, including photocopying, recording, or by any information storage and retrieval system, without written permission of the publisher, except where permitted by law.

Becoming Your Best Self
ISBN: 978-1-7357428-7-8

Printed in the United States of America

EXCERPTS
FROM *BECOMING YOUR BEST SELF*

One of the most important things I teach over and over again is action. Action! It's not enough to have good ideas or the best information. There are a lot of average people who are self-made millionaires.
– Brian Tracy, Iconic Speaker, Author, Trainer

Choices are so significant because they are essential to being true to you! When you are true to yourself, you are being honest with what you feel: your desires, wants, and needs, and in alignment with who you are. Tuning into your higher self makes choosing easier.
– Kim Somers Egelsee, Speaker, 10x Author, Coach, Trainer

Be kind and allow the world to unfold.
– Zach

It's not easy to tell your story. But each time we do, we celebrate it—who we've been, who we are, and who we hope to become.
– Takara Sights, Book Editor, Writer

My mom would push my brother, my two sisters, and me out the door every morning towards the bus stop, and the last thing she would say to us was, "A day without learning is like a day without sunshine." That one phrase instilled in me a want—a need—to learn every day!
– Mac Curfman, Leadership Speaker, Trainer, Coach

More than 2,400 US Military died in the War in Afghanistan. As a Veteran and an American, this deeply affects me. I've memorized the rank, first name, and last name of each of the fallen. Those 2,400 names were made of over 7,000 words, and I memorized each of them using the mind palace.
– Ron White, Speaker, 2x USA Memory Champion

The scars, the uncertainty, and the beauty of this journey transform us. They chisel us not towards a destination but into the person we were meant to become.
– Robert Commodari, Speaker, Podcaster, Author, Top Real Estate Agent

Transformation is a process of destruction and then rebuilding. It isn't linear—it's messy and takes time and effort and often looks like a few steps back and then several more forward. I had to learn to be patient and kind with myself during my expansion and focus on small progression over perfection. I had to remember who I am.
– Clare McKee, Life Coach, Speaker, Entrepreneur

Most people treat freedom as the prize at the end of the race. I treat it as the starting line. Every decision I make, every strategy I run, and every use of AI in my business gets filtered through one question: Will this make me freer?
– Natalie Contreraz, AI Business, Strategist, Marketer

God changed me through my relationship with Lee. What started as obedience because of guilt or obligation ended with me having a softer heart and a new friend. What surprised me most after Lee's death was how much I missed the guy. I'm so thankful that God chose me to be the one to reach out to Lee. I'm thankful for God's grace when He sent me a blessing that I was resentful of at first. I'm thankful for God's patience, love, and the second chances that He gave to Lee… and to me.
– Dr. Eddie Poole, Real Estate Team Leader, Author, Pastor, Marketer

It appeared I'd reached the peak of my career and was staring down the barrel of 40 more years of same. For a while, same had been actually more than okay—it served me well. My corporate career allowed me the opportunity to explore things I enjoyed in my free time—most captivating of all—learning to fly!
– Jenn Shull, Airline Pilot, Real Estate Investor

What I thought was the end of a dream turned out to be the beginning of something bigger. That's the thing about attitude: it changes how you see the map. The road you resist today may become the path that defines your legacy.
– Newy Scruggs, 19x Emmy-Winning Sportscaster

I wasn't just fighting for myself. I was fighting for my future and the life I always wanted. I was fighting for real happiness. I was fighting for the people who had never given up on me, the lights in my life who led me through the darkness until I could see the light.
– Katie Kiliszewski, Mom, Athlete, Speaker, Addiction Recovery Mentor

EXCERPTS

The War Eagle Battalion lived by a simple but powerful motto: To Motivate Young People to be Better Citizens. To the student, it wasn't just a motto. It was a mission.
– Teon Singletary, TSLE WLI Podcast, Motivator of Excellence

You can let an experience like that destroy you—or you can grow from it. I chose the latter. That night changed me. It made me stronger. It gave me clarity.
– Amber Diskin, Real Estate Advisor, Mentor, Survivor

No one should stay in a job they hate.
– Anthony Chara, Educator, Entrepreneur, Investor, Mentor

Here's the truth: becoming your best self isn't about adding more. It's not about more followers, more accolades, more hustle. It's about subtraction. Removing the noise, the distractions, and the false expectations, until what's left is the truest version of you.
– Lauren Donahue, Global Retreat Leader, Wellness Entrepreneur

You are not defined by your past, your bank account, or your last mistake. You are defined by the person God created you to be.
– Tyler Vinson, Real Estate Tokenization Expert

Becoming your best self isn't always about pushing through your challenges. Sometimes, it's about learning to accept the things you can't control and stepping aside from paths that aren't yours to walk.
– Linda Grizely, Personal Finance Expert, Speaker, Educator

We learned to be so thankful for everything coming to us just in time. Not ever early, but just in time.
– Paul Herchman, Educator, Entrepreneur, Investor, Author

Every woman should have the financial ability to walk away from a job or relationship that is not in her best interest.
– Felecia Froe, MD, Wealth B-Hers Founder & Investor

Success is choosing to continually get up, show up, and accept every challenge as a necessary stepping stone to becoming who I was created to be.
– Josh Alexander, Real Estate Broker, Developer, Investor

Family makes a massive impact on everything I do. Having four brothers definitely set the tone for everything I did. With us, it was always a competition, whether it was who could lift more, who could eat more, or who had better grades. You couldn't lose to your little brother and you had to try to beat your older brother. That all-day, every day competition took us all to another level. As we got into high school, we became more friends than enemies, and working together to beat the other team helped us excel on the field.
– Chris Gronkowski, NFL Player, Shark Tank, Founder of Ice Shaker

I lived behind a filter, revealing only what I thought I was supposed to be. Now, I've come to see that my voice, rooted in integrity, and my story, shaped by experience, might be of service to someone else.
– Katrina Delridge, Business Consultant, Life Coach

Ending world hunger isn't just about food—it's about restoring dignity, building community, and sharing the love of Jesus Christ. Hope is the most powerful ingredient we can offer.
– David Lapp, CEO, Blessings of Hope, Feeding Communities

Dare to say yes to the opportunity that scares you. Do it in faith, trusting that God wants to bring something good in you and through you on the other side of that fear.
– Tresa Todd, Founder of WREIN, Inspirational Speaker

True freedom isn't found at the top of the ladder but in living a life aligned with your values. When faith, family, and purpose guide your steps, you discover success that outlasts titles and promotions.
– George Mina, Tech Leader, Real Estate Investor, Mentor

God put me on this Earth to help others heal in their minds, bodies, and souls. Since 2003, that is what I have been doing in my practice. For me, it is all about putting my mind to it and getting it done. We CAN do it!
– Mahealani Trepinski, Natural Healer, Speaker

Consistency is so important. It's so easy to fall off, and when you do, you have to get back into it, and that's a lot harder. If you maintain whatever you're doing and are regularly inspired by it, you achieve more.
– Phil Collen, Lead Guitarist, Def Leppard

EXCERPTS

Becoming your best self requires more than motivation and morning routines. It requires choosing growth, even when it hurts. It means learning to listen to God in the silence. And it demands that you rise again and again until standing becomes second nature.
– Cheri Perry, Leadership Expert, Author, Speaker

Failure was my greatest teacher. After losing my first business, I realized that life's real measure is not financial return but the value we bring to others. Today, in real estate, solar, and energy storage, my mission is to create lasting impact—serving communities, building the future, and staying true to a purpose larger than myself.
– Charlie Yue, Real Estate Investor, Entrepreneur

Yet is a word that brings hope, promise, and possibility. Yet opens the door for a different outcome. It is a bold, powerful act of defiance against your current situation. It's a statement of intent. Use this powerful word as you navigate your personal growth. It will change your internal dialogue, which will inspire new action, build better habits, and change your life.
– Jennifer Marchetti, Chief Marketing Officer, Speaker, Coach

If you can shift your paradigm to recognize that the incentives in the tax code can be one of the most powerful tools in growing your financial freedom, then your whole world can change for the better. It's not about loopholes—it's about recognizing incentives written into the tax code to reward innovation, growth, and investment.
– Mike Pine, Relentless Tax Strategist

Through it all, music remains my anchor. It carried me into healing and being a healer and to lifelong friendships with so many talented, gifted, respected, and sharing artists. Music continues to be the thread that ties my journey together—a journey built on passion, creativity, motherhood, and resilience with all praises to God for the wonderful gifts he has anointed me to share.
– Debbi Blackwell-Cook, Singer, Actress, Writer, Coach

I've learned that we all have a message of value to share. And I'm blessed I get to share others' valuable messages with the world!
– Kyle Wilson, Founder of Jim Rohn Int, Marketer, Strategist

Dedication

To all the mentors and influences that have shaped the lives of each of our authors.

To our families and loved ones who fan our flames.

To the lifelong learners and dreamers who dare to step into their next chapter with courage and wisdom.

Acknowledgments

A big thank you—

To Takara Sights, our writing coach, editor, and project manager extraordinaire, for your endless hours of work and passion in this book! Despite the complexities involved with a project like this, you keep the process a pleasure and always provide first-class results. A thousand praises! You are a rockstar!

To Joe Potter and Anne-Sophie Gomez who have designed this book. Technology plus thoughtful design allow readers to receive the powerful wisdom of these authors. We are grateful!

To Tammy Hane as well as John Obenchain, Adrian Shepherd, Dan Armstrong, Ethel Rucker, Jennifer Stewart, Mark Hartley, Dale Young, Katrina Delridge, Rob Commodari, and Alan Neely for being our second eyes and proofreading the manuscript. We so appreciate it!

And to ALL the amazing mentors and world-class thought leaders for their contributions, wisdom, and insights to make this such a powerful book we're so proud of—thank you!

FOREWORD

by Kevin Eastman

It's not often that someone enters your life and you realize how lucky you are that they did. Kyle Wilson is one of those people for me. He stands up there with some of the best of the best in sports, a world I know well after five decades at the highest levels of college athletics and the NBA.

I was very fortunate to be a coach with the 2008 NBA World Champion Boston Celtics, and we were always looking for ways to become even better. We were always studying what made others successful to see what we could add to our own "success arsenal." That is where this book comes in.

What you will see in the pages that follow is why I say Kyle was a fortunate "addition" to my trusted circle. In these pages, Kyle has gathered some of the best of the best to share with you their "secrets" to success—the behind-the-scenes stories and wisdom that got these people to levels of success they may not have even thought imaginable.

What you will find is that it is not a "secret sauce" but rather a commitment to certain things that these individuals do on a consistent basis. And the beauty lies twofold.

1. No one holds a monopoly on these strategies and mindsets. All of us can insert them into our lives.
2. Each of these successful people will share all they can to help every reader become their best as well. They do not hold back. They give you it all.

It's not often you can get such a wealth of knowledge in one reading, but Kyle has done that for us. I encourage you to read these pages with a learner's mindset and then switch to an application mindset. The formula is here. The decision is now ours, and what we do with it will make all the difference.

I hope you enjoy this read as much as I did. I guarantee you one thing: if you incorporate the lessons shared in *Becoming Your Best Self*, it will potentially take you to places you may not have thought imaginable as well.

Thank you, Kyle, for providing not only insights into success, but also practical tools we can apply immediately, regardless of where we are in our life's journey.

Kevin Eastman is a professional speaker, author, and NBA World Champion coach. His bestselling book *Why the Best Are the Best: 25 Powerful Words That Impact, Inspire, and Define Champions* can be found at www.kevineastman.net. To inquire about speaking engagements, email wendy@kevineastman.net. Follow Kevin on X @kevineastman.

TABLE OF CONTENTS

EXCERPTS
from *Becoming Your Best Self* iii

FOREWORD
by Kevin Eastman ix

KYLE WILSON
Sharing the Messages of Jim Rohn and Other Legends with the World 1

DEBBI BLACKWELL-COOK
A Voice That Inspires. 7

MIKE PINE
Change Your Tax, Change Your Life 13

JENNIFER MARCHETTI
A Present from the Past 21

CHARLIE YUE
From Poverty to Abundance: How an Immigrant Embraced Entrepreneurism and Investing. 28

CHERI PERRY
Becoming Your Best Self: The Refining Fire of Change 36

PHIL COLLEN
Def Leppard, Persistence, and the World's Fittest Rockstar 44

MAHEALANI TREPINSKI
Through Pain Comes Triumph 50

GEORGE MINA
Climbing Down the Ladder to Rise in Purpose. 57

TRESA TODD
Faith Over Fear: How One Yes Became a Movement of Women Thriving in Real Estate and Faith 65

DAVID LAPP
From Buggy to Blessings: A Journey of Faith, Family, and Feeding Nations. 73

KATRINA DELRIDGE
The Leader Within: Showing Up Fully in Business and Life............. 81

CHRIS GRONKOWSKI
From the NFL to *Shark Tank* as the Founder of Ice Shaker 89

JOSH ALEXANDER
Built to Steward..96

FELECIA FROE, MD
Wealth *B-Hers*: Helping Women Have Walk-Away Money 103

PAUL HERCHMAN
Persistence, Lessons, and Faith 111

LINDA GRIZELY
When the Shell Breaks: A Story of Transformation 117

TYLER VINSON
Becoming Your Best Self: The Person You Were Always Meant to Be..... 123

LAUREN DONAHUE
The Cave That Changed Everything 129

ANTHONY CHARA
From Burned Out to Purpose: The Journey to Teaching Real Estate Investing and Building Wealth 138

AMBER DISKIN
The Story Behind the Smile: Resilience, Real Estate, and a
Life Built in Vegas 146

TEON SINGLETARY
SEEDS of EXCELLENCE 154

KATIE KILISZEWSKI
Courage to Endure 160

NEWY SCRUGGS
Home Runs, Heartbreaks, and Pivots: Resilience Beyond the Broadcast ..168

JENN SHULL
The Courage to Fly...174

TABLE OF CONTENTS

DR. EDDIE POOLE
The Reunion I Never Expected... The Lesson I'll Never Forget 178

NATALIE CONTRERAZ
Make AI Your Co-CEO. 185

CLARE MCKEE
Creating Conditions to Thrive: Lessons on Self Love and Transforming
Pain into Power and Purpose 193

ROBERT COMMODARI
CHISELED: A Journey of Perseverance, Resilience, and
Becoming My Best Self 200

RON WHITE
Two-Time US Memory Champion and Creator of The Afghanistan
Memory Wall 208

M. A. MAC CURFMAN
It's a Process 214

TAKARA SIGHTS
Perfect 222

ZACH
Message 227

KIM SOMERS EGELSEE
Allowing My Truest Self to Come Forward 232

BRIAN TRACY
You Can Change Your Life 238

DISCLAIMER

The information in this book is not meant to replace the advice of a certified professional. Please consult a licensed advisor in matters relating to your personal and professional well-being including your mental, emotional and physical health, finances, business, legal matters, family planning, education, and spiritual practices. The views and opinions expressed throughout this book are those of the authors and do not necessarily reflect the views or opinions of all the authors or position of any other agency, organization, employer, publisher, or company.

Since we are critically-thinking human beings, the views of each of the authors are always subject to change or revision at any time. Please do not hold them or the publisher to them in perpetuity. Any references to past performance may not be indicative of future results. No warranties or guarantees are expressed or implied by the publisher's choice to include any of the content in this volume.

If you choose to attempt any of the methods mentioned in this book, the authors and publisher advise you to take full responsibility for your safety and know your limits. The authors and publisher are not liable for any damages or negative consequences from any treatment, action, application, or preparation to any person reading or following the information in this book.

This book is a collaboration between a number of authors and reflects their experiences, beliefs, opinions, and advice. The authors and publisher make no representations as to accuracy, completeness, correctness, suitability, or validity of any information in the book, and neither the publisher nor the individual authors shall be liable for any physical, psychological, emotional, financial, or commercial damages, including, but not limited to, special, incidental, consequential, or other damages to the readers of this book.

ADDITIONAL RESOURCES

 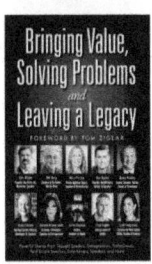  

Order in Quantity and SAVE

Mix and Match

Order online KyleWilson.com/books

"Do the best you can until you know better. Then when you know better, do better."

– MAYA ANGELOU

KYLE WILSON

Sharing the Messages of Jim Rohn and Other Legends with the World

Kyle Wilson is a marketer, strategist, publisher, speaker, and host of the Success Habits podcast and the Kyle Wilson Inner Circle Mastermind. In addition to his 18-year business partner, friend, and mentor, Jim Rohn, Kyle has worked closely with Brian Tracy, Les Brown, Darren Hardy, Denis Waitley, Robin Sharma, Jeffrey Gitomer, and more.

Early Years

I grew up in a small town, Vernon, Texas. I was fortunate to be raised in a loving and supportive family. As a kid, I was always industrious and would go around the neighborhood selling different things. I got my first job at age 14, and I've been working ever since.

Unfortunately, as a teenager, I got into drugs for a few years. But, at age 19, I had a significant emotional experience that radically changed my life.

That led me to start my first business at age 19. It was a detail shop washing and cleaning cars. Then, I added oil changes and eventually took over running a service station. That led to opening Wilson's Texaco, a full-service station located on a high-traffic freeway. I had 10 employees and was open 24/7.

Things were going well. But, by age 26, I really wanted something different. I felt compelled, a God Whisper, to sell my house and business and move away from the town I was born and raised in. I didn't have much of a plan, I just strongly felt the desire to move to a new and bigger place.

Plant a Tree

While making the decision to move, a friend shared with me a quote by Martin Luther. In response to the question, "If you were going to die today, what would you do?" Martin Luther said, "Even if I knew that tomorrow the world would end, I would still plant a tree today."

That hit me hard. So, I bought a peach tree, and I planted it in the front yard of the house I was selling. At the time, I had almost a fatalistic outlook. I felt our world was in some turbulent times. And, at times, I thought, *What's the use?*

Planting that tree symbolically helped lead me to a more long-term mindset that I still have today.

Getting into the Seminar Business

I moved to Dallas, and after several serendipitous events over the course of two years, I got a job working for a seminar company. The job entailed making 50-100 prospecting phone calls a day to book myself to speak at a company's weekly or monthly sales meeting. The presentation was designed to bring value to both salespeople and managers, and at the end of the talk, I invited those in the audience to buy a ticket to an upcoming seminar.

The thought of getting up and speaking in front of a group was terrifying to me, but I really felt I was supposed to give it a shot. I did everything I was taught to do. I made the phone calls. I followed up. I learned the presentation. I learned the close. And I went to work and gave it 100%!

After just one year, I became the company's top guy, but I was hardly making any money. The model was broken. So, I decided to go out on my own. I convinced Heidi, my wife at the time, to leave her job, and we began to travel the country putting on events. After a few years, we got really good at it, eventually getting 2,000-plus people in each city. We would hire Jim Rohn, Brian Tracy, and Og Mandino to speak at our events. We also enjoyed an amazing lifestyle traveling and exploring new places.

Launching and Growing Jim Rohn International

In 1993, Jim Rohn and his business partner split up. I told Jim I really believed he was the best speaker in the world and that I was a pretty good promoter, and I asked him for exclusive rights to promote and market him and his products. In two of Jim's previous partnerships, he had lost over a million dollars combined, so when considering another partner, he was reluctant. So I proposed the idea of it being my company. I would cover all the expenses and overhead, pay Jim's speaking fee off the top like a speakers bureau, plus give him a royalty on all the products I would create and sell. That way it was all profit for Jim with zero overhead and no risk of losing money.

Jim said yes. We did a handshake agreement which lasted for over 10 years until we finally put our agreement in writing in 2003. In the beginning, Jim did not have a customer list and had only a handful of products to offer. I knew I needed to go to work on both.

I now had exclusive rights to book Jim to speak and create new products. Within the first 12 months, I took Jim from 20 speaking dates a year to over 110 dates a year while tripling his fee.

Also, I wanted to create new products to take to the marketplace. The first was a viral quote booklet that went on to sell over six million copies.

My focus was to build the product line and a customer list using what I call The Wheel. Within two years of launching and building Jim Rohn International, business was booming, and I had grown a team of 20 people. I found that Jim was the gateway to personal development for so many people.

With my focus on list and customer building, I decided to also launch Your Success Store where I could market other speakers' products and book them to speak at the companies where I was booking Jim. The speakers included Brian Tracy, Les Brown, Mark Victor Hansen, Bob Burg, Jeffrey Gitomer, and many more.

I found each speaker and product would attract new people onto the overall marketing wheel. Then in 1999, I dove headfirst into the internet and was one of the first people to build a 1,000,000-plus email list. By 2002, I had multiple publications and over 300 different products (including digital) by Jim Rohn and other authors and speakers I was working with.

Working with my mentor, friend, and business partner, Jim Rohn, for 18 years (he passed away in 2009) as well as Brian Tracy, Denis Waitley, Mark Victor Hansen, Les Brown, Darren Hardy, Tom Ziglar, Robin Sharma, Bob Burg, and many more, going on 30 years now has been one of my life's greatest honors.

They have been the catalyst for much of the success I've had.

Selling It All in 2007

In 2006, one of the few companies that I felt could steward Jim's message and also take the other speakers and authors I managed to the next level wanted to buy me. They were also in the process of buying *SUCCESS* magazine.

I had over 20 employees, plus I was representing several speakers. Things were going well, but I was tired and burnt out, and my kids were growing up fast. I felt maybe the timing was right to hand it all off. I was able to negotiate a great deal for my team to stay on plus pay them profit sharing on the sale of the company. It felt like it was a win/win for my team, the speakers, and the company wanting to buy me. So, in late 2007, I sold the companies. I stayed on to help them transition up until the unexpected passing of Jim Rohn in December 2009.

Coming Back Out of Retirement

In 2013, I started getting the itch. I tested the waters a bit and knew it was time to get back into the industry that had changed my life. Being the promoter and marketer for others was my comfort zone. I didn't want to be the talent. But I found it necessary to come out from behind the curtain and start to share my knowledge and experience with others.

Today, I focus on three core things.

The first is my Kyle Wilson Inner Circle Mastermind, which is something I love. I started the group for me. Jim said who you spend time with matters. We have the best members who travel to Dallas, SoCal, and Philly from all over the country. It's an incredible community of heart-centered entrepreneurs, small business owners, investors, and speakers.

Second is publishing books like this one, *Becoming Your Best Self*, where Takara Sights and I get to connect amazing thought leaders with the marketplace.

And third is coaching, consulting, speaking, and my podcast.

I still get to be the promoter and shine the light on others and their talent through my Inner Circle, books, and podcast. But I'm now also the face (reluctantly at first) of the platforms.

I've learned that we all have a message of value to share. And I'm blessed I get to share others' valuable messages with the world!

Q&A WITH KYLE

What are a few of your favorite quotes?

In addition to curating and publishing *The Treasury of Quotes* by Jim Rohn as well as quote booklets for Brian Tracy, Zig Ziglar, Mark Victor

Hansen, and Denis Waitley, I also had a daily email to 250,000 people: "Quotes From the Masters." So, I do love quotes!

Here are a few from Jim Rohn that changed my life.

"The major key to your better future is you." This was so powerful when I realized that the biggest influences in our lives are the things I can control. My health, my finances, my attitude, my work ethic, and who I spend time with, I get to control! Not the government, the economy, my job or boss, negative friends, or family!

"Be a student not a follower. Take advice, but not orders. Make sure everything you do is the product of your own conclusion." This gave me permission to take it all in, find what was valuable and applied to me, and leave the rest. There is no cookie-cutter. Get the principle that applies to you and personalize it to your unique gifts, skillset, and calling.

"If you want to be successful, learn to bring value to the marketplace. And if you want to be wealthy, learn to be valuable to valuable people." I caught that pass. And I realized for me to become wealthy, I had to be valuable. This dramatically changed my life. I became good at putting on events that connected talent with the marketplace. That made me valuable to both sides. I now build platforms to do this including podcasts, events, books, and more, connecting talent with an audience where both sides win. In everything I do, I want to always answer first, "How will this provide value?"

And one more that I'm not sure where I heard but I've always loved it. "Speed bumps keep out the tourists." It's just a reminder that everything in life that is valuable will have some obstacles along the way to make sure only those that are serious and committed keep going.

What is your favorite movie?

By far, the movie that impacted me the most going back to when I saw it on my birthday in 1993 and many times since is *Groundhog Day*. When Phil tried to get everything he wanted by beating the system or shortcuts, he only ended up frustrated, depressed, and hopeless. But when he started serving others and working on himself, he then became the person who attracted all that he wanted, including getting the girl at the end.

How do you recharge?

Alone time. Meditation and prayer. Nature. Playing sports and music.

Who are your mentors and greatest influences?

Over the past 30 years, I've had the incredible good fortune of knowing and working intimately with Jim Rohn as well as Brian Tracy, Darren Hardy, Les Brown, Mark Victor Hanson, Denis Waitley, Phil Collen, Paul J. Meyer, Bob Burg, Tom Ziglar, and so many more amazing thought leaders and humans. I'm beyond blessed.

Have you had any past challenges that turned out to be blessings?

All of them!

What hobbies do you enjoy?

Tennis, pickleball, basketball, guitar, hiking in nature, concerts and sporting events, and travel.

What books do you often recommend?

I've given away thousands of books by Jim Rohn and so many authors in this book. Giving away books has the power to change someone's life.

What would you tell your 18-year-old self?

That self-care is different from self-indulgence. Have health and spiritual routines while growing your business and being there for those in your life.

To learn more about Kyle Wilson's Inner Circle Mastermind, the #1 Bestseller Book Program, and The Strategic Marketing Wheel and to access over 100 blog posts and podcast episodes, go to KyleWilson.com. To receive over a dozen interviews by Kyle with Darren Hardy, Les Brown, Brian Tracy, Phil Collen, and more, email info@kylewilson.com with **Interviews** in the subject. Follow Kyle on Instagram @kylewilsonjimrohn.

 Kyle Wilson Inner Circle

DEBBI BLACKWELL-COOK

A Voice That Inspires

Debbi Blackwell-Cook is an international singer, award-winning Broadway actress, and spiritual light whose voice blends soul, gospel, rock, and house. Dubbed the Queen of House Music in Germany, she has sung background for Def Leppard, Michael Bublé, and many other legendary artists. She is also the creative partner of Def Leppard's Phil Collen in their acclaimed group Delta Deep. A devoted mother of five, and mentor to many, Debbi continues to inspire and uplift through cooking, music, acting, speaking, and coaching.

Born to Sing Out

I was born and raised in Paterson, New Jersey. One of my earliest memories is walking about three miles to church with my grandmother, partly because she did not drive.

I also remember my grandmother singing. She reminded me of Bessie Smith. When I started singing, my voice was very, very soft. My godmother Annie Mildred Stancil would say, "Sing out, Debra!" She'd be on that organ and that look she gave me.... I knew she meant it, and so I did.

My mother said I'd been singing since before I could walk. She said I was standing in the crib mimicking playing the piano, humming, and dancing around. I'd say it was in my DNA.

My sixth grade teacher had me narrate "The Night Before Christmas" for a school play. He told my mom I should either be a journalist or an actress. I was 11 then. At 13, I wrote two songs for the church choir I sang with. We won a contest and were able to record those two songs.

Later on in life, I would win another contest singing Stephanie Mills' "Feel the Fire." I was grown with children when I won that contest, but I wasn't supposed to be singing secular music because I was in the Church, and that was frowned upon. However, the prize was to do a demo singing with a live band, which I had never done before. That live band of gentlemen would introduce me to become a prominent background singer in New York. I met many people like Luther Colonel Abrams and had the esteemed pleasure of working with very talented artists like Cissy Houston, Tesla, Michael Bublé, and Gregory Hines, to name a few.

Growing up, in the Church, they would say we couldn't wear pants, we couldn't wear makeup, we couldn't wear lipstick, we couldn't go to the movies, and we couldn't sing the devil's music. Everything was the devil's music if it wasn't Gospel. But, even as a grown woman with children, I would sing Gladys Knight songs and, my favorite, Aretha Franklin's "Ain't No Way" in the mirror holding my hairbrush. However, I'd also sing my Gospel to Miss Shirley Caesar's "God Don't Want No Coward Soldiers." It was so fulfilling.

One day, as a young girl, while watching *The Ed Sullivan Show*, I happened upon Diana Ross. She was absolutely beautiful—a goddess. She made me realize a little girl like me could be beautiful. As an adult, I went to Barbizon and Grace del Marco modeling schools and learned grace and poise. I also went to school and earned my licenses for cosmetology, barbering, and aesthetics. I am proud to have done hair and makeup for movies. Some of my makeup even made the cover of magazines.

Diana Ross was my sweet inspiration. I'd hoped to meet her one day, and I did, though she didn't know it. I would sit across the street from The Sherry-Netherland because I'd read in a magazine that she stayed there, just hoping to catch a glimpse of her. I found out later that a friend I had met in Germany years afterward used to do the same thing. We laughed because Diana was probably getting into her limousine in the back of the hotel, but back then, we had high hopes.

I married at 16 and had my first child at 17. I read Dr. Spock cover to cover at least five times, determined to raise my children with love and wisdom. I was blessed to have five beautiful children. I grew up alongside them, encouraging each of their passions—music, sports, dance, and education. My oldest son became a minister of music. My second son was an NFL football player and a NYC police officer and is currently assistant commissioner of probation in New York City. My third son graduated from NYU and was a dancer for the second largest ballet company in Canada. He had the opportunity to perform in *Riverdance* on Broadway, among so many other things. My only daughter was the first Black Huggies baby. I recently found out that the character she played, whose name was Jennifer, was the inspiration for Jennifer Hudson's mom to name her Jennifer. My daughter is also a dedicated one-on-one teacher of children with special needs. My baby son, who moved to Heaven after his life was taken by gun violence, was a sound designer and had the opportunity to do sound for Michelle Obama when she was first lady, as well as so many other celebrities. He also sang at a World Series Yankees game and was a graduate of The Boys Choir of Harlem.

I was blessed to sing with Bill Clinton's inauguration choir with Cissy Houston. And in the '80s, I was the lead singer of a group called The Jammers. We had a number one hit in England. I toured Germany with The Original USA Gospel Singers & Band. Then, I met Germany's famous DJ Cambis, and we collaborated to write and perform house music. In Munich, Germany, I am dubbed Mah Dee Vah, Queen of House Music. On one of my Gospel tours in Europe, on the same bill with Dionne Warwick and Dee Dee Bridgewater, I had the prestigious opportunity to sing at the Vatican for Pope John Paul II. Back in New York, I landed a role in a play with Clarice Taylor, Bill Cosby's TV mom. She was so kind to me and became my surrogate mother. Well, my sixth grade teacher called it—I wound up becoming an award-winning actress!

I've been blessed in my musical career to work with wonderful people, including Phil Collen of Def Leppard, who also happens to be my godson-in-law. I was blessed to sing at his and my goddaughter's wedding and to sing Motown songs around the table. Later, we ended up singing for a cancer facility where people asked, "Where can we get this music?" This would ultimately birth Delta Deep. What a blessing Delta Deep has been.

The Hardest Day

Tragedy struck on Easter Sunday. My youngest son, D-Roderick—known as D-Rock—was walking to church to prepare sound for sunrise services. He was robbed, shot, and killed at just 28 years old. I was at the Hard Rock Hotel in Las Vegas with Def Leppard, and he was in Baltimore. When I got the call, the shock dropped me to the floor, and Phil caught my fall as I collapsed.

Grief consumed me—it still does, even now.

Sitting at a Starbucks with Phil and his best friend, Louis Armstrong's "What a Wonderful World" and Earth, Wind & Fire's "Sing a Song" were the first songs I heard. I sincerely felt they were messages from my son sent straight from Heaven. In a dream, my son came to me and said, "Mommy, sing my life."

Music saved me. Performing music, I saw it saving others. Watching faces light up in the audience gave me strength to keep going. And my son kept sending me signs—pennies on the ground and flickering lights (he had also been a lighting designer). I had dreams so vivid they felt like visits. No matter where I was in the world, even overseas, if my son was traveling from New York to Baltimore, he would Skype me, text me, or call me and let me know he made it home safely. In one of his Heavenly visits, he smiled and said, "Ma, I made it. I'm in the light." Even in death, he let me know he was home, *really home.*

Loss has not been a stranger in my life—I've lost my father to dementia and so many dear friends in the AIDS era. I've lost my dearest sister-friend Phyllis Hyman to suicide, my best friend Wayne Brathwaite, and my dear friend Cambis in Germany, who was my writing partner for house music for 25 years. Each passing deepened my empathy and my call to serve. People began to call me a "singing therapist" because I brought my voice into hospitals, mental health facilities, prisons, churches, and even intimate one-on-one spaces.

As a certified life coach, my training gave me tools, but it was love—the heart of a mother—that gave me purpose. Along the way, I am told because of my nurturing nature and mothering energy, so many who I call my children adorned me with beautiful titles. Jenelle called me Mama D. My beautiful choreographer, Rhapsody James—who reminded me that I helped her when her parents moved to Heaven—calls me Mama Deb. Even Mama Hattie, my goddaughter Helen's grandmother, who was almost 100 years old, would call me Mah. My godson, Jesse Hamilton Jr., dubbed me MahDeb, and that stuck and is now trademarked.

Before every performance, I pause and call on my ancestors. I take one step back, step out of myself, then step into God, and whisper, "Have Your way." My nerves quiet when I remember: if I can touch even one person, help them forget their troubles for a moment, then my living will not be in vain.

Through it all, music remains my anchor. It carried me into healing and being a healer and to lifelong friendships with so many talented, gifted, respected, and sharing artists. Music continues to be the thread that ties my journey together—a journey built on passion, creativity, motherhood, and resilience with all praises to God for the wonderful gifts he has anointed me to share.

Q&A WITH DEBBI

What is a motto or mantra you live by?
Change your mind, change your world.

How do you celebrate your wins—big or small?
A little dance, a lobster dinner, and serving fried fish. I love sharing time with others, seeing people happy and smiling. And buying myself a little perfume.

What are a few of your favorite quotes?
- Each one teach one.
- Live and let live.
- If you don't deal with reality, reality will deal with you.

Who are your mentors and greatest influences?
There have been so many supports and mentors in my life. I would really be fooling myself if I even began to think I could name them all, so here's special mention: my mom Dorothy Jefferson Brown, my grandma Jennie, my godmother Annie Mildred Stancil, Woodie King Jr., André De Shields, Theresa Merritt, Barbara Ann Teer, Micki Grant, Helen Brodie Baldwin, Dwight R.B. Cook, Kyle Wilson, Phil Collen, Jadina Jaguar, Monica McKinney Lupton, Simone Black, Professor Edward Boatner, Odell Padgett, Sarah Bolden, Anna Stewart, D. Deas, Net Perry, McKinley Winston, Ria Alexander, Shirley Black-Brown, Randy Flood, Chaye McCrary, ALL of my children, as well as life's lessons good and bad that I've learned and grown from. There are so many—and if I've left out anybody's name, forgive me. You know who you are.

What is some of the best advice you've received?
As said in *The Wizard of Oz*, "It was with you all the time."

What do you consider your superpower?
Transmuting pain into power through music—that's what allowed me to stand after the murder of my baby son.

What is one thing you hope people remember about you?
That I loved out loud—and helped them love themselves.

What would you tell your 18-year-old self?
Never, ever give up or second guess yourself. Trust the voice inside.

What has been your greatest lesson?
You're never too old to begin again.

What makes you feel inspired or like your best self?
When I'm onstage connecting souls through song. And when I'm gathering with people with food and games. And even in the toughest times, never forgetting that I'm God's girl.

How do you define success?
Success, to me, is living in alignment with your purpose and your truth. It's when your soul feels at peace with what you're doing, how you're showing up, and who you're becoming. It's not just about accolades or applause—it's about impact, integrity, and joy.

If I can look in the mirror and say, "I stayed true, I gave love, and I left light in the room," then I've succeeded. Success is also waking up with gratitude and going to bed with peace. And it's knowing in my soul, if I've helped somebody, my living is not in vain.

Debbi Blackwell-Cook is proof that the voice can heal, humor can lift, and love can carry us through anything. She weaves music and story into medicine for the soul, leaving audiences braver, lighter, and ready to walk in their own power. From Popes to paupers, from grand stages to quiet corners, Debbi's gift has traveled the world reminding us that we all share the same heartbeat. She is not here to impress—she's here to bless.
Website: Debbiblackwellcook.com
TikTok: mahdebsboootea
Instagram: debbiblackwellcook
Youtube: Mahdeb Boootea

MIKE PINE

Change Your Tax, Change Your Life

Mike Pine, CPA and founder of Revo Taxpayer Advocacy, is on a mission to help clients keep more of what they've earned through smart, strategic tax planning. A former Big Four tax specialist turned taxpayer champion, Mike believes changing the way you think about tax can change your life.

A Practical Path

I chose accounting in college for two main reasons. First, my grandfather, who was raised during the Great Depression, said there were only three professions that had no problem putting food on the table in hard times: doctors, lawyers, and accountants. Well, my father was a doctor, my stepmom was a doctor of pharmacy, and my mother was a registered nurse, and I saw how hard they worked—too hard. As for lawyers, it appeared to me that they had all sold their souls. So, accounting it was.

Second, during my sophomore year at Montana State University – Bozeman, I noticed the College of Business had the highest concentration of beautiful women on campus, especially up on the fourth floor... where the accounting program was. That solidified my major choice!

PricewaterhouseCoopers

In my senior year, I began to have serious doubts about my major. I was struggling with a 400-level class, Accounting – Advanced Business Combinations and Consolidations. It was all about accounting principles, and I hated it. I didn't know a lot in those days, but I knew that a life focused on applying the correct Generally Accepted Accounting Principle in all types of detailed things would not bring me contentment.

I was 99% ready to choose a new major and add another one and a half years to my college experience, but the night before I was going to officially switch, fate intervened.

I was an officer in the accounting fraternity Beta Alpha Psi, and that night, a recruiter from PricewaterhouseCoopers' Venture Capital and Private Equity Group, Silicon Valley, gave a presentation about an internship they were recruiting for. All I could hear was "prestigious," "very little to do with accounting," plus the chance to work with some of the largest dot-com companies in the world. I immediately wanted it.

With my less-than-stellar grades, I did not receive an offer after my first interview. However, I badgered the recruiter relentlessly until he agreed to fly me down to meet the group and their partners at their Silicon Valley office.

After my visit, I still did not receive an offer. But, I did get the email and numbers for the two primary partners and a couple of other managers. I relentlessly badgered them until they finally relented and gave me a shot during the tax season of 2000.

In those first two weeks of my internship, I fell in love with tax.

Proving and Pivot

Partnership taxation is a weird and amazing beast. A small percentage of CPAs understand it well, but it made sense to me. For the next five years, I learned about the taxation of some of the largest and most complicated partnerships in the world. It was in this environment that I got my training wheels and a foundation in CPA taxation that serves me well to this day.

I got hired full-time at PricewaterhouseCoopers (PwC), but eventually, I began to resent the 100-hour weeks. However cool and intricate, I was growing weary of working on billion-dollar funds at the partnership level. I wanted to see my work benefit the actual investors, the individual taxpayers who ultimately pay the tax in any partnership.

Change the Way You Think About Tax

So, I got serious about my profession. I earned my Master of Professional Accountancy with a 3.8 GPA and passed the CPA exam on my first attempt—something only about 13% of candidates did that year. In those days, the exams were two grueling days of pencil on paper, and we had to wait nearly half a year for our results. I killed it with amazing scores, and in all honesty, I only studied so hard because I knew if I didn't pass the first time, I wouldn't ever want to try again. It sucked! Since then, one of my mantras is "CPA stands for 'couldn't pass again!'"

I left Silicon Valley, moved to the Dallas-Fort Worth area in Texas, and joined a much smaller regional firm where I could work directly with small business owners and higher net worth individuals.

One day at work, I had a disagreement with one of my partners. One of his clients, husband and wife business owners who were finally selling their service company for just north of $3 million after 30 years of grinding to create and grow it, were going to pay nearly half of that $3 million in taxes. My boss told me that's just how it goes and $1.6 million was a great amount for our clients to retire on. But it broke my heart to see half of their hard-earned money go to the black hole of the US Treasury via the IRS.

So, I dug into the tax code, and I found a way to help them reduce their tax burden to just under $300,000. When I shared the good news, the clients both had tears in their eyes. I was able to change their lives! And I have been hooked ever since.

Short note: We lucked out with their particular facts. Also, I realized that if I'd had a chance to meet with them years before, not only would they have not needed the luck I found for them, but they may have been able to keep even more of their hard-earned money.

This impressed on me the power and absolute need to always be proactive with tax planning.

Most CPAs live by a mantra, "the more you make, the more you pay in taxes." I couldn't disagree more. I believe, and have proved time and again, that the less you know about the tax code, the more taxes you will pay. If you can shift your paradigm to recognize that the incentives in the tax code can be one of the most powerful tools in growing your financial freedom, then your whole world can change for the better. It's not about "loopholes"—it's about recognizing incentives written into the tax code to reward innovation, growth, and investment.

I left that regional firm to start my first practice in 2008.

Fighting Faith

On the outside, it looked like things were finally coming together—I had left Silicon Valley, found a professional path I believed in, and was striking out on my own. But inwardly, my early 30s were a different story. Despite all the success, I found myself profoundly empty, directionless, and depressed.

I had survived and even excelled in what many Christians might call a life far from God. My sister, a devout follower of Christ, would gently try to nudge me toward faith, but I thought of Christianity as nothing more than the "JC fairytale." I planned to put my gift at finding loopholes in large legal documents, like the Internal Revenue Code, to work and prove the Bible wrong—especially the part about Jesus.

After several humbling, and honestly dejected, months, I became convinced that my sister was right and I had been completely wrong. This JC fairytale was not only true, it was statistically crazy and stupid to not believe.

Though I still had plenty of doubt, on December 28, 2008, I offered my first, real, honest prayer to God. That day, my life experienced a tectonic shift and would never be the same. Five years later, on December 28, 2013, I married Bekka, and the best part of my life's journey began.

A Different Kind of CPA Firm

Starting my first solo practice was hard. Although I had a wonderful dream of changing the way CPAs serve their clients, building a different CPA firm was a nearly impossible uphill battle.

The hardest part was cash flow. When just starting out, the "typical" CPA fees we charged were not enough to keep a team of highly-skilled CPAs who had the capacity to provide the value I knew we could provide. I was married, raising my first child, and couldn't afford a home. It felt like my peers were passing me by.

After working much harder than I ever had for a couple of years and barely getting by, another national CPA firm made me an offer for an 18-month commitment I couldn't refuse. I accepted, and just after 18 months, I left.

I really gave it a shot, but I just had to go back to the grind of building my own practice. The typical CPA paradigm was not for me—not anymore. That fact finally gave me the grit to do whatever I had to do to make it work. I was all in.

Making it work took nearly a decade of barely skating by, my life savings, and financial support from my father while I fought bankruptcy. Then came a blessing: a single appearance as a podcast guest went "viral," and the phones started ringing off the hook!

I have grown to absolutely love what I do at Revo Taxpayer Advocacy. Not only does it provide a good living for my family, I also get to change the world by helping people take back what is rightfully theirs.

I believe we should always pay every dollar we are legally obligated to, but we should never pay a penny more. That is my life's vocational mission. Changing the way you think about tax will change your life.

Lessons and Inspiration

I learned that even when experiencing failure after failure, if you know you are right, you cannot ever give up. Sweat and tears, and lots of "failures" will pay off, or at least you won't ever have to regret giving up. For me, they have paid off, but there is so much further to go. We have a thriving practice, but it's a long road to hit my goal of saving clients $1 billion in taxes per year. I am sure there will be many more failures, lots more hard work and tears, and a lot of sacrifice—but I have faith that God will get us there… or at least, I will never have to regret giving up.

My wife, Bekka, is by far the greatest blessing I have ever received, only second to Christ. She is one of the few people I have ever met who is more determined and stubborn than I am. She is also fiercely loyal and loving. She homeschools our three amazing boys, Elijah, Josiah, and Jethro. We're learning how to grow as parents and as partners, even through struggles. We are, in every way, blessed—but still human, with daily challenges, especially as we try to live by faith and serve others, especially each other.

I won't sacrifice family time—my father's greatest regret was not being around enough while my sister and I were kids. I will not make that mistake, and so far, I can count on my fingers how many times I have missed putting my eight-year-old son to bed. I will keep my priorities without sacrificing them: God first, Bekka second, kids and family third, and business fourth.

I know it is hard. It may seem insurmountable, but I am confident that nothing is impossible. It is actually true when people tell you, "This too shall pass." Focus on love, servant-heartedness, integrity, and honesty—it will prove to be worth the cost.

Q&A WITH MIKE

If you could have dinner with three people, living or deceased, who would they be?

Obviously, Jesus, but beyond that, Paul, who wrote the greatest number of books in the Bible. He spent an inordinate amount of passion and dedication to grow and succeed as a Pharisee of Pharisees, only to become what they hated most, an unapologetic and fierce disciple of Christ.

Elon Musk – Oh, to pick that guy's brain on how to truly be a revolutionary change agent in this current world! And just hang out. As well as ask him on some occasions, "What the heck were you thinking?!"

My great-grandfather, Max Pincus – He fled growing antisemitism in Austria to come to the US in the early 1900s for abject poverty in New York City. Because of him, I got to grow up and live in the greatest country in the history of the world so far. Why did he do it? Who was he really? And to tell him about the legacy he left and to thank him.

What are you passionate about?
- My family – They are what is most important.
- Jesus Christ – He chose and blessed me even though I flaunted my rebellion against him.
- My vocation – The typical paradigm is wrong! I must educate and convince enough people that tax is a powerful asset to truly change the world.

What is a guilty pleasure that you love but don't always admit to?

Waffle House hashbrowns—scattered, smothered, covered, chunked, capped, and burnt!

What are a few of your favorite quotes?
- "Those who do not learn history are condemned to repeat it." – George Santayana
- "The definition of insanity is doing the same thing over and over again and expecting different results." – Albert Einstein
- "There is therefore now no condemnation for those who are in Christ Jesus." – Paul, Rom 8:1 ESV

What is something most people don't know about you?

I was a fly fishing guide and horseback riding guide.

I played college football as a lineman on scholarship. I wasn't the most talented athlete, but through desire, I learned that we can accomplish nearly anything we set our minds to as long as we are willing to put in the effort.

I received athletic appointments to West Point, The US Air Force Academy, and a few D-1 schools, as well as a plethora of smaller schools. I ultimately chose University of Tennessee – Chattanooga and played for just over a year before being injured out.

Instead of quitting at life like I wanted to, I chose to follow my love of downhill skiing and fly fishing by transferring to Montana State University – Bozeman, which incidentally happened to have one of the best CPA programs in the country at the time, which was pivotal to getting me to where I am today.

What do you consider your superpower?

Thinking outside the box and not giving up until you find the right answer.

What philanthropic causes do you support?

Rays of Hope – Mumbai. They have multiple ministries, including an orphanage, elder care, and the Hope Center for education. They feed and provide for the well-being of children of sex workers in the red light district of Mumbai's second-largest slum and rescue victims of sex trafficking. Plus, they are building the future City of Hope, an oasis for everyone above. My wife and I honeymooned in Mumbai and fell in love with the ministries of Pastor Manoj Magar. We have never felt such peace, such joy, and such belonging as we have when spending time with those children and people. We even named our first son after him, Elijah Manoj Pine.

What hobbies do you enjoy?

My kids take up nearly all my time not at work, but hobbies I hope to get back to enjoying are scuba diving, fly fishing, amateur (ham) radio, reading fiction, and camping.

What has been your greatest lesson?

Humility and humbleness are incredible strengths.

What makes you feel inspired?

Experiencing life from my kids' perspective. Changing people's lives with tax savings. Bekka, my wife.

How do you define success?

Accomplishing your God-given and most-dedicated mission while helping others and improving the world.

Ready to rethink your tax strategy and reclaim what's yours? Contact Mike Pine at Revo Taxpayer Advocacy at www.revotaxpayer.com to learn more. For smart, actionable solutions to all your tax-related questions, tune into *Hidden Money*, co-hosted by Mike, at www.hiddenmoney.com.

 Mike Pine - Relentless Tax Strategist

JENNIFER MARCHETTI

A Present from the Past

Jennifer Marchetti is a chief marketing officer who helps companies grow through branding, marketing, and competitive positioning. She is an author, coach, and speaker on topics including leadership, career and life transitions, the importance of branding, and winning growth strategies.

Doing the Math

Birthdays bring excitement about the future and a chance to reflect on what we want to accomplish in the coming year. I love birthdays.

Usually.

I remember the night before our twins' eleventh birthday. In the midst of wrapping gifts and writing their cards, I did something I had not done before. I started doing the math.

How could they be 11 already? I remember being 11 like it was yesterday. I'm about to turn 48. When my kids are 48, I will be 85 years old! It's going too fast!

I was beginning to panic.

I used to think time was a renewable resource. My twenties and thirties raced by, but it didn't bother me. When I turned forty almost ten years ago, I welcomed it. I had a thriving career and was fortunate to have a personal life filled with family and a vast network of friends.

As I write this, I have eighteen months left in my forties. It seems impossible.

The decade I greeted with such excitement is the first decade of my life I fear ending. The thought of another ten years of my life rushing by hits me differently.

Have you ever done the math? It could terrify you or drive you to make the most of this gift of life.

Me? It terrified me—at first. Then, it gave me the push I needed to think clearly about the life I wanted. A life lived deliberately. A life grounded in experiences and values I could be proud of.

I remembered I had a map to guide me through this exact type of journey. It was created for me twenty-eight years ago by someone I hadn't thought about in a long time.

The Leadership Map

My senior year at Duke University, I was fortunate to take a class called Leadership Development taught by the remarkable professor, Tony Brown. Our final project was a Leadership Map. The assignment seemed simple: What does leadership mean to you?

In reality, it wasn't simple. That is what made it brilliant.

Tony espoused and promoted Socrates's belief that the unexamined life is not worth living. He wasn't challenging us to write about the concept of leadership. He was challenging us to examine our lives: who we were, who we wanted to become, what our values were, and how we wanted to present ourselves to the world.

If I had been assigned this project in my freshman year, I would have written an academic paper, traditionally structured with a thesis, supporting points, and a conclusion. As a freshman, I would have been unable to contemplate the stakes of the questions he was asking. I would have written it at arm's length.

Thankfully, I wrote it the second semester of my senior year. Graduation was looming. I would soon be leaving the cocoon of Duke, where I grew as a person, cultivated my intellectual curiosity, and developed precious friendships.

I had abandoned the idea of medical school the year before. Working with blood made me lightheaded, as did the thought of the punishing years of medical school. In my last semester, I changed course and prepared to enter the corporate world. I had accepted a job at a dynamic software company in Austin, Texas, for which I had no practical skills. I was playing defense instead of offense with my next chapter. This would be the first time in my life that I wasn't correctly prepared for something, and I knew it.

Against this backdrop, I prepared my Leadership Map.

Knowing I would be inevitably shaped by my new career path, I was desperate to maintain a tight grip on the best parts of the person I was but was also curious about the person I would become. My Leadership Map reflected this. Instead of a traditional paper, my Map was crafted as a dinner party conversation between me at ages nine, twenty-one, forty, and eighty. Those personas individually represented defining life stages. I chose them for my Leadership Map because, collectively, they represented a life.

The dinner party provided a framework for what was to come. As my life progressed, I would be in situations that would test my values and stretch my perspective. On the precipice of graduation, I knew that real impact would come from living a life my past and future selves could be proud of, a life where my values and actions were aligned. I imagined all versions of me—child, graduate, adult, elder—sitting around the same table. If they could all respect the life I was building, I'd know I was on the right path.

At age nine, my tiny world revolved around the simple yet powerful concepts of kindness, optimism, and discerning right from wrong. Would the nine-year-old me respect the way I would live up to those values in the future?

Would my twenty-one-year-old self—so full of hope and excitement about the future—admire that I preserved, grew, achieved, and contributed no matter what situations I faced?

Would my forty-year-old self—who would look at the world with more realistic eyes but keep showing up every day—be proud that I course corrected, protected my values, and tried to bring my best self to all aspects of my life?

And finally, would my eighty-year-old self—reflecting on life—feel that I lived a life of value and impact? This persona was the hardest to write when I was twenty-one. She would have the greatest benefit of hindsight on my life, but my life hadn't been lived yet. She would also be the person most invested in how I chose to live. Would she appreciate how I took care of the health, body, and mind she inherited? For all of us, our eighty-year-old selves have an incredible stake in the decisions we are making right now.

The Litmus Test

When I dusted off my Leadership Map at age 48, I didn't know if it would be useful to me. After all, I had written it nearly thirty years prior when I had relatively few life experiences. I was most nervous to read my personal mission statement again. If it varied greatly from the way I live my life now, it would mean I had become a fundamentally different person. That alone would require a level of reflection I may not have been prepared for.

As I read it, I was happy to discover that if I were writing a personal mission statement today, I wouldn't change a word.

*To live life as an active participant rather than a passive observer.
To recognize that personal development is found as much in the learning process as from the achievement.
To always keep integrity at the center of my character.
To never sacrifice my values for the quicker route to a personal goal.
To remember that happiness and a positive mindset are contagious.
To surround myself with family and friends, enriching their lives as much as they have enriched mine.
To earn respect and to give it.
To devote time and energy to philanthropy, particularly those that benefit children.
To be open and honest in dealing with others.
To have the ability to look at myself objectively.
To have the strength to accept and learn from my mistakes.
To continuously strengthen my faith.
To never stop learning.
My legacy will be my family, my children, and the many friends I care about. For it is in them that the best parts of me will live on.*

The pillars of relationships, integrity, intellectual curiosity, impact, faith, and personal growth are what I hoped to build my life upon when I was first starting out in the world at age twenty-one.

They are the same pillars I hope to build upon as I continue my journey. If I can continue to be honest and curious like the Child, energetic and hopeful like the Graduate, strong and balanced like the Adult, and wise like the Old Woman, the math no longer scares me.

A Broken Compass

Later in my forty-eighth year, my Leadership Map helped me walk away from a role I'd served in for only a few months because it was misaligned with my values.

I had been at my previous job for twelve years, in a career-defining position working with and for people I respected. I had been very careful about selecting my next opportunity. Over two years, I turned down other jobs because they weren't a good fit for my career or life.

When I was offered the opportunity to lead marketing at a growing private company, the role seemed perfect. It was presented as a strong business model with tremendous upside, an accomplished leadership team, exciting potential for a lucrative exit, and the chance to learn a new area of marketing. I did my homework. I interviewed the company's clients, board members, leadership team, and some employees before accepting the job.

It took less than a week to realize I had made a tremendous mistake. The business was on the precipice of failure. The culture was toxic from the top down. At best, they had no idea how bad things were inside the organization. At worst, they had lied to me. I am not sure which is worse. I should have walked away immediately. Instead, I gutted it out for four excruciating months, enduring the wrath of a CEO who seemed incredible during the interview process but who led with a draconian style of threats and insults. I was working around the clock, trying to bail water out of a ship that had hit its iceberg years earlier—fighting a slow sinking that was impossible to hide as the market changed.

Perhaps I stayed because I didn't consider myself a quitter. Perhaps I thought I could fix it. It was likely a little of both. I reread my Leadership Map. I imagined my younger self, clear-eyed and confident, glaring at me and saying, "What the hell are you doing there?" It was time to go.

The instant I left, everything else came into focus. I restarted my brand strategy and executive coaching practice. I was once again working on things I love, helping many different companies and people. I was learning every day. I again had time for the pursuits and priorities I outlined so earnestly for myself decades before.

I will be forever grateful for that misadventure, as my father so beautifully categorized it. It was the smack in the face I needed to reframe my approach to my career and make the most of my life.

A New Rhythm

When I was younger, I didn't feel the pressure of time. Decades—not years or months—were the standard unit of measure of my life. Now that I have a different awareness of time, I have a tighter view. What goals can I accomplish in one month? One year? Two years? When the timeline is tighter, my daily actions have more weight and more impact on my personal growth. I am more accountable to the person I want to become.

This practice prevents the math from scaring me. A lot can be accomplished and experienced when you treat each day, week, or month as a distinct opportunity for real growth and progress.

The Leadership Map gave me a framework I didn't realize I needed when I matriculated at Duke. All of these decades later, I am so grateful for its centering wisdom. I wish I could take my twenty-one-year-old self out to one final dinner to thank her.

Q&A WITH JENNIFER

What is the best advice you have received?

I was a world-class worrier. I thought worrying was a form of strategic preparation or defense. I falsely believed that worrying could stave off bad outcomes. Worrying doesn't prevent bad things from happening. Instead, it wastes your time and energy in the present. My dad consistently shares advice his mother gave to him: "Ninety-five percent of what we worry about never happens. Most of the rest you eventually forget about." She lived to be 100.

Healthy food, good sleep, consistent movement, and spending time in nature are all medicine. The more of these you incorporate into your life, the fewer actual medications you will need.

Lift heavy weights multiple times per week. Stretch every day. You will be surprised how much you need muscle mass, strength, and balance later in life.

Instead of keeping track of the things that have gone wrong in a day, keep track of all of the things that have gone right. If you look for the small bright spots in your day—even days that don't go well—you will be amazed how you can tip the scales in favor of more enjoyment, gratitude, and joy.

What are some mottos you live by?

Excellence Is Found in the In Between

I used to treat excellence as a one-way pursuit: work harder, get better. Once I got there, I would work even harder and improve again—sometimes by miles, mostly by inches. It was a never-ending chase without the commensurate feeling of accomplishment.

Our culture seems to value the arrival more than the process. Over time, I realized that excellence is more nuanced. It is a process, a mindset, and a practice. It's more than what we achieve by arriving. Excellence gives beauty, purpose, and dimension to our lives because it's also found in the in between.

I remind my children that excellence is found in the invisible moments when you are striving, learning, failing, succeeding, and growing. This progress mostly happens when no one is watching. Now that I truly understand this, I prioritize training, learning, and mentorship with a fervor I haven't felt since my youth.

I strive to notice and value the thousands of small moments between the milestones. This is where the real growth occurs.

Yet Is a Powerful Word

You may be reflecting on your life, and you may feel unsatisfied or unfulfilled. You may have called the ballgame on one or more aspects of your life: *I am not a success. I am not financially secure. I am not the type of parent I want to be. I am not making healthy choices. I haven't lived up to my potential.*

Yet.

Yet is a word that brings hope, promise, and possibility. *Yet* opens the door for a different outcome. It is a bold, powerful act of defiance against your current situation. It's a statement of intent. Use this powerful word as you navigate your personal growth. It will change your internal dialogue, which will inspire new action, build better habits, and change your life.

To connect with Jennifer, go to jennifermarchetti.com to schedule a 15-minute introductory call for executive and life coaching, fractional CMO work, strategy workshops, and speaking opportunities on topics including branding, strategy, having a growth mindset, finding your purpose, and leadership. Follow Jennifer: linkedin.com/in/jennifermarchettimarketing
Instagram: @marchettijennifer

 Scan to schedule a consultation with Jennifer.

CHARLIE YUE

From Poverty to Abundance
How an Immigrant Embraced Entrepreneurism and Investing

Charlie Yue is a real estate investor and entrepreneur specializing in multifamily properties and renewable energy ventures. As a general partner, he has invested in over 5,000 multifamily units across the US and is now applying his experience to launch clean energy projects that support long-term sustainability and growth.

Humble Beginnings Outside Beijing

I was born in 1968, in a small suburb outside Beijing, China. At that time, China was still a very poor country. My parents earned only five or six US dollars a month, and the four of us—my parents, my older brother, and I—shared a single room as our home.

My father was an engineer in a factory, and my mother had once been a high school teacher. But during the Cultural Revolution, educated professionals like them were viewed with suspicion. My parents were sent to the countryside for "re-education," which meant losing their careers and returning to menial work far beneath their capabilities. When they came back to the city, my mom could only teach elementary school.

Despite the hardships, my childhood was filled with simple joys. Life was safe. From the age of six, I walked to school alone. After homework, we played in the streets with friends. We didn't have store-bought toys, and new clothes came only once a year—at the Spring Festival. That was the happiest day of the year, with good food, fireworks, and a fresh outfit to wear.

I wouldn't call myself a genius, but I was always among the top students throughout my school years. Even in hard times, I had hope.

First Taste of Business

I studied Japanese at a foreign language institute in Beijing during a time when China had just opened to the world. Speaking a foreign language gave me rare access to good jobs. During our long summer breaks, my brother and I launched our first business: we bought a pool table.

We'd haul it outside and charge people 15 cents a game. If two kids played, the loser paid. If only one came, they'd play against me. I wasn't very good—but I worked long hours and made great money. I was hooked. I didn't even want to return to college.

After graduation, I became an interpreter at Nippon Electric Company (NEC), then the sixth-largest company in the world. They paid me $200 a month—a huge salary compared to my mother's $30 which she was earning after a lifetime of teaching.

I eventually became the Beijing office manager for a Japanese trading firm. Life seemed stable, but I didn't yet know how radically it would change.

A Life-Changing Journey to America

Most Chinese people dreamed of going to the United States—but few ever made it. The first time I had the opportunity, I passed it up, thinking I'd never be selected. The second time, I applied with a friend. She got rejected. I got in.

Speaking very limited English, I landed in Vernon, Texas—a town of just 12,000 people. But on my second day in America, I met the people who would become my American parents: Nelson and Johnie Hilliard. Johnie was our group's English teacher at Vernon Regional Junior College, and they took me in as family.

Though I was 26 and couldn't legally be adopted, they even asked a lawyer about adopting me to help with my green card. I've spent every Thanksgiving with their family ever since.

After two years in Vernon, I transferred to Midwestern State University. After graduation, I followed the Hilliards to Rockwall, Texas and settled in nearby Dallas.

From Tech to Tofu

I started out as an engineer, but it didn't suit me—I loved people, not code. Even at lunch, I'd switch tables between my Chinese and American coworkers because I got along with everyone.

"Charlie would be a great salesperson," people kept saying. They were right.

I had spent four years waiting tables on weekends while in school. Through that job, I built friendships with countless customers. One of them, Peter Axt, a physics teacher at Shepherd Air Force Base, even let me sleep at his house on weekends to avoid long, late-night drives.

That's when I began thinking about opening a restaurant. Food is recession-proof. People always eat.

My former boss moved to Dallas and opened a successful noodle restaurant. He invited me to co-found a second location in Plano, Texas. It was in a large shopping center across from Sam's Club and Walmart.

But our spot was tucked far from the main road. The rent was high. And the foot traffic never came. After 18 painful months, we had to close. It was 2004, and I hit rock bottom.

Breaking Down—and Breaking Through

Ten years into my American journey, I had lost everything. I moved into a $300 a month bedroom in someone's house. I ignored all phone calls. I even considered ending my life.

But then… a knock at the door.

It was my American parents.

"Charlie, you didn't answer our calls. We know you're hurting. Come stay with us."

I did. We spent time together, and one day, while browsing at a bookstore, I picked up *Rich Dad Poor Dad*. That book opened my eyes. I devoured it. I realized: I could still build wealth. I wasn't finished. I was just getting started.

Real Estate: The Path to Freedom

I dove into real estate education. I read *Nothing Down* by Robert Allen, studied lease purchase options with Ron LeGrand, and learned owner financing and wholesaling. With no money and no credit, I started investing part-time.

Inspired by Robert Kiyosaki's story of selling for Xerox, I got a full-time sales job: whole-house water filtration systems—100% commission, door-to-door, every evening. During the day, I made calls for real estate deals.

In my first week, I gave six or seven sales presentations—and made zero sales. I couldn't even pay rent. But then I found Over the Top by Zig Ziglar, and everything changed.

The next week, I closed five out of six presentations. By the end of three years, I was the company's top salesperson.

In 2006, I became a licensed Realtor and investor, bought a house in Frisco, Texas, met my wife (who also owned a home in Plano), and married her six months later. Four years later, our son was born.

From Single-Family to 5,000+ Units

By 2009, I let my Realtor license go and became a full-time real estate investor. I did everything—wholesaling, flipping, rentals, short sales, subject-to, and owner-financing.

Eventually, I narrowed my focus. If the house was in a great area, I'd use owner financing. If not, I'd wholesale.

A typical deal? I'd borrow $100,000 from a Chinese investor at 8% interest, buy the house, then resell it for $250,000 with $50,000 down and 9.5% interest. I earned income in three ways: upfront, monthly cash flow, and backend.

As my network grew, I moved into larger commercial projects.

In 2012, my wife and I began passively investing in multifamily. By 2016, I became a general partner and acquired my first multifamily asset. Since then, I've invested in over 5,000 units as a general partner or limited partner.

In 2015, my entrepreneurial journey caught the attention of *The New York Times*. I was honored to be interviewed and featured in an article highlighting immigrants who had overcome adversity to succeed in America. It was a proud moment—not just for me, but for everyone who supported me along the way.

The Next Chapter: Solar, Storage, and Global Growth

In 2022, with interest rates rising and the market cooling, we stopped new real estate projects. I began exploring other industries—import/export, franchises, and renewable energy.

That's when I partnered with Andrew Li. Together, we launched a new business focused on solar and battery solutions. We've built strong relationships with top-tier Chinese manufacturers and now supply both residential and commercial energy systems.

One of our clients is the globally renowned hot pot restaurant with 1,300 locations worldwide. We're helping them scale their solar installations affordably across the US.

Looking Back, Moving Forward

From a one-room home in Beijing to a portfolio of 5,000 units and a growing solar business—I've lived the journey from poverty to abundance.

Along the way, I've learned:
- Adversity is part of the process.
- Education is the most powerful investment.
- Relationships are everything.

And most of all—when life knocks you down, someone might knock at your door and help you get back up. Be ready to answer.

Q&A WITH CHARLIE

If you could have dinner with three people, living or deceased, who would they be?

I'd choose Jim Rohn, Tom Cruise, and my American mom.

Jim Rohn was a legendary motivational speaker whose wisdom on personal growth and success has inspired millions, including me. I'd love to hear his insights firsthand and learn more about how to live a meaningful and disciplined life.

Tom Cruise is not only a phenomenal actor but also someone who embodies dedication and pushing limits—both professionally and physically. It would be fascinating to hear about his approach to his career and the mindset behind performing such incredible stunts.

And lastly, my American mom, because she's been a huge influence in my life. Having dinner with her would be a chance to share stories, express gratitude, and enjoy the warmth and connection that family brings.

What is your favorite movie?

If I had to pick one, it would be the Mission: Impossible series. The plots are gripping and well-balanced, combining spy intrigue, deception, and tech-based espionage with high-energy action. I also love the variety of exotic and culturally rich locations featured—from Prague and Dubai to Paris and Rome.

What are a few of your favorite quotes?
- "己所不欲，勿施于人." Don't do to others what you don't want done to yourself. This classic reminds me to always treat others with respect and empathy.
- "Success is not final, failure is not fatal: It is the courage to continue that counts." – Winston Churchill. This quote motivates me to keep pushing forward no matter the obstacles.
- "The best way to predict the future is to create it." – Peter Drucker. It inspires me to take initiative and be proactive in shaping my path.

What is some of the best advice you've received?
One of the best pieces of advice I've ever received is: "Focus on what you can control, and don't waste energy on what you can't."

This simple idea has helped me stay grounded during challenging times and make more effective decisions. It reminds me to prioritize my efforts on actions that truly move the needle, and to let go of unnecessary stress over things beyond my influence.

What is one thing you hope people remember about you?
I hope people remember that I showed up with integrity—that I did what I said I would do, treated others with respect, and tried to leave things better than I found them. Whether in business or in life, I want to be remembered as someone who cared deeply, built trust, and helped others succeed along the way. At the end of the day, character outlasts achievements—and that's what I'd like to be known for.

What do you consider your superpower?
I'd say my superpower is strategic thinking—the ability to see the big picture, anticipate outcomes, and navigate complex situations with clarity. Whether in business or everyday problem-solving, I enjoy breaking things down, spotting patterns, and finding creative paths forward. It helps me stay calm under pressure and make decisions that balance both short-term action and long-term vision.

It's also something I bring into my hobbies, like strategy games, and even into how I approach relationships and leadership—always trying to think a few steps ahead while keeping people aligned and empowered.

What books do you often recommend?
Think and Grow Rich by Napoleon Hill. *Rich Dad Poor Dad* by Robert Kiyosaki. All of Jim Rohn's books.

What philanthropic causes do you support?
I care deeply about causes that create long-term impact, especially in education, clean energy, and community development. I believe access to knowledge and opportunity can change the trajectory of someone's life, so I support programs that empower young people through mentorship, scholarships, and skills training.

I'm also passionate about sustainability and renewable energy. Supporting clean energy initiatives—especially in underserved regions—aligns with both my professional work and personal values. It's about building a better future, not just for us, but for the next generation.

Ultimately, I believe in giving back where I can make a meaningful difference—whether that's through time, resources, or connections.

What is a habit or ritual that has significantly improved your life?
Getting up early to start the day. I find that beginning my mornings with intention gives me a sense of control and focus that carries through the rest of the day. Reading *The Miracle Morning* by Hal Elrod helped me understand how powerful this practice can be. It's not just about waking up early, but about creating a calm, productive routine that sets me up for success.

What would you tell your 18-year-old self?
I'd tell my 18-year-old self to trust the process—you don't need to have everything figured out right away. Take bold steps, but be patient with yourself. Don't be afraid to fail; the lessons from those moments will shape you far more than your wins. Surround yourself with people who challenge you to grow, and remember that character matters more than image. And most of all, enjoy the journey—time moves fast, and the relationships, risks, and resilience you build now will define the life ahead.

What has been your greatest lesson?
One of the greatest lessons I've learned is that growth often comes through discomfort. Whether in business, relationships, or personal development, the moments that stretched me the most were the ones

that taught me the most. I've learned not to fear challenges or failure, but to see them as part of the process. They've also taught me the value of humility—to listen more, ask better questions, and surround myself with people who challenge and inspire me.

What makes you feel like your best self?

I feel like my best self when I'm fully engaged in something meaningful—whether it's working on a project I believe in, supporting others to succeed, or exploring a new idea that challenges me to grow. I thrive in moments when I'm both focused and curious, when I can contribute value and keep learning at the same time. Being surrounded by people who inspire me, and having the space to think creatively and act decisively, really brings out the best version of me.

How do you define success?

To me, success is about alignment—when my values, actions, and goals are in sync. It's not just about outcomes like wealth or recognition, but about making consistent progress toward meaningful goals, growing along the way, and doing so with integrity. Success means having a positive impact on others, maintaining strong relationships, and waking up with a sense of purpose. It's also about balance—being able to pursue excellence without losing sight of health, family, and joy in everyday life.

To connect with Charlie Yue about real estate investing, renewable energy, or strategy games, email Charlie@BlueHawkProperties.com or call 214-923-0561. To learn more about Charlie's mission to deliver life-changing, affordable, reliable, and sustainable energy solutions with exceptional customer experience, visit www.lumo-battery.com.

CHERI PERRY

Becoming Your Best Self
The Refining Fire of Change

Cheri Perry is a certified coach, speaker, and trainer passionate about guiding individuals and teams through transformative growth. With decades of experience in leadership and personal development, she empowers others to embrace change and become their best selves.

Reveal

Becoming your best self isn't about arriving at some perfect destination. It's about becoming, especially in the uninvited, unplanned, and unwanted moments—the kind of moments that show up without warning and turn your world upside down. They don't ask for permission. They don't knock gently. But here's what I've learned: those moments don't destroy you. They *reveal* you. And, if you allow them, they will *refine* you.

> *"I will refine them like silver and test them like gold. They will call on my name and I will answer them."* – Zechariah 13:9

I didn't know I was becoming my best self when I sat alone in the quiet of a house that used to be full. I didn't know it when I was signing legal documents that confirmed my 35-year marriage had ended. And I certainly didn't know it the first time I had to handle the things in my life that had been taken care of by my husband. But I know it now.

Pain is a powerful teacher. But only if you let it teach. Change can be relentless. But, only when you face change with faith does it become transformational.

Becoming your best self requires more than motivation and morning routines. It requires choosing growth, even when it hurts. It means learning to listen to God in the silence. And it demands that you rise again and again until standing becomes second nature.

If there's one thing I've learned, it's this: becoming your best self means learning to expect change, embrace it when it comes, and eventually employ it to move forward with purpose. It doesn't necessarily mean you like the change. It just means you choose to walk through it with your faith intact and your heart open to what God can do through the refining.

Reflection Prompt: *What moment in your life didn't ask for permission but changed you anyway? Can you see the refining, even if it's still unfinished?*

The Unmaking That Made Me: *Expecting Change*

When we think about personal growth, we usually picture rising, stretching higher, stepping forward, soaring. But for me, the *unraveling* came first.

I had built a life I was proud of: a marriage that had weathered decades, a family that felt rooted and steady, and a business that mattered. But slowly, and then all at once, that picture began to blur.

Change came like a thief in the night. It didn't take everything, but it sure felt like it at the time. It took the version of life I thought I could count on. It scribbled across my carefully written script with thick, black ink and dared me to keep reading. At first, I felt stripped. Exposed. Unmade.

But when the shock began to settle, I heard something deeper rising beneath the ache: a whisper of truth that said, "This is not the end. This is the beginning of becoming."

> *"Therefore we do not lose heart. Though outwardly we are wasting away, yet inwardly we are being renewed day by day. For our light and momentary troubles are achieving for us an eternal glory that far outweighs them all."* – 2 Corinthians 4:16–17

That verse became a thread I clung to in the unraveling.

The world will tell you your best self is polished, powerful, and productive. It sounds great, but I believe your best self is the one who can walk through a storm, feel every raindrop, survive every lightning strike, and still find the strength to love, to lead, and to believe. That's who I was becoming.

Not because I had it all together, but because I refused to let it all fall apart without finding the meaning in the messy middle.

Reflection Prompt: *What part of your story felt like an ending… but may actually have been an invitation to begin again?*

Faith Is Not a Backup Plan: Embracing Change

To find that meaning, I had to return to my foundation. I've always believed in God. But believing in God and *trusting Him* are two very different things.

My best self didn't emerge when I felt strong. She showed up when I had no plan B—when my carefully created plans were ripped from my grasp and my "perfect" world fell to pieces.

> *"But those who wait on the Lord shall renew their strength; they shall mount up with wings like eagles, they shall run and not be weary, they shall walk and not faint."* – Isaiah 40:31

I love that part about soaring. About strength and running and rising. But what we don't talk about is the waiting. The stillness. The ache in between the life you had and the one you didn't ask for.

That's where I met God all over again or, should I say, that is where He found me; in the space between the *no longer* and the *not yet*.

There were nights I sat in bed with my Bible open but couldn't read through the tears. Days I poured coffee with shaky hands, wondering how I would make it through a meeting, a phone call, or a simple decision. Moments I whispered prayers not for answers, but just for peace and hopefully to feel His presence. That peace came, eventually. Not in the form of fixes but in the form of presence.

> *"And the peace of God, which transcends all understanding, will guard your hearts and your minds in Christ Jesus."*
> – Philippians 4:7

It didn't always make sense. But it was enough. And in that quiet reliance, I started to rise, not because the storm ended, but because my roots were growing deeper than the winds of change could reach.

That kind of faith became my oxygen and my calm in the storm.

Reflection Prompt: *When have you discovered that faith wasn't your fallback, but your foundation? What do you know about God now that you didn't know before the storm?*

Leadership in the Mirror

The storms of life find a way to test who we really are! In the middle of grief and dramatic change, I still had a company to run. A team to lead. Clients who didn't need my tears. They needed my steadiness.

Leadership had always been a part of my life. But in this season, it became something else entirely. Richer. Fuller. More meaningful.

It wasn't about influence or strategy or being the strongest person in the room. It was about showing up: honest, humble, and real. Leadership wasn't a title anymore. It was a mirror. And in it, I saw who I really was when the foundation cracked beneath my feet.

There were days I answered emails while wiping tears. Days when my team could see the heaviness in my eyes even though I was smiling through the Zoom call.

One afternoon, I apologized to a team member for being distracted during a leadership meeting. Her response stopped me in my tracks:

"You're teaching us how to lead through hard things. Not by pretending you're fine but by being real and still showing up."

That's when I realized: Your best self doesn't arrive when the storm is over. She rises *in the middle of it*. Not perfectly. Not easily. Not all put together. But powerfully.

"If any of you lacks wisdom, let him ask of God, who gives generously to all without finding fault, and it will be given to him."
– James 1:5

I stopped trying to have all the answers. I listened more intently. I let my team see my humanity. I let them help me. I lived what I had taught and believed for years: that people matter more than performance. And somehow, through all that vulnerability, we got stronger. Not just as a company. As a community. As humans navigating life with one another, supporting each other and standing in the gaps that chaos and unexpected change inevitably create.

Reflection Prompt: *What kind of leader are you when things don't go as planned? Who might be learning from your courage to show up honestly?*

The Gift of Becoming

It takes courage to find the silver lining in the chaos. Becoming your best self isn't a one-time event. It's a continual unfolding; a quiet, gritty, revealing journey that happens in the in-between places. Sometimes it's visible. But often, it's not. It's the quiet resolve to get out of bed when everything hurts. The whispered prayer when no one else is listening. The decision to believe that healing is still possible, *even here*.

> *"Not only so, but we also glory in our sufferings, because we know that suffering produces perseverance; perseverance, character; and character, hope."* – Romans 5:3–4

Growth is rarely glamorous. It's not always found in the breakthrough moments.

It's found in the consistency of showing up broken, tired, unsure—and choosing not to give up. I've had days when I cried in the morning and led a meeting in the afternoon.

I've had nights where I questioned everything I thought I knew about love and trust, followed by mornings where I still showed up to serve and lead with integrity. That's the gift of becoming. It's messy. Sacred. Unseen by most. But God sees everything.

> *"The Lord sees not as man sees: man looks on the outward appearance, but the Lord looks on the heart."* – 1 Samuel 16:7

You don't become your best self because the world claps for you. You become your best self because you chose to trust God when no one else was watching.

Reflection Prompt: *What quiet, internal decision are you making right now that no one sees? Could that be part of your becoming?*

Anchored in Purpose: *Employing Change*

Purpose doesn't always show up like a thunderclap. Sometimes, it's as quiet as a whispered prayer. Sometimes, it's the decision not to quit.

In the beginning, I thought my purpose was about building a business. And in some ways, it was. But the storm redefined that for me. It wasn't just about building a company. It was about building people. Loving deeply. Leading with integrity. Becoming someone whose life said, "You can rise again."

> *"Many are the plans in a person's heart, but it is the Lord's purpose that prevails."* – Proverbs 19:21

That verse held me steady when my own plans crumbled. When I had to figure out who I was—not as part of a "we," but as a whole "me."

And when I finally embraced the reality that my life would look different, I also embraced the truth that *different could and would be better.* Not easier. Not pain-free. But better. Because it would be *more* honest. *More* aligned. *Deeply* rooted.

Employing change doesn't mean forgetting the pain. It means using what the pain taught you to live with deeper clarity, stronger faith, and a softer heart for others who are still in their fire.

Reflection Prompt: *Has your purpose shifted or deepened in the middle of a season you didn't ask for? What does "different could be better" look like in your life?*

Becoming Your Best You

If you're walking through a season of loss, transition, or uncertainty, I want to whisper a few things into your ear:
- First – You are going to be A-OK.
- Next – Becoming your best self isn't about perfection. It's about alignment. It's about aligning your heart with God. Your actions with your values. Your pain with your purpose. It's about choosing to believe that the fire didn't come to ruin you. It came to *refine* you.
- Finally – You got this!

> *"Being confident of this, that He who began a good work in you will carry it on to completion until the day of Christ Jesus."*
> – Philippians 1:6

I don't have it all figured out; and maybe you don't either. But I know this:
- God is faithful.
- You are stronger than you think.
- And becoming your best self isn't about changing who you are. It's about returning to who you were created to be.

Here is a little mantra that I created—feel free to borrow it!

> *Each day I look in the mirror,*
> *Amazed at the person I see.*
> *Handling challenges and life's every curve*
> *With the passion inside of me*
> *With faith and leadership driving each step*
> *With patience and love as my guide,*
> *I'll face every mountain, thrive through each storm*
> *And enjoy the journey as I RISE!*

Final Reflection Prompt: *Who are you becoming in this season? And what truth are you ready to return to?*

Q&A WITH CHERI

What is your core business?

I've owned a national credit card processing company for 29 years. As a result, I also do a tremendous amount of business and personal coaching using all of the experience and lessons I have learned.

What are your products or services?

We help businesses improve their cash flow and interaction with their clients through credit card processing, gift cards, and business growth tools.

How would you describe what you do in just a few words?

We remove the frustration and lack of trust from a critical part of every business: CASH FLOW! In the process, we develop relationships and end up helping business owners with their team dynamics and other areas of their business.

Who do you associate with?

I love to associate with difference makers, thought leaders, and individuals dedicated to leaving a lasting and powerful legacy.

What are you passionate about?

I am passionate about taking care of the people God gives me. Every day we are given opportunities to engage with others, and our presence leaves a mark—being intentional with that mark is definitely my passion!

What are your highest values?

Integrity, Love, Enthusiasm, Contribution, Growth

How do you relax?

I LOVE kayaking, reading, spending time with friends, and finding wonderful new adventures to try out!

What is your self-talk during challenging endeavors?

I hear myself saying SUCK IT UP BUTTERCUP a lot! I also remind myself of previous life challenges where I was able to step up—so STEP UP! You got this! YES I CAN!!

What have you learned along the way?
- I am stronger than the storm.
- People are good!
- Change is typically opportunity dressed in work clothes.
- We are WIRED for community.
- God is ALWAYS near!

What do you feel is the most important part of your day?
MORNING for sure! Each morning, I do a 2 Chairs moment where I ask God what He wants me to do today. I ask for guidance and the wisdom to see whatever path he wants me to be on. I also plan for the tasks ahead of me and spend some time writing in my gratitude journal!

Whether you're navigating life changes or seeking to strengthen your work culture, Cheri Perry offers coaching, speaking, and training to guide your journey. Visit www.CheriPerry.com or email Cheri@CheriPerry.com to connect.

 Visit Cheri's site to learn more and see her Gratitude Journal.

PHIL COLLEN

Def Leppard, Persistence, and the World's Fittest Rockstar

Phil Collen is a world-class musician and the lead guitarist for the band Def Leppard which has sold over one hundred million albums. In addition to music, Phil is highly committed to fitness, personal development, and making a positive impact on the planet.

Learning Guitar and My First Band

I was born in Hackney, a borough of London, England, and grew up in a place called Walthamstow. As a child, I loved music but thought it was completely out of reach, until I got a guitar at age 16 and started to play.

I left school and worked in a burglar alarm factory and then as a dispatch rider on a motorcycle while I was in a band called Girl until we got a record deal. We only got about $50 a week, but suddenly, I was a professional musician, and I could concentrate on that. I had something I had to get out. My artistic expression was so rewarding and still is today.

Def Leppard, Joe Elliot, and Mutt Lange

On tour with Girl, we played the British clubs and pubs. When I met Def Leppard, they already had two albums out.

Joe Elliot and I became friends. One day, he called me and said, "Pete is not in the band anymore. Do you want to play some guitar solos on this record?" I agreed and ended up on *Pyromania* playing songs like "Photograph," "Rock! Rock! (Till You Drop)," "Rock of Ages," and "Foolin'" and singing backing vocals. That album exploded. It all changed from that point onward.

Robert John "Mutt" Lange had just come off of an AC/DC album, and our management was fortunately able to hook him into Def Leppard's production. He saw something in the band, that we were malleable and something he could improve on. Unlike some musicians who would let their egos get in the way, we listened to Mutt and his suggestions.

Mutt Lange is, without a doubt, the most influential person in my musical career. He is totally inspiring with the highest intellect of anyone

I've ever met. This guy is a giant, but he's humble and modest. We learned so much from him.

Singing, Songwriting, and the Muse

Mutt is the reason I learned how to sing and how to play guitar properly. He had a way of introducing you to concepts so you would excel. It was an amazing way to do things that was almost spiritual.

There's no more complete way to express yourself than through singing. It also improves your confidence. A lot of people pick up a guitar because they're a little intimidated by performing, and guitar is a great way to get out of your shell. When you're singing, it's entirely different, especially if you sing in front of people with no effects or band. If you can get up there, sing with confidence, and not really care what others may be thinking of you, it will improve other areas of your life. If you're a musician, it takes you somewhere else.

When you add writing, you're not just a songwriter, producer, or singer, you can be all of the above. I have songs going through my head all the time. I can't ignore them. I could sit down and write all day every day. Music can be so many things, and I find inspiration everywhere. It can be a drumbeat, the sound of a car going by, or any sound that comes to you out of open windows or on the street when you walk around the city. One sound or phrase makes you sing and think of another phrase, word, or memory. I don't even look for inspiration. It practically comes through the air. When the inspiration hits you, it's fantastic, and you're grateful for the muse, whatever it was.

In 2020, I signed with Sony Publishing, and they have been great, hooking me up with a couple of different songwriters. We've been on a storm, working on stuff I wouldn't normally do. It's very inspiring to get into a different type of music. I'm also always writing Def Leppard stuff and am excited about where we are going.

"Pour Some Sugar On Me"

The album *Hysteria* was hard work. Rick had lost his arm in a terrible accident, among many other things. We were moving through different studios in different countries for two and a half years. We went into so much debt that it brought tears to my eyes when I read the breakdown. I thought we would never be able to pay it back to the record company.

The album was almost finished, and we had to sell a ridiculous number of albums to break even.

One afternoon, Joe was sitting in the hallway singing something while playing his guitar, Mutt Lange said, "What's that?"

Joe said, "Oh, I don't know."

Mutt said, "Play that again." Over the next 10 days, we wrote and recorded the song "Pour Some Sugar On Me." It was the last thing to go on the record that we had already poured so much into, almost as an afterthought, and it broke the album.

We had three singles out before it and we hadn't broken, even by a long shot, and then that one came out. Dancers in strip clubs would request the song, and then it started getting popular by request on local radio. It became this massive song in Florida, and we had no idea. From there, it just exploded.

Rick Allen's Accident

On New Year's Eve, 1984, our band's drummer Rick Allen had a terrible car accident that resulted in him losing an arm. Our band loves and supports each other like a family, so we asked him what he wanted to do. Mutt Lange went to see him in the hospital and said, "There's all this technology, and you've got amazing kick drum, bass pedal technique. You can use your foot and keep playing." He would have to change one limb for the other and would do double the work with his feet.

Rick was practicing in bed with his one arm and his foot when Steve Clark and I went to visit him in hospital. The three of us lived in a house together in Donnybrook just outside of Dublin. I remember that it was very frustrating for him. He would practice from eight in the morning till about 10 at night, swearing and cursing. Then one day, there was no cursing, and we heard a cool rhythm that was in time. It just got better from there. He got to that next level and was able to keep taking it to another level until it was second nature.

Health and Fitness

I believe if you're going to be constantly traveling and experiencing high levels of physical and mental stress, you need all the help you can get. The best thing anyone can do, especially in this environment, is to nurture and protect their body. This usually has a knock-on effect mentally, too. I try to keep a consistent workout routine going, which really helps, especially when on tour. Diet is as important as a workout routine and serves as a fountain of youth. I feel better than I did when I was 30, and I love the energy my routine gives me in my 60s.

I've been a strict vegetarian for 38 years and have practiced a vegan lifestyle for many years. Becoming a vegetarian was a moral decision because I couldn't eat a dead body. I stopped drinking 34 years ago. I was able to stop, but my best friend Steve Clark wasn't, and it ended up killing him.

Recognizing Addiction and the Benefits of Being Sober

I recognized I had an addiction when I realized I couldn't remember things. There were times I drove blind drunk. I finally understood that I could have hit someone. That really weighed on me, but I couldn't quit cold turkey. I had tried a few times before. I tried things like bringing just one glass of wine with me to the social gathering, but I couldn't do it. I'd bring the bottle instead. And then it was Jack Daniels by the end of the week.

On my ex-girlfriend Liz's birthday in April 1987, we were in Paris having a glass of champagne, and I said, "I'm not drinking after this." We went to India the next day, and I quit cold turkey. That was it, actually. It was easy, and she did it with me.

The benefits were outrageous. I got two extra hours a day that I wasn't spending recovering or just feeling not great. That's when I started working out, because I actually had time to burn. I started running, and it inspired me to do more. I'd run along the shoreline just south of Dublin, even in the cold weather. It wasn't the running itself I enjoyed, it was being in nature and the fact that I just felt different because I wasn't nursing a hangover. I was this clear, cleaner version of me.

Adrenalized Life, Def Leppard, and Beyond

Chris Epting encouraged me to write a book because he thought I had some great stories to share. He received some interest from a few book companies and then Simon & Schuster agreed to publish it. I worked back and forth with their editors, and my wife Helen helped me as well. At one point, we sat down and re-edited the whole thing. When you write it down, you wonder if it's right, if you are getting the point across, if it sounds too highbrow or lowbrow.

I've started writing short stories and plan on writing more. But writing a book, writing a story, or writing a song is a lot more difficult than people think.

Q&A WITH PHIL

What have been some of your musical influences?

Coming from London, the hotbed of the music industry, I grew up on The Rolling Stones, The Beatles, and later the Sex Pistols. All the great bands would come through London. I also love reggae music. Then, I got to America, where they created rock music, which comes from the blues. So I got into the blues, funk, soul, rock and roll, and jazz. I'm a huge fan of Motown!

Do you enjoy touring?

Touring can be challenging for many musicians, but I love the chance to be a tourist. Everywhere we go, I get up early in the morning, find somewhere to have a coffee, and absorb the local vibe. Traveling can get to be a bit much, but if I'm on a tour bus, I'm asleep before we leave the parking lot and usually wake up in the next town.

I have a wonderful wife and five kids, and I'm grateful that my family comes out at different parts of the tour. It may be Europe, Australia, Florida, or Fargo. I remember playing chess in Fargo with my son, Rory, when he was nine. It was winter and cold, and we were playing in a coffee shop, and it's just a beautiful memory. I really enjoy touring and being in new places.

What is something most people don't know about you?

I'm always busy creating and am part of two other bands. One is Delta Deep with Robert DeLeo of Stone Temple Pilots, Debbi Blackwell-Cook, and Forrest Robinson, and the other is Man Raze with Paul Cook of the Sex Pistols and Simon Laffy. I'm always having fun writing and recording. At some point, I might do a solo album.

I did the G3 concert tour with Joe Satriani and John Petrucci from Dream Theater with Delta Deep. Robert DeLeo couldn't make the tour, so Craig Martini stepped in and played bass. Those guys are over-the-top musicians, yet they are so humble.

How did you build confidence?

When I was a kid, I was told I was asthmatic. My doctor said, "I'm not going to give him an inhaler. I want him to go swimming." When you're swimming, you're thinking about other things, and after a while, I would forget that I couldn't breathe, and my lungs would open up. When I started playing guitar, I gained confidence in myself and started feeling different, and the asthma more or less went away.

I think every little thing you learn creates confidence, an ability to deal with stuff and not feel embarrassed. When I first became a vegetarian, I felt bad because I felt my dietary restrictions would put people out. At some point though, I decided I wasn't going to compromise my beliefs to please others. My vegetarianism became empowering for me. It wasn't ego. It was confidence. You have to accept yourself and your limitations, then make your limitations your strengths. Actually, when you are aware of your limitations, they often become your strengths.

Do you have daily rituals?

I think consistency is so important. It's so easy to fall off, and when you do, you have to get back into it, and that's a lot harder. If you maintain whatever you're doing and are regularly inspired by it, you achieve more.

One of the hardest things to do is meditate and think of nothing, especially if you've got songs running through your head and a toddler running around. I struggle with it, but I do it. Meditation is very powerful because it gives you time alone to escape.

I like to have flow in my day and not be rigid. You don't have to fix things. It is what it is. You're on a trajectory. When you're not in that mode, you can overthink things. You can go, *My God, I haven't got any money coming in. I'm not doing this. I'm not doing that. My songwriting has dried up.* You overthink. When you avoid this but keep all the moving parts going in a successful routine, your life runs itself.

Phil Collen is the lead guitar player for Def Leppard. For more information on Phil and Def Leppard, go to defleppard.com. To learn more about Phil speaking for your organization, contact info@kylewilson.com.

MAHEALANI TREPINSKI

Through Pain Comes Triumph

Mahealani Trepinski is a natural healer who specializes in mind-body wellness through craniosacral therapy, neuro-linguistic programming, IASIS neurofeedback, integrative and clinical nutrition. She empowers others to restore balance and vitality through holistic treatments, nourishing food, and mind renewal—believing it's never too late to reclaim your health.

Healing of Mind, Body, and Soul – Learning and Teaching

God put me on this Earth to help others heal in their minds, bodies, and souls. Since 2003, that is what I have been doing in my practice.

In 1995, I was studying to become an athletic trainer, hoping to make a difference in the lives of teens and young adults. I also enrolled in EMT school to support that goal. But in 1999, everything changed: I became a single mom while leaving a very abusive marriage. I knew then that I couldn't pursue this career and still be the kind of mother my child needed.

I began searching and praying about what I could do to financially raise my son and still physically be there for him. I felt that God was leading me to massage therapy. I thought, *Massage? That is just fluff and buff. Why, Lord, would you have me do that? ... If I am supposed to do this, then Lord, you need to provide everything to make it happen.*

He did just that, and I am so glad that I listened because massage has opened many doors for me. I was able to work on Olympians and pro athletes from football, baseball, and hockey, and I also worked in very prestigious spas in the Dallas-Fort Worth area.

When my dad became sick with cancer for the second time in 2010, I went back to school to study nutrition. I wanted to help him and others naturally heal with food. Since then, I have become both an integrative and clinical nutritionist.

At the school for integrative nutrition, they also had a life coaching program and a program to learn to be a nutrition-focused chef who cooks and meal preps for people. I took these added programs so I could help people with the full spectrum of issues—the outer body and what goes into the body: nutrition, what we listen to, and what we think about. It all affects our well-being, how we live, and how we age.

I absolutely love what I do: helping people and learning new ways to help people.

A Major Health and Life Turn

In 2018, I was diagnosed with a black mold fungal infection which caused all kinds of neurological issues in my body. It started with my legs going numb. While shaving my shin, I cut my leg deep, but I didn't feel anything. By the end of the week, my whole body was numb.

I went to the ER. They sent me to a neurologist and other doctors, and eventually, I got the diagnosis. Even though I was sick and worried, I was able to function well and could hide that I had issues. After nine months of dealing with symptoms and appointments, the doctors and I were able to get rid of the infection.

After three months of feeling like I was back to being myself, I started having symptoms again. I went to doctor after doctor, and no one could tell me what was wrong with me. I didn't know whether this was related to the original black mold infection, and neither did they. Test after test, doctor after doctor, and disappointment after disappointment, the symptoms kept coming and getting worse.

In 2019, my father passed away from cancer. In 2020, my mother moved in with us—me, my husband, and our kids. Then, COVID-19 happened. All of that stress made my symptoms worse. Since I was stuck in the house, I began researching more about what I could do to improve my symptoms naturally. I tried everything you could think of with limited success.

Once COVID finally lifted to where I could start going out to see doctors, a natural doctor had me do all kinds of tests, and... bingo, I was finally diagnosed with Lyme disease and many co-infections that can come with this disease.

I finally knew what was going on with me, but now I needed to figure out what to do about it. I saw multiple doctors and tried multiple treatments with no improvement. It was horrible and costly. We were not exactly sure what to do.

By this time, this disease started messing with my short-term memory, and eyesight, and I started to experience pain in my whole body that felt like knives stabbing me everywhere or vice grips on me everywhere. This was debilitating, and running my practice became very hard.

Over the next couple of years, my body's systems became so out of whack that it was hard for me to climb stairs or get out of bed some days. My kids would have to push me up. It was embarrassing and frustrating. *Here I was helping other people heal their bodies, and I couldn't heal mine, no matter what I did or tried.*

A Ray of Hope... So I Thought

In 2022, I finally found a treatment center that I thought could get me into remission. My husband and I visited and thought this was the place. So, we packed up our fifth-wheel camper and traveled with our daughters to Florida, where they dropped me off. I lived there on my own from October 20 to December 22. This was one of the hardest things I have ever done on my own.

Unfortunately, my time there was an experience I never want to go through again. I did all kinds of intensive treatments, mostly alternative, including one where they took my blood out, cleaned it through a filter, put ozone in it, and then put it back in me. It was a tough treatment that was physically intense and left me feeling drained. I was also taking tons of daily supplements and undergoing tests. I had to get a PICC line put in, which they barely monitored, except for the fact that my skin was blistering from the bandage adhesive on my arm. They paid more attention to small blisters than the fact that I was not doing well with the PICC itself.

On December 4th, I had planned to fly home for the weekend to see my daughter's first gymnastics competition. But, my gut told me to talk to the nurse to make sure I could fly. I went in for sonograms and found out that I had a serious condition: thrombosis—blood clots blocking blood flow. Actually, I had three thromboses: a one-inch thrombosis in the jugular vein in my neck and two more in the axillary vein in my armpit. They sent me to the hospital. I am so grateful I listened to my gut, or as I like to say, God's whisper.

The hospital discharged me with a prescription, so I planned to start the medication, return to the center, and finish my treatment. But when I went to fill the prescription, the pharmacist said, "Why did they discharge you? You need to be admitted and receive continued care with meds that only a hospital can administer."

I am so glad I listened. When I went to one of the best hospitals in the area, two doctors told me that if I had gotten on that plane, I would have gotten off in a body bag. That really scared me and made me wish my family was with me. I stayed in the hospital for what felt like the longest four nights of my life.

On my second night, the charge nurse yelled at me, "Do not rub your neck! You could cause the thrombosis to become a brain embolism!" I was terrified! As a massage therapist for over 20 years, it was instinct to rub anything that hurt—I did it without thinking. That night, I was scared to fall asleep. All I could do was pray and ask for peace.

I did have a sweet angel, who I met at the center, visit me in the hospital. She helped get me things like shampoo and a book for the stay. I also called a friend who lived an hour away, and he came to pray with me. He was once my pastor, and we had gone on a mission trip together. This was a scary time when God and I became a lot closer.

During those four days, the hospital put me on a drip protocol that helped drastically shrink the thrombosis and thinned my blood to allow my body to start healing. By the fourth day, I was able to drive back to my camper and rest. I tried to finish my treatment at the center, but I was not able to do everything. I had no choice but to finish what I could and go back home. I went home better, but not in remission as I'd hoped.

I am still struggling with this very expensive disease and pray that I will be able to get into remission one day.

New Knowledge from the Experience

Through all of this, I worked as best as I could. Because of my new limits, I had to learn new ways to work and help people. I also learned a ton at the center which I added into my practice as a natural healer.

One treatment that truly helped me was IASIS microcurrent neurofeedback. I found it so helpful that I found someone at home who did this treatment so I could continue. After what I went through, I was experiencing PTSD, and this treatment helped me get through that in four sessions. It also helps with my pain, memory, eyesight, sleep, plus much more.

I love this treatment so much that I went to school to receive my certification to learn how to do it. I love what I have seen in the past two years in my IASIS microcurrent neurofeedback practice. I have helped people with depression, anxiety, sleep, ringing in the ears, learning disabilities, ADHD, headaches/migraines, and much more. After learning this, I was excited to learn even more, so I decided to go back to school to get my doctorate in Holistic Medicine.

This journey has led me to a bold vision: to build a transformative healing retreat center—a sacred space where traditional and alternative therapies unite to restore the whole person. Where people can come, relax, retreat, or get healing from cancers, Lyme, mold, or other diseases. I envision a full-service spa, a wellness treatment center with doctors, nutritionists, counselors, and pastors, and a peaceful campus with a chapel, a farm-to-table restaurant, and accommodations for individuals and families to retreat or receive care. My dream includes a nonprofit to uplift single parents and survivor battered women—offering them meaningful work, affordable housing, counseling, and a fresh start. Rooted in faith and guided by prayer, I trust that the right land, name, and people will come together to bring this vision to life.

Meanwhile, I have bought a franchise with Carico. Their longevity products allow people to live healthy, longer lives. This company has helped me with my health issues. I intend that as this company grows, so will my capacity and opportunity to build my BHAG–my big hairy audacious goal.

I have been dealing with this disease and co-infections all while I maintain my practice, and my two young girls, husband, and aging mother with dementia. I am very active in my church, I sing on the praise team, and I am a co-lead for the ladies' ministry. Through all of this, I have come to believe that no matter what I am going through in life, I can get through it and rise above it. No matter what the circumstances are!

I am praying that my story has inspired you to be able to do anything that you want to do. For me, it is all about putting my mind to it and getting it done. We CAN do it!

Q&A WITH MAHEALANI

If you could have dinner with three people, living or deceased, who would they be and why?

First would be Jesus. I would love to ask him all kinds of questions and get a better understanding of things.

Next would be my mother-in-law. I never was able to meet her, and I would love to say thank you for raising such an amazing man.

My third would be Einstein. I'd love to see how he overcame early language delays and learning challenges while becoming one of the greatest scientific minds in history.

I also would not mind sitting down with Ronald Reagan. In my opinion, he was one of the best presidents in our country's history. I would love to talk to him about his decisions, how he stayed level-headed, and how he helped change history, because I would love to be a history changer myself in some way.

What is a motto or mantra you live by?

May everyone who leaves my presence feel better than when they arrived.

What are you passionate about?

I love helping people. I love to help heal them in body, mind, and soul. The word "heal" is in the middle of my name, and I feel that God put me on this Earth to heal and help people in the ways they need help.

Who are your mentors and greatest influences? How have they impacted your life?

Kyle Wilson. Being in his Inner Circle has helped shape my mind and how I carry myself. I have more confidence, and I am now doing things I would never have thought of doing. Like buying a Carico franchise or property. I am reaching higher and doing more amazing things in business and life.

The other person would be my husband. His work ethic is crazy; not like anyone I have ever seen before. He is a true one-percenter with all of his jobs (senior vice president of safety and security for a major airline, in the police department, and teaching masters students at three different colleges), and he strives to be the best that he can be in all of them.

Have you had any past challenges that turned out to be blessings?

My first marriage. Even though it was abusive in every aspect and my ex cheated on me, it has made me into the person I am today.

What is something most people don't know about you?

I have a love for horses, and I ride. I used to be a professional singer and have also trained to sing opera.

What is a habit or ritual that has significantly improved your life?

Meditation time, gratitude journaling, and vision boards.

What books do you often recommend?

Switch on Your Brain by Dr. Caroline Leaf, *The Power of Now* by Eckhart Tolle, *The Prime* by Kulreet Chaudhary, and *The Strangest Secret* by Earl Nightingale.

Mahealani Trepinski shares her story as an inspirational speaker and author. She has lead retreats and spoke at events since 2008, earning recognition as a two-time #1 bestselling author and artist. To invite Mahealani to speak at your event, email Mahealani@HealingMasters.net or phone the office 214.336.5425 or cell 469.215.0075

HealingMasters.net
HealingMastersCarico.com

GEORGE MINA

Climbing Down the Ladder to Rise in Purpose

George Mina is a tech leader, real estate investor, and mentor helping others find purpose beyond the 9-to-5. With 750+ multifamily units across his portfolio, he blends business acumen with deep faith, a love of family, and a mission to lift others up, especially burned-out professionals who are ready to rewrite their story.

Waking Up to What Really Matters

I spent decades in the corporate world chasing titles and promotions, thinking that's what success was all about. But eventually, I hit a wall where I had to ask myself: *Was I living a life that mattered?*

I'd been with the same company for nearly 30 years. On the surface, I had the steady job and a solid income. But deep down, I was exhausted from constantly trying to prove I'd "made it."

That's when the questions started: *What am I here for? How can I use my gifts to help others? Am I living the life God wants me to live or just the one that checks all the boxes?*

From Egypt to a Better Life

Let's back up a bit. My story starts in Egypt, where faith, family, and community were woven into every part of who I was. As Coptic Orthodox Christians, "Copt" for short, which literally means "Egyptian," we were a minority there. My family wanted a better life and more opportunities, so we moved to the US when I was just a kid.

I vividly remember taking speech therapy classes to lose my accent. I especially struggled with pronouncing the "th" sound. I knew the therapy would help me fit in, but it also felt like I was losing a piece of who I was… like I was slowly trading my identity for acceptance. That tension of wanting to belong but not wanting to lose myself shaped me more than I realized at the time.

My dad landed a job at a well-known company that became part of our family DNA. My mom worked at the company's daycare, where my brother and I spent summers at camp, playing ping pong and basketball for hours. Those memories still stick with me.

Years later, that same company became the core of my career. My dad once said, "Become an electrical engineer, and you'll be set." So I did, earning my degree and spending nearly three decades growing, learning, and supporting others there.

It wasn't just a job. It funded my MBA, helped me buy my wife's engagement ring (thanks, stock options!), and gave me the flexibility to work remotely and relocate. That company helped me build the life I wanted for my family.

But here's the thing: sometimes, even when you're grateful, you can still feel stuck or unsatisfied, like there's something more you're meant to be doing, even when you're not sure what it is.

The Corporate Climb and the Plateau

I was always the employee who played by the rules: work hard, deliver results, get promoted. And for a while, it worked... until it didn't.

An executive promotion, one I spent years chasing, kept slipping through my fingers. Company reorganizations, budget cuts, shifting priorities, there was always a reason it didn't happen.

But it wasn't just about wanting the title or the pay raise. I had a nagging feeling that I was chasing a version of success that didn't feel like mine.

I felt like I was on a treadmill, running hard but getting nowhere.

That's when the questions started: Am I really living my purpose? Or am I just going through the motions?

A Getaway from Burnout

When COVID hit, life changed fast. Like many, my wife and I were juggling remote work, our kids' online schooling, and family life. Luckily, I was prepared for the shift since nearly half of my career had been spent working from home.

We bought a cabin in the North Georgia mountains, a place to unplug, reconnect, and make new memories. It became more than a second home; it became our sanctuary.

We hiked, swam, and celebrated birthdays and New Year's. At the top of the stairs was a cozy nook, "the conversation room," as my kids called it, where we'd sit and talk about everything and nothing.

As we settled in, we saw the property could be more than our retreat. It could be a place for other families to make memories. So we turned it into a short-term rental.

But the biggest question that kept coming back was this: *What if this was the bridge to something bigger?*

Real Estate as a Bridge, Not the Destination

At first, real estate wasn't just about building wealth. It was about giving back and creating extra income to give our family more flexibility.

Then, I attended a real estate conference for physicians and spouses, like me and my wife, a dermatologist, seeking more than just career success. What struck me most was that it wasn't solely about financial wealth. The focus was on freedom: spending time with family, giving back, and building a life aligned with your values.

It was a mindset shift. The people there were building lives of purpose, impact, and balance. And, that's when it clicked for me.

Real estate wasn't the end goal. It was the bridge: a way to build a life grounded in faith, family, and service to others. It offered true freedom, not just life on autopilot.

Remembering My Why

Growing up, my faith was always my compass. I still remember church trips to New York City, where I saw people living on the streets and feeling this deep pull to help. My priest would remind us of the words from the Bible: "Truly, I say to you, as you did it to one of the least of these my brothers, you did it to me." – Mathew 25:40. That verse has always stuck with me.

One of my greatest joys is taking long walks before conferences, picking up food, and sharing it with people in need. I often sit and chat with them. It's not about recognition, but about connection. It's a humbling, grounding experience that brings me real joy.

The Pay Off

When that long-awaited executive promotion did come my way, seemingly out of nowhere, I should have been thrilled.

My manager said I probably wasn't qualified for the promotion but encouraged me to interview anyway. True to form, I prepared thoroughly and honestly, ready to face any weaknesses. I took the call from my hotel room before a small real estate retreat, and by the end, I had the offer.

That moment turned out to be a pivotal decision point in my life. At the retreat, surrounded by people who were building lives that aligned with their values, I found myself wondering: *Is this really the life I want?*

I asked a physician what I should do. She listened, then asked, "Are you afraid that if you turn down the promotion, you'll lose your job and can't support your family?" That question hit hard.

I prayed, reflected, and true to my engineer mindset, built a spreadsheet to rank my values. The result was clear: taking the promotion meant putting my priorities on hold... maybe forever.

So I stayed in my current role to focus on what mattered most: my faith, my family, and building my real estate business. It wasn't just a career choice. It was me choosing to live my why.

Living My Best Self, On My Terms

These days, I'm still in the corporate world, but on my own terms. Alongside it, I've built a real estate portfolio of single-family and multifamily properties. I'm a general partner, co-owner, or operator on over 750 units, all while managing a demanding, rewarding day job.

But the real win isn't the unit count. It's what those investments make possible. Along the way, I've learned a lot about myself and about what truly matters. And now, I've been able to put those lessons into action to:
- Mentor burned-out IT professionals who feel stuck and are seeking a better path forward
- Show people it's never too late to reinvent yourself
- Remind them that progress is enough, you don't need it all figured out to move forward
- Lead with empathy, humility, and trust, and help others build that same mindset

I know firsthand how scary it can be to take that first step. I've asked myself all the same questions:
- *What if I don't know how to get started?*
- *What if I lose money?*
- *What if I fail?*

I've had my share of ups and downs, and I've made plenty of mistakes along the way. But I kept moving forward.

My faith keeps me grounded through it all. It reminds me that it's not about me, it's about using the gifts God has given me to serve others, to lift them up, and to make a difference in their lives.

Living Your Best Self, Your Way

Here's what I've learned: living your best self isn't about titles or wealth. It's about aligning your actions with your values and using your God-given gifts to serve others. You don't need all the answers to begin, just the courage to take the first step and keep moving forward.

I've also learned that success looks different for everyone. For me, it's about building a life of faith, family, and service. It's about using the blessings I've been given to leave this world better than I found it.

None of us knows how much time we have. But what we can do is use each day to make an impact, to live with purpose, and to bring light to the people around us.

Q&A WITH GEORGE

What is your favorite movie?

Back to the Future is my all-time favorite. It shows how even the smallest decisions can change your whole future. What I love most, though, is how it's about discovering who you are and who you can become. We're all on a journey, making mistakes, learning, and growing.

Who is your favorite musical artist?

Keane, a British pop-rock band. I love how they explore themes like love, hope, fear, and finding your way through tough times. It's the kind of music that makes me think on life's bigger questions about purpose, resilience, and navigating the ups and downs.

What is a motto or mantra you live by?

Progress not perfection. I believe in moving forward, one step at a time, rather than waiting for everything to be perfect. Perfection can be paralyzing; progress builds momentum and confidence.

We all die and will go up or down. I want to go up, and I believe my purpose is to lift people up and support them, no matter their status, upbringing, or circumstances. That's my why.

How do you recharge?

Family time comes first, whether it's watching *The Middle* or walking the neighborhood with my wife. Orangetheory workouts keep me sharp, and sleep is key (shoutout to my Oura ring). Sometimes all I need is a good cup of coffee and a porch swing to reset.

What are a few of your favorite quotes?

"Do not love the world, nor the things in the world, for the world passes away, but he who does the will of God shall endure forever." – 1 John 2:17

"Self-care is never selfish." (Something I tell my wife when I go a bit too long on a Peloton workout!)

The first quote grounds me in what matters. The second is a gentle reminder that taking care of ourselves is part of taking care of others.

Who are your mentors and greatest influences? How have they impacted your life?

My parents are at the top of the list. Their work ethic, faith, and commitment to family shaped so much of who I am today. My dad, even as he battles Parkinson's, remains a source of wisdom and kindness. I'm writing down his story now, while he can still see the impact he's had. My mom's strength and steady love anchored our family, and I carry that with me every day.

What is some of the best advice you've received?

In my first week at my IT job, I was so eager to learn that I was barraging my mentor with questions without even letting him finish a sentence. He paused, looked me straight in the eye, and said, "Shut up and listen." Learning to listen first was a game-changer.

What is something most people don't know about you?

I was baptized at the Monastery of Saint Mina near Alexandria, Egypt, a place close to my heart. Our family name comes from Saint

Mina, known for his faith and miracles. The monastery was revived by a modern-day saint deeply connected to him, Pope Cyril VI. I still cherish a photo taken after my baptism, sitting beneath a large image of Pope Cyril.

What are some favorite places you've traveled to?

Italy – especially the Dolomites. The beauty and splendor there are unreal, and I love feeling one with nature. That trip was an epic backroads adventure with incredible food, people, and culture.

Zion National Park – some of the most beautiful hikes I've ever seen. It's a place where I can be alone with my thoughts and connect with nature.

What hobbies do you enjoy?

I've always loved baseball history, especially the 19th century. It started with opening Topps packs in the '80s for the gum and grew into a passion for the game's roots in 1840s New York and New Jersey. I love the hunt for rare lithographs, woodcuts, and photos from that era.

What books do you often recommend?

- *Unbroken* by Laura Hillenbrand
- *A Gentleman in Moscow* by Amor Towles
- *Screwtape Letters* by C.S. Lewis
- *The Pilgrim's Progress* by John Bunyan
- *The Everyday Hero Manifesto* by Robin Sharma
- *All the Light We Cannot See* by Anthony Doerr

What would you tell your 18-year-old self?

I'd tell him not to let cultural norms and expectations hold him back, because they kept him playing it safe. I'd encourage him to push past those boundaries and chase what's possible. You're capable of more than you think, but you have to take that first step and tune out the noise.

How do you define success?

Learning something new every day, growing through discomfort, and building deep relationships. I define success by feeling with my heart, knowing that God is guiding me. When I'm aligned that way, the financial success and other "freedoms" naturally follow.

George Mina is a tech industry veteran and real estate investor helping professionals find freedom and purpose through faith, family, and intentional investing. He mentors others seeking more than just success. He helps them live their why. Learn more or connect at www.wfhinvestor.com or george@wfhinvestor.com.

 WFH Investor Mastermind

TRESA TODD

Faith Over Fear
How One Yes Became a Movement of Women Thriving in Real Estate and Faith

Tresa Todd is the founder of the Women's Real Estate Investors Network, the largest and fastest-growing community of its kind. At 50, she chose faith over fear, leaving a 25-year career to build a movement empowering thousands of women to thrive in real estate and faith.

The Call

"Mom, I've done the math. If you want to spend your retirement as a greeter at your friendly neighborhood Supercenter, you're on the right track."

This is a phone call I'll never forget. It didn't feel too good at the time, but oh, how grateful I am for it. That call changed my life forever.

Just a few weeks prior, Kelton, my youngest son, had reviewed my finances. He wanted to know about my savings, mortgage, 401(k), and other accounts. At the time, he didn't say much about it, but when he called me that night, he had quite a bit to say.

"I want you to quit your job, sell your house, and move to Dallas so we can teach you how to invest in real estate."

I would have laughed if it had not been for the seriousness in his voice. Before I could protest, he began to spell out my future. If I worked until I was 65, I would enjoy about seven years of retirement before I would need to take that job as a greeter.

Proud Mama

My three sons were a pretty big deal. They had become wildly successful real estate investors in Dallas, Texas. They had completed over 100 real estate transactions in two years, putting them in the top 2% of real estate investors in the nation. When your kids are in business together, flourishing, and not killing each other, you kind of feel like you have hit the mom jackpot. Several times in the past three years, they had asked me to join them.

I had always answered, "I'll think about it," but honestly, I had brushed off these conversations. It was ridiculous. I was 50 years old, and they wanted me to leave my career, my home, my friends, and my ministry—for what? I knew nothing about investing.

I had been in the medical field and living the same life for 25 years. It was familiar. It was predictable. I wasn't unhappy. I wasn't particularly stressed, because I knew how to live in the predictable status quo.

On top of that, I didn't have some big stash of money that I could invest. My son should know that. He had just taken a glimpse into my finances. To be honest, I had never really understood how they had gotten started. They had put themselves through college, and they certainly did not have capital. When I asked, they simply said, "Mom, we use other people's money." That sounded a little scary to me. Why would someone give you money to invest? I asked a lot of questions but thought it all sounded too good to be true.

However, they had done it, and I was proud of them. I was content to be their cheerleader. I did not need to uproot my life for something I didn't understand....

But tonight felt different!

To Be Brave

My sons had no idea what was going on behind the scenes.

I had been teaching a Bible study on the book of Joshua for several weeks. In the story, God called Joshua to lead the children of Israel out of the wilderness and into the promised land—a luscious and prosperous place, known as the land of milk and honey. However, this would require going up against giants and many other great feats.

One scripture, Joshua 1:9, kept jumping out at me: "Have I not commanded you? Be strong and courageous. Do not be afraid; do not be discouraged, for the LORD your God will be with you wherever you go."

As I studied these scriptures, I felt God was saying those words to me. Those words had so much impact on me that I recall vividly making a commitment. I was going to live the rest of my life being brave. I would stop playing it safe. If I had a decision to make, I would always make the brave one.

I started immediately. There was a difficult conversation that I had put off for more than a year because I was afraid of how it would go. I made that call! Then I said yes to a project that seemed overwhelming, as well as a few more silly things that felt brave. And, I was sure God was so proud.

But, after hanging up the phone with Kelton that night, I sat on the side of the bed and said out loud, "God, surely this is not what you meant. You really want me to leave everything I know behind? For me to start over, completely?"

But I had made a promise to God. I was determined to keep it.

Big, Bold Moves

Within days, the FOR SALE sign was in my yard. I submitted my resignation at work. The following Sunday, I shared my plans with the Bible Study group I'd been leading for years. And in less than a month, I packed up everything and moved into a tiny apartment in the heart of downtown Dallas.

It was the scariest thing I had ever done. My new job was learning real estate investing through experience. Truthfully, it didn't come easily for me. I was not a natural like my sons. But I had walked away from everything. I had no choice but to make this work.

For some strange reason, as they taught me all the ways to find deals, I chose to start knocking on the doors of people who were facing foreclosure. I knocked on 57 doors before I got my first contract. 57 DOORS. That's a lot of doors. After knocking on 27 with no results, I really started doubting myself. After 37, I started thinking I had made the biggest mistake of my life. By 47, I was humiliated and felt like a loser. I thought, *Should I go begging for my job back?* BUT THEN, on door number 57, I got my first deal and profited $20,000. What? $20,000! I was only making $65,000 a year at my job after 25 years of climbing my way up.

This first contract set a precedent. It told me it was possible. It assured me I could do this. But, it wouldn't be my last call to courage.

After Door #57

As my business exploded with contract after contract, I would often think back to my days as a single mom, raising three boys and living paycheck to paycheck. As my boys grew, God provided for our needs time and time again: shoes, homes, cars, sports gear, and even a few vacations on a budget, as I called them. Every time I had a need, I'd add it to a list that I kept on my dresser and pray over it. When God met that need, I'd cross it off and give thanks. That didn't mean it wasn't hard. It could be lonely. It can feel daunting to be a female raising all boys.

After all that, God had brought me into a place of plenty. I knew it wasn't so I could hoard it all and sit on the blessings He had poured out. I was here to share it with other women. He had given me two things that I was compelled to give to others:

    1) Inspiration to believe God loved them and wanted good for them

    2) The specialized knowledge that I'd acquired to help women change generational cycles through financial independence. If I were going to impact anyone, it was time for another step of faith.

I rented a space that seemed like too much money. I ask my sons, "If I start a women's network, will you help me? Will you teach these women everything you taught me?" They said yes.

With that, I scheduled my first event. I'll be honest. I was trembling. I'd only been in this business for 16 months myself—who did I think I was? *What if no one came? What if they didn't take me seriously? What if they asked questions I couldn't answer?* (They did, and I learned!)

We served cookies and coffee, wore our smiles, and that first night, 40 women walked in the door. I was scared and excited. *Is this really happening?* I asked myself every week as the group grew. It was the start of a movement—the very first milestone of the Women's Real Estate Investors Network.

The women were thrilled to find a place where they could connect with others, learn from each other's experiences, and draw strength from the inspirational stories of women facing similar challenges. The in-person events grew all over the Dallas-Fort Worth metroplex and eventually Houston, Texas. I traveled from one city to the next, raising an army of women who were capable, inspired, and driven.

Watching these women step into their power and take hold of what they needed to transform their families' futures filled me with joy and a sense of purpose. I wasn't just witnessing growth—I was experiencing it too. With every breakthrough they had, I found myself growing right alongside them—in confidence, in skill, and in the clarity of my own vision for what was possible.

Divine Alignment

In January 2020, I felt an undeniable pull toward a training program. It came with a hefty $15,000 price tag—an investment that gave me pause. I couldn't explain why I felt so strongly about attending, but the impression was clear: I had to go.

So, I boarded a plane, spent days immersed in learning how to host digital training sessions, and returned home with a notebook full of strategies and ideas. Then I set it aside, returning to my usual rhythm of traveling and leading in-person events.

Just a few weeks later, the pandemic hit—and everything stopped. We could no longer host our events in hotel ballrooms.

I watched as people were losing their jobs, even their retirements, and I knew women needed the specialized knowledge that my sons had taught me more than ever.

While the world scrambled to adapt to a new digital reality, I remembered the seminar from January. I already had a playbook waiting on my shelf, filled with insights.

I pulled the notebook off the shelf and handed it to my sons and my team. That training—once just a nudge that I couldn't ignore—suddenly became our roadmap. It guided us as we scaled, reaching far beyond the circles I could have never touched through in-person events alone.

We launched our first digital training, and 699 women signed up. The most we had ever had at our in-person events was 180. Today, our online training sessions regularly draw thousands. And, every time, I'm in awe. I had no idea what God had planned when I said yes to walking away from everything I knew.

Now, I get to witness transformation unfold in real time—women breaking out of debt, building retirement plans, and creating legacies that will outlive them. It's one of the greatest blessings of my life.

Life of Courage

We blended my calling to share Jesus with my specialized knowledge of real estate investing, and it became what is now the largest and fastest-growing Women's Real Estate Investors Network in the world. We have had over 250,000 women register for our online training.

To fully grasp the absurdity of that sentence, you need to understand where I started.

My mom loved Jesus, and she was unwavering in her commitment to raise me in faith. But outside her influence, I grew up in the shadow of generational cycles—addiction, poverty, and fear. Those patterns wrapped around the people I loved and knew so well.

Ironically, it was fear that left the deepest mark on me. Fear of water. Fear of sickness. Fear of the unknown. Fear of risk. Fear of people. My world was blanketed in fear.

And I carried that mindset with me into adulthood. The "what-ifs" constantly crept into my thinking, pushing me to overanalyze, second-guess, and shrink back from anything that might disrupt the status quo.

But over time, I learned that the status quo is a cheap and gaunt version of the thriving and abundant life God invites us to live. That's why Joshua 1:9 became my battle cry. Fear kept the Israelites wandering in the wilderness—until Joshua stepped forward with courage to take the land.

I knew that if I wanted to lead others out of their own wilderness—whether financial, emotional, or spiritual—I had to face mine first. And that's where everything began to change.

I started asking myself a new question: **What decision will require more courage?**

Whichever option rose to the top—that was the one I knew I was called to choose.

So here's my challenge to you: Dare to say yes to the opportunity that scares you. Do it in faith, trusting that God wants to bring something good *in you and through you* on the other side of that fear.

Maybe you've tried before. Maybe you've failed. But what if that failure was just "house #56"? What if the next try is where it all turns around?

Faith requires perseverance. It requires vision beyond your current reality. It requires change. Love. Steadfastness. Above all, faith requires courage.

So, what's holding you back?

If I could share anything from what I've learned, it would be this: Listen to God instead of your fear. As I was saying no to my sons when they invited me to join them as real estate investors, it felt like being responsible. I could not fathom walking away from a steady job where I knew exactly what that paycheck would look like. Becoming an entrepreneur was too risky.

But I know now, you weren't created to live a quiet, retreating, safe life. You were built to take on hard things. To stretch beyond your own limitations. To step into a life of abundance that's waiting on the other side of your "yes."

It's so worth it! It won't be easy. You will probably cry every once in a while, but, oh, the victory, the thrill, when you experience all that God has for you.

My heart is so full of gratitude to not only my sons who mentored me, encouraged me, and helped me to grow this amazing network of women, but to God, who is so faithful that when I decided to be strong and courageous, He truly was with me every step of the way.

Have you ever imagined a life of abundance where you could write checks to ministries, nonprofits, friends, or family in need? Have you ever imagined that you could thrive and not just survive?

I am here to tell you it's possible.

Be brave.

Dream big.

Q&A WITH TRESA

What are you passionate about and why?

I'm passionate about helping women break generational cycles—spiritually, emotionally, and financially. Because I've lived through what it means to be bound by fear and limited by lack. I know what it's like to pray over a list of needs, unsure how they'll be met. And I've seen firsthand how faith, knowledge, and community can change a woman's life—and her legacy. That's why I do this.

What is your guilty pleasure?

I'm not sure if this is a guilty pleasure, but I am addicted to black ice tea with light water and three stevia. I have one 365 days a year.

What is something most people don't know about you?

I love adventure. I have been rock climbing, sky diving, and ziplining every chance I get.

What is one thing you hope people remember about you?

That I didn't let fear have the final say.

I hope people remember that I chose to live *without* fear, and that I used my story—and everything I've been given—to pour into others. I want to be known as someone who said yes to God, even when it was hard, and helped other women do the same.

How do you define success?

Success is knowing I did what God asked of me.

It's not about the numbers, the titles, or the outcomes—it's about faithfulness. Did I show up with integrity? Did I pour into others? Did I keep going even when it was hard? If I can say yes to those things, I'm at peace.

Tresa Todd empowers women to overcome fear and build generational wealth through real estate investing. She's on a mission to help women rewrite their legacy with courage and confidence. You could be the one to change the trajectory of your family. Ready to take your next brave step? Visit wrein.com or withoutfearmasterclass.com, and connect with us on Instagram @womensrein.

DAVID LAPP

From Buggy to Blessings
A Journey of Faith, Family, and Feeding Nations

David Lapp is the CEO of Blessings of Hope, a nonprofit food logistics organization that has distributed millions of pounds of food across the US. He is a former Old Order Amish farmer, and he left everything to follow God's call. Now, David empowers communities to bridge food waste and hunger with the Hope of Jesus Christ.

Life as an Amish Child

I grew up on a 70-acre dairy and produce farm in Lancaster County, Pennsylvania, in an Old Order Amish family of my parents and eight boys and two girls. I was number eight of ten. Life was simple. We didn't have things like electricity or modern cars. Instead, we used horse-drawn buggies to get around and gas lamps to light our home.

I went to school in a one-room schoolhouse with about 35 other students. All eight grades shared the same teacher, who focused on teaching us how to learn, not just what to learn. I loved that because it helped me understand the principles of learning. Even though my formal education ended after the eighth grade, I have been able to use the tools she taught me to learn about any subject that pertains to my life to this day.

As a child, I spent most of my days helping on the farm or playing outside with my siblings. We lived close to nature, and the work we did was hard but rewarding. I remember how my family worked together to grow food, take care of animals, and keep the house running. We didn't have things like TV or computers, but we always found ways to have fun. Life was busy, and while it was simple compared to what most people know today, it was full of good memories and strong family bonds.

One of the things I appreciated most about growing up Amish was the strong focus on community. There was value in everyone working together to support each other, whether it was helping with chores, building a barn, or sharing meals during gatherings. Our community was close-knit, and that made me feel secure and valued. Looking back, those early years taught me the importance of hard work, family, and sticking together no matter what.

Excommunicated

When I was 13, my family moved from Pennsylvania to a new Amish settlement in Wayne County, Indiana. We were the 15th Amish family to move into the new settlement. Today, there are almost 400 Amish families living in that area. My father wanted to give all eight boys the opportunity to farm, and with high land prices in Pennsylvania, he didn't see that happening unless he moved to a new settlement where land prices were only a fraction of the cost.

When farms that were connected to our farm came up for sale, dad would buy them to hold until my siblings got married or were ready to start their farming careers. After a few years, we had accumulated multiple farms and, for two or three years, my unmarried siblings and I, along with a few hired boys, farmed over 400 acres using horses (we were not allowed to use tractors to do field work). It was a big challenge but also something I look back on and realize helped to shape my future.

In 2003, I married the love of my life, a beautiful young woman named Fannie! At that point, Dad was ready to retire from farming and offered us the opportunity to move onto the home farm and establish our family there.

We had lifelong dreams on the farm. Fannie and I dreamed of building a life that would last for generations, where we'd pass the farm down to our children. But God had different plans for us. Around 2004, we (along with a few of my siblings) started experiencing supernatural miracles and a desire to know God more deeply. It was exciting, but also confusing, because it challenged the core of what we had been taught by the Amish church.

As our faith grew, we gained a Biblical understanding about God that simply didn't fit with the teachings of our church community. This led to a difficult decision—either ignore what God was showing us to maintain peace with our Amish community or obey God and risk excommunication.

We knew we had to follow God's calling. It wasn't easy to give up our dreams, our way of life, and the community we loved, but we knew we had to follow what God was showing us. Leaving the farm, the culture, and even strong family relationships behind was heartbreaking. But, it was the start of a new chapter that would change the trajectory of our future forever.

Through this upheaval in our family, my parents and nine of my ten siblings ended up being excommunicated from the Amish church.

After being excommunicated, Fannie and I moved back to Ephrata, Pennsylvania, where we still reside with our twelve children. We have since been able to restore a lot of family ties with my in-laws and are able to bless and respect each other's different beliefs.

The Early Years of Ministry

In 2006, after leaving the Amish church, Fannie and I (along with four other couples) co-founded Light of Hope Ministries. We wanted to help others who were going through difficult times, just as we had experienced during our own journey. The ministry focused on providing counseling, sharing God's love, and offering practical help to people who were struggling. Though it wasn't always easy to keep pouring into others while still wrestling with our own questions and needs, we trusted that God would bring hope through our path.

During this time, we began to hear about how much food was being wasted—while so many people around us were in need. Aaron Fisher (one of the co-founders) started helping at an outreach in Harrisburg, Pennsylvania, that was giving away food, and he would usually bring some of the extra food home. This was a huge blessing to our families. With five families living in community, and over 20 children among us, we constantly struggled to make ends meet. I remember weeks when we had a $30 grocery budget for all of us (outside of what we got at the food bank).

Before long, we found ourselves with more food than we needed, so we began sharing with a few neighbors and families we knew were struggling. As time went on, the food kept coming—so much that we could no longer store it in our pantries. Eventually, it overflowed into a three-car garage. By 2010, we were receiving enough food on a consistent basis that we felt led to step out in faith and commit to giving seven boxes of food each week to a local pastor. That simple act—just seven boxes of food—became the seed that would grow into what is now known as Blessings of Hope.

The early years of Blessings of Hope were a time of learning and trusting God to guide us. We had no big buildings, no trucks, and no extra money, but we had a vision to bridge the gap between food waste and hunger.

From the beginning, what made Blessings of Hope special was that it wasn't just about food. It was about empowering individuals to share the Hope of Jesus Christ. We didn't just want to meet people's physical needs; we wanted to remind them that they were loved and cared for. Each box of food we gave out was also a way of sharing the message of Jesus Christ. As the food ministry grew, we began to see how God could use even the smallest efforts for something much bigger than we ever dreamed.

From 2012 to 2018, our growing family lived in an RV and traveled to different communities with Light of Hope Ministries as we brought the message of Hope and God's love. The RV served as our home, and I pulled a travel trailer that served as the base of operations. We traveled from coast to coast, usually staying in southern states for a few months in the winter. With our growing family, living in such a small space required creativity and teamwork, but it also brought us closer together. We often parked in church parking lots, or someone from the community would host us at their property.

Looking back, those early years were filled with miracles. From operating out of a tiny garage to eventually serving tens of thousands of families and nonprofits, God has been with us every step of the way. Those humble beginnings remind me that no matter how small a start might seem, great things can happen when you trust in God's plan and take the next step in faith.

Rather than trying to educate God on what was possible, we decided that we would always say "yes" when we knew He was calling us to something—then ask Him how to carry out the details.

Stepping into the CEO Role at Blessings of Hope

In 2018, we moved out of the RV, and I officially stepped into the role of CEO at Blessings of Hope. By then, we had already outgrown the garage and moved into multiple larger facilities that we had leased. But, the opportunities for growth were far greater than we had imagined. We began to realize that world hunger wasn't the result of a food shortage—it was a management and logistics problem. Every day, tons of perfectly good food is being wasted, often ending up in landfills simply because that is the easiest option. There was no efficient system in place to connect surplus food with the people who needed it most. We believed that if we trusted God and followed the steps He laid out for us, we could grow Blessings of Hope into a ministry capable of making a significant, far-reaching impact.

One of the first major challenges I faced as CEO was expanding our infrastructure. In 2019, we purchased our first large facility, a 44,000-square-foot warehouse (three times the size of the previous facility). We took this leap of faith with no extra money in the bank, relying on God to provide what we needed. Within six months, the warehouse was already too small to handle the growing volume of food donations and distributions.

By 2020, as the COVID-19 pandemic hit, the demand for food skyrocketed. Because we had stepped out in faith and invested in growth earlier, we were uniquely positioned to meet the crisis head-on.

During the pandemic, we saw God's provision in extraordinary ways. While food insecurity rose across the country, Blessings of Hope grew rapidly to help meet the need. We distributed millions of pounds of food to families, food pantries, and outreach programs—partnering with local churches and nonprofits to extend our reach. The pandemic showed us how important it is to have systems in place that can scale quickly. It also reinforced our mission of not only to feed people, but also to bring Hope to communities during their most challenging times.

Over time, we developed a "Handling Fee" model at Blessings of Hope, where nonprofit organizations contribute a small fee when selecting food. This fee helps offset the operational costs of making food available to them. By doing this, we empower trusted local organizations to serve the needs of their communities, while supporting our sustainability and allowing us to build a scalable, community-funded, long-term solution. Operating on a privately funded model has also allowed us to avoid many of the limitations and restrictions that typically come with government funding.

We also grew to have a strong and passionate volunteer base, filling over 1,200 volunteer positions weekly. Volunteers sort food, pack boxes, stock shelves, and help ensure everything gets distributed efficiently. This team effort became one of the ministry's greatest strengths, showing how much can be accomplished when people work together for a common goal.

In the years approaching 2025, we started to broaden our vision. What would a national organization look like? We started looking at food waste and hunger as national issues, not just local ones. According to the USDA website, we live in a nation that wastes 30-40% of all food produced. This equates to a semi-truck load of food every 13 seconds.

In 2023, we initiated an exciting development: food dehydration. Food dehydration allows us to turn fresh produce into shelf-stable meals. This process retains over 90% of nutritional value, shrinks food to less than 20% of its original volume, and can give fresh produce a 5+ year shelf life which allows us to distribute internationally to developing countries.

In 2024, Hope RE Funding was established as a creative and innovative solution to address the capital financial challenges of expanding the Blessings of Hope infrastructure while staying true to our mission of stewardship and impact. By utilizing private capital, we can efficiently purchase and develop the facilities necessary to distribute surplus food to those in need. This approach ensures that Blessings of Hope can grow sustainably while maintaining its commitment to stewarding resources for God's Kingdom.

From Hunger to Hope

Ending world hunger is not just about providing food; it's about giving Hope. Hunger is often accompanied by despair, isolation, and hopelessness. When we meet physical needs, we also have the opportunity to address emotional and spiritual needs. Through partnerships with churches and community organizations, we can offer more than just meals—we can provide education, encouragement, community, and a sense of purpose.

Our vision is to not only fill stomachs but also to literally change the way we address food insecurity, all while sharing the love of Jesus Christ.

- What if we could privatize welfare by empowering the community to take care of the community?
- What if we could implement Kingdom-based, strategic, real-life teaching and equipping programs as a part of the welfare system?

- What if we could help people overcome dependency on government funding, and reshape their future?
- What if, through a Kingdom-driven strategy and a community-funded model, we could reduce the $1.2 trillion America currently spends annually on welfare—with an infrastructure investment of just $12–15 billion?

We believe we could serve the nation with 18-20 strategically placed, large food distribution centers (approximately one million square feet each) and a food selection center in every major city (30,000 to 40,000 square feet each) that would empower the nonprofit organizations of that region to restock their food pantries and serve their community with excellence. Our proven, community-funded model in Lancaster, Pennsylvania, draws nonprofit organizations from hundreds of miles each direction.

We know this vision will require significant resources and collaboration. Governments, corporations, nonprofits, and individuals all have a role to play. At Blessings of Hope, we believe that no effort is too small. Every donation, volunteer hour, and partnership moves us closer to the goal of a world where no one is hopeless and hungry. Together, through faith and collaboration, we can turn the dream of ending world hunger into reality.

The challenges have been tremendous—from creative funding solutions, to finding enough space for our growth, to managing logistics on a massive scale—but the rewards have been even greater. Seeing lives changed, communities strengthened, and faith restored makes every obstacle worth it. Our mission continues to grow, and I firmly believe the best is yet to come as we follow God's leading into the future.

Q&A WITH DAVID

What is your favorite movie?

The Ultimate Gift – It shows the power of going through trials and learning what it means to do something beyond what you can get.

What is a motto or mantra you live by?

If I believe God called me to something, my answer is, "Yes, Lord, how?" I do not believe it's beneficial to try and educate God about what is or isn't possible.

What are a few of your favorite quotes?

"I am only one, but still I am one. I cannot do everything, but I can do something. And I will not let what I cannot do interfere with what I can do." – Edward Everett Hale

What books do you often recommend?

Excellence Wins by Horst Schulze, *Rooting for Rivals* by Peter Greer and Chris Horst, *Chasing Failure* by Ryan Leak.

How do you define success?

At the end of my life, if I hear the words, "Well done, good and faithful servant! You have been faithful with a few things; I will put you in charge of many things. Come and share your master's happiness!" – Matthew 25:23

David Lapp invites you to be part of the mission of sharing Hope with our communities and ending world hunger through stewarding excess resources that have already been produced and crafting strategic, community-driven solutions. Learn more, get involved, or support the vision. Check out David's personal website at dlapp7.com and follow along on his journey.

KATRINA DELRIDGE

The Leader Within
Showing Up Fully in Business and Life

Katrina Delridge is a proud wife, mother, and grandmother, as well as a business owner and real estate investor. She's been an athlete, a leader in family business, a start-up contributor, a hospitality consultant, and more. For years, she worked diligently behind the scenes. Through challenge, reinvention, and surrender, she is now open to sharing all sides of herself and to helping others realize their full potential.

Saturdays

Growing up, Saturdays were special—they meant game day. I played soccer from age five to 40, including a year in college. On the field, I didn't need words. I didn't need internal walls of protection. I could be my true self—strong, fierce, and free. Soccer became a great outlet—a place to release the emotions I didn't know how to express in a childhood shaped by divorces, stepfamilies, and re-divorces.

After my first year of college soccer, burnout hit me hard, and I decided to retire from college soccer and transfer schools. For the first time since early childhood, I wasn't anchored by my identity as an athlete, and I felt a little lost.

Why Not?

At my new university, I worked concessions at the school's sporting events. From the concession stand, I watched our university's talented volleyball team lose a critical playoff game that ended their season.

I felt compelled to help. I wasn't sure what I had to offer, but I knew I could contribute a little fire towards winning.

Was I actually thinking about playing volleyball? I couldn't be. I'd only played in school growing up, no competitive or travel teams. However, some inner voice inside me wouldn't let it go, and I respected how I saw the coach lead with high standards and technical knowledge.

It took a few weeks to get my courage up, but I called the head coach, Frank Lavrisha, and asked for a meeting. I'm not usually a person who perspires from stress, but before that meeting, I sure did! I was about to tell a successful, respected coach that even though I hadn't played much volleyball, I thought I could help his team.

Bless Frank for not laughing at me. To start, he let me participate in the off-season workouts and practices with the team. Then, junior year, I played back row in each match and even earned an athletic scholarship. In the end, with me as the only senior, our team went to the Div 2 Elite Eight at Nationals, and our team was later inducted into the school's Hall of Fame. At the time, it was cool and fun, and the older I get, the more I appreciate what a unique experience that was.

Lesson: I may not have had the answer to "Why?", but I was beginning to recognize the quiet force within, urging me to ask, "Why not?"

Steady

A year after college, I got married and we moved to a small town where I worked full-time waiting tables while launching a small bookkeeping business. I also earned my real estate license, though I only ever sold one house.

With encouragement from a mentor and support from our family, my husband and I took a leap and bought a duplex. I had always been a saver, but that $3,000 investment was everything I had. I nearly backed out more than once.

Advice from my dad kept me steady: "Live on your college budget as long as you can—even when you start earning full-time income."

That mindset made all the difference. We'd continue to save until we had enough for the down payment on the next property. In two years living there, we bought a place about every six months. We didn't keep that pace up later in life, but this was a solid foundation to build from.

Surrendering

When my aunt was ready to retire from the family business, her position was mine to fill if I wanted it. So, my husband and I moved from Colorado to Montana.

My grandparents were all entrepreneurs, so I think entrepreneurism is in my DNA. I started by computerizing the manual bookkeeping. Eventually, I was overseeing the operation.

Running a busy operating business provided an invaluable education that I'm so grateful for. With my dad's mentoring, I was able to figure things out, find the right resources and people. I always want to help people, and I had the opportunity to learn firsthand about company culture.

Family business is complicated—you mix love for your relatives with analytical business decisions. Sometimes, looking at a decision from different perspectives gives you different answers. What takes priority? I learned that we all answer that differently.

While we had much of the business structure and governance well-positioned, we did not have an exit strategy in place for any family member who wanted out. My dad had successfully led the family businesses, but he was done. He wanted to retire, AND he wanted to be bought out.

Figuring out how to value assets and the financing terms for buying someone out, while you're in the middle of an exit event, is not a good idea. At the time, there was only a 3% success rate in transitioning a family business from the second to the third generation. We were part of that 3%, but the transition took its toll. Not every relationship between family members made it through that transition intact, but I'm grateful mine did.

I learned early on to rely on myself, convinced that asking for help always came with a cost. The truth was that juggling the responsibilities of three young kids, managing our rental properties, running the business by myself, and what became a long and difficult business ownership transition all pushed me to my breaking point.

Alone in my upstairs office, in total desperation and humility, I prayed. The relief was immediate—like something beyond me had stepped in. It felt like a miracle. That moment redefined my understanding of faith, strength, and grace.

Lesson: What I took from that season—more than any lesson in leadership, finance, or resilience—was the quiet strength in surrender. Letting go meant I could stop carrying it alone. Surrender opened me to a peace I couldn't manufacture on my own.

Staying True

After the multi-year transition, I was emotionally and mentally exhausted. The whole family was. After some time had passed, I decided to leave the family business. I had poured myself into it, and now I needed some space to heal and find myself again—both personally and professionally.

Next, I had a consulting contract with a tiny start-up company planning to mass-produce biodegradable chemicals. The business was mostly a vision at that time, and the simple tasks, and less responsibility, they had for me were just what I needed. The creativity and bootstrapping of a start-up were thrilling to me.

As we grew to needing series B funding to build up production, we also grew to about 25 employees, including chemical industry leadership. Personnel shifts created an opening for a full-time position that fit my skill set. I always want to professionally grow and contribute, but I was also managing our portfolio of rental properties, and being available for my three kids was top priority for me. While I believed the start-up phase could accommodate me getting the work done part-time, the business didn't agree. I was also starting to see business decisions that I didn't think were good for our long-term success, so I had a decision to make. After some thought, I saw it was time to move on.

Lesson: I learned to trust my business perspective and to stay true to my values.

Resilience

As it has seemed to happen for me, the next opportunity fell into my lap. A group of investors had bought six hotels, including their first and only full-service hotel, and it needed renovations. The owners and their accounting firms needed help with how to best set up the accounting structure and systems. With my ownership perspective, this was a perfect fit for me.

I enjoyed the creativity of deciding how to track revenue centers and presenting information in ways that would be most helpful to the owners. Once the financial systems were in place and the data caught up, I gradually uncovered new ways to improve and contribute. I'm grateful to work with owners I genuinely respect—both professionally and personally.

Throughout my life, other than a few sports injuries, I have been blessed with good health. However, for more than five years while I was working with the hotels, my health was on a roller coaster ride. I was easily overwhelmed and foggy—I think I even had some social anxiety. I wanted to drink alcohol most nights, and my body was a mess, so it was hard to hold onto my usual healthy habits.

The change in my health was such a slow transition that I didn't see the full impact until I got so tired of one continuous physical symptom that I went to two different doctors.

As it turned out, all of these symptoms could be attributed to hormones. *This is real. Why didn't I know?* After just a few months of working to rebalance my hormones, I was amazed by how much better I felt.

Walking through this opened my eyes to how strong women truly are. We learn to live with discomfort as though it's ordinary, yet it takes extraordinary resilience. That ability to keep showing up through shifting seasons is a quiet power woven into the fabric of women's lives.

Head Up

Over the years, I mostly kept my head down, tried to over-deliver at work, and settled for dishonest harmony—mistaking keeping the peace for being at peace.

Why did I self-censor for so long? I trusted my heart and my intentions. But, I lived behind a filter, revealing only what I thought I was supposed to be. Now, I've come to see that my voice, rooted in integrity, and my story, shaped by experience, might be of service to someone else.

As I keep growing into my own imperfect fullness, I find the paradoxes aren't incongruent. Those are the sweet spots: quiet and bold, ambitious and simple, servant and leader—being both big and small.

Q&A WITH KATRINA

What sport do you most enjoy watching?

Hockey. Especially the NHL playoffs. I've never played hockey, but I can imagine the physical and mental demands of what looks like wrestling and boxing on ice skates while working as a team to win.

How do you recharge?

Time in nature—alone and undistracted. Sleep—everything about me works better when I get good sleep. Exercise—especially helpful when I need to get out of my head.

What are you passionate about?
Health and wellness—without it, what we have to offer life is diminished.

How do you celebrate your wins—big or small?
Now, I share them with people—different people, depending on the type of win—because it amplifies the effect and is motivating to continue to try uncomfortable things.

What are a few of your favorite quotes?
- "In a race that you can't win, just slow it down." – Thomas Rhett
- "The kingdom of God is within you." – Luke 17:21
- "Your life does not get better by chance, it gets better by change." – Jim Rohn
- "And the day came when the risk to remain tight in a bud was more painful than the risk it took to blossom." – Anaïs Nin
- "When you change the way you look at things, the things you look at change." – Wayne Dyer

Who are your mentors and greatest influences? How have they impacted your life?
My dad for his wisdom and belief in me.

My husband's deep, unquestionable love and similar core values, and also how he challenges me.

My kids inspire me to live with that same excitement of creating the future you want, and I respect the care with which they choose who they let into their lives.

Have you had any past challenges that turned out to be blessings?
All of them so far—I think it's my choice. I believe life will continue to present similar challenges until change happens and the lesson is learned. Sometimes you have to be patient to see how it unfolds. Other times, you must do the work.

What is some of the best advice you've received?
You can't control other people—all you can control is yourself and the actions you choose to take. But at times, I took that too far and allowed myself to be disrespected.

What is something most people don't know about you?

I think music speaks straight to our soul—it can bypass language. Emotionally, I'm pretty even-keeled and controlled, but when I hear the song "Amazing Grace," I usually tear up. I learned to play that song on the piano in middle school and hearing it takes my emotions right back to then.

After my heart broke from reading *Where the Red Fern Grows* in grade school, I decided I just won't like books. So, as I got a few years older, I chose to read *The Kiplinger Letter*. (I love books now.)

What is a skill or quality you're currently working on improving?

Being at ease showing up fully—sharing my thoughts, values, flaws, and all.

Reaching my most effective and highest potential as both a business consultant and coach for developing business leaders.

What do you consider your superpower?

Kindness, positivity, and deep faith.

What philanthropic causes do you support?

Watson's Children's Center, St. Jude's, because kids are powerless in their situations.

What are some favorite places you've traveled to?

- The churches in Spain—from huge and ornate to the tiny shell of a building with a cross in it
- The Bob Marshall Wilderness in Montana
- The Dominican Republic: I was affected by seeing both the poverty and the resorts within the same country (on separate trips), and every beach; I set my alarm to see the sunrises and sunsets over the water.

What would you tell your 18-year-old self?

Don't compare your insides with everyone else's outsides. All the differences that make you you are the most special things. Lean into these, own them, nurture them, and share them—you never know which people will resonate with it.

What has been your greatest lesson?

Forgiveness: People hurt you and that's okay. My strength doesn't come from them.

What makes you feel inspired?

Stories about other people, especially when it's a difficult win in life, whether it's a book, documentary, movie, or music. I believe we are all capable of more than we can imagine. It's inspiring to learn of anyone tapping into that.

How do you define success?

My whole life: time freedom, which quickly led me to financial freedom.

Now: Giving back. Using my unique gifts and experiences to the highest potential I can to make the most positive impact possible.

Showing up fully means honoring the quiet nudge to share. Katrina Delridge helps business leaders who want clarity, effective strategy, and a grounded thought partner. She also coaches the person behind the business, too—because both matter. If you would like to learn more, please reach out to Katrina by emailing kdelridge72@gmail.com or visiting katrinadelridge.com.
Instagram: @KashBusinessServices

 To connect, visit katrinadelridge.com

CHRIS GRONKOWSKI

From the NFL to *Shark Tank* as the Founder of Ice Shaker

Chris Gronkowski played four years in the NFL along with his three brothers, Rob, Dan, and Glenn. Chris graduated from the University of Arizona. After leaving the NFL, Chris appeared on Shark Tank with his company Ice Shaker in 2017 and made a deal with Alex Rodriguez and Mark Cuban. Chris lives in Southlake, Texas, with his wife, Brittany, and three kids.

Growing Up in Buffalo with Four Competitive Brothers

My parents raised five boys. In Buffalo, New York, we lived in this awesome neighborhood. Every couple of houses there was another kid our age. We had that house where everyone came over, and we would make up games in the backyard and play against each other. Every sport you can imagine, we competed in. I believe that bred competition among us brothers and the neighborhood kids.

As we got older, we started playing competitive sports in leagues, mostly hockey, baseball, and football.

My dad started a fitness equipment company from scratch and worked long hours. My mom was in charge of getting all five of us to school and sports events. Five boys. We all played multiple sports for multiple teams and were on travel teams. I still don't know how she got all of us to all our practices. She physically could not bring us all to every practice and game. Plus, we were going to church and other functions too. She had to bring in coaches, friends, and family from other neighborhoods. Thinking back on it, she did all that without a cell phone.

Ivy League or Football Scholarship

My dad played college football, and at one point, he had a Bills contract hanging on the wall at home. He was a good player but then got injured.

All five of us brothers grew up wanting to go to college and play pro sports, and all of us did.

I wanted to play college football but wanted to make sure I also got a good education so I could become a CPA and make good money if pro sports didn't work out.

I committed first to the University of Pennsylvania. My dad was excited. I would be the first Ivy League son in the family. We wouldn't just be the family of dumb jocks. And I was the one to prove it.

At the last minute, I ended up getting a full scholarship offer to play for the University of Maryland. I wanted to play at the highest level, but at the same time, I also didn't want to pay for college. At the University of Pennsylvania, I would probably graduate with $200,000 in debt. So, two weeks before the summer ended, I accepted a full D1 scholarship to Maryland.

That scholarship really came about because a bunch of their players were about to go on academic probation and some of the incoming players didn't make it because of grades. So, they gave it to the guy who had good grades that could bump up the GPA for the football team a little bit. I tell people all the time, I got my first athletic college scholarship by having good academics.

I ended up transferring to the University of Arizona where my younger but much bigger brother, Rob, had also decided to go play. He was a coveted 4-star recruit. I was just hoping to make the team. Since I was a transfer, I had to sit out a year. So, that first year, I played baseball, and after two years, I went full-time in football.

I never thought I'd make it to the pro level, but I got my chance.

NFL for Four Years

I was undrafted. I was fortunate to have an agent believe in me and sponsor me to train for several months in Miami for the NFL Combine. That led to an opportunity to try out for the Dallas Cowboys. My wife is from Buffalo, but her dad got transferred to Dallas-Fort Worth six years before I went to the Cowboys, and everyone fell in love with the area.

I made the team. I hoped I would be playing for the Cowboys forever. It lasted a season before I started bouncing around to other teams.

I made it four seasons in the NFL, which locked in some nice benefits. After I retired, we came back to the Dallas area. We love it here. It's a great business environment and having family around is really important.

Life After the NFL That Led to *Shark Tank*

I wasn't rich by any stretch, but I had a pension and a nice 401K built up (the NFL offers a nice double match). Plus, you get severance pay and healthcare benefits. So, I had a good chunk of money without debt. I had gone to school and only had to pay for one semester. At age 26, I was leaving the NFL far ahead of everyone else my age.

I had this money that I could invest into whatever I wanted. I first went into business with my wife. She had started a business and Etsy shop while I was playing with Denver so she could work from home. She did really well. I helped her, and we ended up making more money than when I was playing in the NFL.

It was a good transition for me, but having grown up in fitness and having played football my whole life, making wedding gifts wasn't really me. After five years, I thought of the idea for Ice Shaker.

I love a shaker bottle, but the shaker bottle wasn't perfect. I took what I loved, like being able to blend powders and an easy-open pop top, and added insulated, kitchen-grade premium stainless steel to keep drinks cold or hot and a handle to make it easy to carry. Through my wife's business, I could customize Ice Shakers and fulfill bulk orders fast.

I could go to the gym, and I could call it work by making product videos around my workout. It was awesome. I thought, *Let's start this as a side hustle. Let's see if it gets to a place where we can make this a full-time thing. Let's go all in and see where it goes.*

Lessons from the Tank

I remembered getting an email in 2012, when I was with the Broncos, that said ABC's *Shark Tank* was looking for current or former NFL players to pitch them. Four and a half years later, I emailed back. That spark got me the opportunity to pitch to the Sharks.

That was about three months into the company's life. We only had $20,000 in sales, but at least I had proof of concept. They asked me to submit a video. I did, and they liked it. They said I had three months before we would film and that I should get ready. My focus became to get all the revenue I could so I could get the best valuation possible.

When I went on the show, we had around $80,000 in sales, and I was asking for $100,000 for 10% of the company.

After I did the initial pitch, I had all my brothers come on. They brought a lot of energy, and we had fun with the Sharks. One of the big lessons is to just show up with confidence, have fun, and know what you're talking about!

I watched every episode. I wrote down every question they ever asked. I felt like I was best friends with each Shark. So, when I walked out there, instead of being nervous, I could say, "Hey, I feel like I know you guys."

I ended up getting a deal with Mark Cuban and Alex Rodriguez. Later, my brother, Rob, bought Alex's position.

With their help, I was able to get Ice Shaker into The Vitamin Shoppe, Lifetime Fitness, GNC, and Walmart as well as to appear on QVC, *Good Morning America*, and many other outlets.

We then secured a licensing partnership through Wincraft, which was purchased by Fanatics, bringing Ice Shaker into the NFL, NBA, NHL, and MLB! With that new audience, we realized the power of licensing. We now have a license with the US Army license and many more.

Learning from My Dad

I have a family, a wife, and kids, so working a hundred hours a week doesn't work for me anymore. That forced me to put people and processes in place, which takes time!

My dad has more than 30 years in the fitness industry, and in that time, he built 17 retail stores. When he wanted to be a mentor to me in sports and business, at first, I didn't listen. It took time for me to realize the value of his wisdom.

When the pandemic hit, things slowed down. There were no processes in place. There was no budget. I could only come in the store when half of my employees were there because of the COVID restrictions and my kids at home. I realized I had better figure things out pretty quick.

It was time to figure out how to do this the right way and to build the team. I went to my dad and said, "How'd you build your business to 200 employees? That's insane." At the time, I was trying to manage eight employees.

My dad said, "From day one, I asked you, what's your game plan? What's your budget? What's your forecast? How are you incentivizing people? Tell me that first, and I'll tell you how to fix it."

That's exactly where I was going wrong. First, there was no team. It was me making every decision and me with all the responsibilities. I thought that was how it was supposed to be because it was my business. When it couldn't be like that anymore, I was forced to delegate, which was one of my dad's keys from day one.

When I started to share the responsibility, I realized that people responded well. They felt like they were part of a team. They could make their own decisions. They loved it and wanted more.

Next was figuring out how everyone could win. I had to figure that out with the whole team. We had a fulfillment team that wasn't feeling the win when we made sales. They didn't have a piece of that pie or input on the goals we set. We had to realign all the goals, and rather than incentivizing certain individuals, we had to incentivize everyone as a team.

Once we did that, I would walk in with a big sale, and everyone in the entire company was pumped. That's when I knew we had figured this thing out.

Q&A WITH CHRIS

Is working out and nutrition important to you?

When you own a company that's all about health, fitness, and protein shakes, being fit is part of the brand image, so you better live that image. But also health and fitness were ingrained in me growing up and playing sports. It feels like an accomplishment to get a workout in every day, and without it, I feel like the day hasn't really been completed. A workout is a mental release for me as well, to help get the stress out.

I think fitness is also an opportunity for me to be a role model. I coach kids in football and baseball, and the first thing they say when I walk out there is, "Man, let me see your muscles!" It earns immediate respect, and I think being in shape sends a good message for these kids.

My real journey with nutrition started after I was done playing football. I had to figure out how to eat healthy and what healthy eating really was. Because you can say eating a banana is healthy, but eating two or three bananas before bed is not always the best choice.

After the NFL, I dug deep into what to eat and when to eat it—breaking down the macros of protein, carbs, or fat—helped me fuel my body. On average, I'm burning 3,500 calories a day. Since I'm not trying to gain or lose weight, I eat right around that mark most every day.

What is a major priority in your life?

Family makes a massive impact on everything I do. Having four brothers definitely set the tone for everything I did. With us, it was always a competition, whether it was who could lift more, who could eat more, or who had better grades. You couldn't lose to your little brother and you had to try to beat your older brother. That all-day, every day competition took us all to another level. As we got into high school, we became more friends than enemies, and working together to beat the other team helped us excel on the field.

Now that I have a family, I see my boys already competing. It's a lot of fun to watch, and I'm here all day, everyday coaching them on how to be the best they can be and how to be great teammates like my dad did for my brothers and me all those years.

Do you have any philanthropic causes you support?

We started the Gronk Nation Youth Foundation about 10 years ago. Through that organization, we do fundraisers every year and give to youth sports programs and children's hospitals. My brother is building a new playground in Boston, MA, which is a more than a million-dollar project. Some of the youth sports programs we helped might have shut down if someone hadn't stepped in to buy the football and weightlifting equipment they needed.

If you purchase Ice Shaker through our website, you have the opportunity to choose between three different foundations to give money to. It's 1% of the sale, and it comes out of our end. We've donated thousands of Ice Shaker bottles to active military members, made a Guinness World Record to raise money for a local youth football program, and donated to local schools because we love representing and helping kids live an active and healthy lifestyle.

How do you recharge?

Definitely with a gym session. Also playing pickleball. Having a big workout on a weekend morning is definitely my go-to for a recharge.

What is something most people don't know about you?

I got accepted into the University of Pennsylvania's Wharton School of Business. I also took an official visit to Harvard and missed only one question on the math part of the SAT.

How do you define success?

It's about the whole team winning. If everyone on my team has the opportunity to win and we're winning as a team, to me, that's success. It's like winning a Super Bowl.

You can follow Chris Gronkowski on Instagram @chrisgronkowski and go to Iceshaker.com to order your own Ice Shaker. You can also order in bulk and have your order customized with your logo. You can order from Chris's wife's company at EverythingDecorated.com.

 Snag the best, ditch the rest. Ice Shaker's 26oz Shaker bottle is third-party tested to hold ice for over 30 hours, and the patented twist-in agitator will help mix your favorite drinks and powders.

JOSH ALEXANDER

Built to Steward

Josh Alexander is a real estate broker and principal of a multifaceted real estate investment firm in the Dallas–Fort Worth, Texas area that focuses on multifamily portfolio management, residential property development, and commercial private credit. Passionate about business and leadership, Josh is driven to help others seek purpose and develop their God-given gifts.

Connections

I grew up in the Texas suburbs—first in Katy, outside of Houston, then later in Southlake, within the Dallas–Fort Worth metroplex. Naturally relational with a passion for sports, my favorite thing to do as a kid was spend afternoons playing pick-up games with friends in the neighborhood. That love for community and competition—and an ability to connect with others who loved it too—led me to meet some of my closest friends and helped open the door to life-changing opportunities.

A few of those close friends, after we grew up and attended the University of Oklahoma together, presented one of those opportunities by introducing me to the business of residential real estate and inviting me to join their start-up house-flipping company.

In the process of growing from purchasing foreclosed properties at the courthouse steps to developing single-family houses, condos, and townhouses near downtown Dallas and downtown Fort Worth, we went through years of ups and downs before finding our stride and eventually building a successful company that we were all proud to be part of.

A New Road

Rather unexpectedly, there came a day when I started to feel unsettled. The most likely path forward for my role within the partnership was not something I felt at peace with, and while I cherished and was grateful for the memories, experiences, and relationships that came from our time together, a new vision began to unfold.

After a year of deliberation and seeking the counsel of close and trusted advisors, I left to pursue a new venture.

Initially, I was confident, excited about endless possibilities, full of passion, and ready to take on whatever lay ahead. Although I was leaving talented and trustworthy partners and an established, proven process, I knew that I could do more and go further if given the freedom to fully pursue my own ideas on my terms. Rather than focus on building and selling, I wanted to start a dynamic, multi-faceted real estate investment firm with the ability to underwrite multiple cash-flowing real estate asset classes across Texas and eventually beyond.

Looking back, it is humbling to think about my naivety. I had no clue what it was going to take to build something new without my former team. Naivety and pride served their purpose in getting me to walk away from a comfortable and established situation, but the weight of my decision soon set in. What I thought was a professional pursuit focused primarily on financial upside quickly became a revealing, relentlessly demanding, exhilarating, and ultimately, purpose-filled personal journey.

Helpless

In March of 2022, I sat by a pool watching my oldest son in swimming lessons when notifications from some of my go-to financial apps started going off one after another. I felt dread sink into my chest. The 10-year treasury yield, the foundational benchmark rate for many real estate lending products, was jumping higher—at an alarming rate. Members of the Federal Reserve Board were acknowledging that the recent surge in inflation was not transitory as previously thought and stood to pose a significant, long-term problem. Market participants were realizing this in real time and selling off their treasury holdings as a result.

I stared at my phone thinking, but more like hoping, that the yield run-up was an overreaction that would work itself out and quickly subside before too dramatically affecting commercial real estate lending and property values.

But that's not what happened. The Fed went on to raise the federal funds rate at the fastest pace in recent history, and Treasury yields kept climbing. For me and the team—managing sponsors of commercial multifamily real estate investments—this had a major impact. We had just purchased one property and had others under contract or in the loan application process. Our plans, our projections, and our near-term future all changed.

It quickly became clear that my focus had to narrow, and my leadership needed to improve. Originally, my primary role centered on acquisitions and deal structuring while third-party property managers ran the on-site day-to-day operations and reported to our internal asset manager. With new transactions stalled and operating expenses surging, we all turned inward and began the tedious process of evaluating current management methods—from how to make them better to how to scrap and rebuild them altogether. We increased communication with property staff, directly managed select property-level processes, and built better systems that closely monitored real-time results.

Influence

With our reality changing rapidly, I had to dig deep—not just operationally, but personally. The challenges exposed new areas where I needed to take notice and grow as a leader.

While we felt our way through the uncertainty, I struggled with investor and lender communication. My pride would persuade me to wait until I felt more certain before sharing thoughts or strategies to avoid possibly being wrong or looking bad. But silence only added stress. We discovered that most stakeholders just want to know you're paying attention, that you care, and that you're working on the problem. We learned that giving timely updates was more important than having the right answer and now strive to communicate regularly with the data, possibilities, and strategies we are currently working with.

As a husband, father, and entrepreneur, I've realized the hard truth that I'm not in control. As much as I'd like to act or think otherwise, macro and circumstantial factors are beyond my direct influence. I don't get a say regarding global relations, pandemics, economic shutdowns, supply chain interruptions, government monetary policy, runaway inflation, market conditions, and countless other things.

What I do know, however, is that I have free will. I get to make choices and am accountable for the thought process and intentions behind those choices. What is my mental framework and underlying intention? As a husband, am I committed to sacrificially loving and serving my wife? As a father, am I determined to protect, provide for, and encourage my kids? As a business owner, am I leading with humility and an unwavering commitment to stewardship and my responsibility as a fiduciary? If my belief system and decision-making process are rooted in a "bigger than me," purpose-driven perspective, I can be at peace with the uncontrollable unknowns and the consequences of the choices I make.

Three Career Impacting Lessons

Out of that period came some of the most formative professional lessons of my career. Here are three that continue to shape how I lead today:

1. On-site, day-to-day personnel have a disproportionate impact on success. The best laid plans mean little without a competent, committed, and caring team executing them. The necessary skill set, experience, and personality must be identified and represented in every operational position. When the right people are in the right seats, plans get implemented, results are measured, accountability works, and problems are solved more effectively.

2. Work towards immediate progress, and plan long-term. Well-intended but short-sighted actions can yield positive results, but often don't last or cause more difficulty in other areas. For example, one solution for a commercial property with a vacancy problem is to lower rents and relax tenant screening. But while occupancy and gross potential revenue may immediately look better, this strategy potentially puts collections, rent roll stability, and net cash flow all at risk, which can be painfully detrimental when it comes time to sell or refinance.

3. Diversify wisely within complementary pursuits. When commercial real estate transactions basically came to a halt, so did our business. We made it a point never to be caught so singularly focused and dependent again. Knowing our passion and talent revolved around deal facilitating, capital structuring, and financial analysis, we decided to bolster our realty business and launch a private credit fund for commercial real estate lending. Within our core competencies, we now have several additional ways to stay solvent and grow.

Breakthrough and Real Impact

I hold the business lessons dear, but undoubtedly more important are the personal takeaways. Recent revelations regarding how I respond to difficult, out-of-my-control situations have taught me more about myself than anything else in my life.

For as long as I can remember, I thought a sustainable breakthrough was just one major accomplishment away—that life would somehow be easier and more meaningful after. In the midst of the years-long professional challenges, I have learned that success and meaning are not about passing a milestone or achieving a predetermined level. Success comes from living on purpose through one season to the next, regardless of what each season brings. Success is choosing to continually get up, show up, and accept every challenge as a necessary stepping stone to becoming who I was created to be.

Difficulties, whether one-off or relentless, will always be a regular part of my life, just like they are for everyone else. But, while they naturally feel negative, persevering through them is key to unlocking what's on the inside. A big part of who I become is how I allow what I go through to shape me. If I believe that everything in my life works together towards my growth, my development, and participation in a greater purpose, I can face whatever comes with hope and resilience—knowing the struggle is necessary for increased promotability that waits on the other side of overcoming.

For me, achieving real impact and lasting influence demands persistent refinement and that I keep the questions that matter in plain view. What do I believe? What do I believe about myself? Who or what am I putting my faith in? What is my default mindset? What are my priorities? Am I willing to hang in and fight when I feel like giving up?

I am and always will be a work in progress, but how far I go and my impact on others will be determined by my authentic, lived-out answers to those questions. Well, that, and more so, by God's grace.

Q&A WITH JOSH

What is a motto or mantra you live by?
"This is my command—be strong and courageous! Do not be afraid or discouraged. For the Lord your God is with you wherever you go."
– Joshua 1:9

Fear and anxiety are unavoidable, but how I manage and persevere through those feelings is a choice. This verse reminds me to keep things in perspective—God is greater, and He goes with me. If God is for me, who can be against me?

Who are your mentors or greatest influences?
Jesus is my greatest influence. I want to better understand every day how he loves and sees me, so I can better serve and love others. The more I understand and receive his love, the more peaceful, meaningful, and impactful my life will be.

My dad taught me to work hard, never get too high or too low, and be generous. He told me from a young age, "Money is a tool to be used, not coveted," and "If you err, err on the side of generosity."

My mom taught me the importance of family, what it looks like to care for others, and how to live responsibly with a focus on what's important. She always puts others first and authentically lives out her faith.

What is some of the best advice you've received?
You are not as important to the outcome as you think.

This may sound harsh, but the truth in it brings freedom. If I show up, give my best, and treat others well, I can let the outcome go. I am learning to take responsibility for what I can control and accept results, always striving to be a good steward while maximizing resources and opportunities.

Never take credit or blame yourself for things you can't control.

This is a good reminder to stay humble and maintain a healthy perspective. I am responsible for my words and actions, but not for market conditions or the behavior of others.

What do you consider your superpower?

The ability to encourage genuinely and accurately. I believe that I have been given a gift to perceive unique strengths and personality traits in others, and it is my responsibility to share what I see to lift up and inspire confidence.

What would you tell your 18-year-old self?

The things you think are most important today are not. Status and success are not bad, but they should not be pursued for the sake of having them. If they come, it should be the result of hard and honest work over time. The true treasures in life are the experiences had and relationships made along the way. Put and keep faith, family, friends, community, and business in the right order, and things will go well.

ALX is a DFW-based real estate investment firm that believes in and supports the entrepreneurial spirit of developers, builders, and property renovators. Contact Josh Alexander to learn about exclusive investment opportunities built on providing capital, expertise, and support to qualified project sponsors.
Email: josh.alexander@alxland.com
LinkedIn: www.linkedin.com/in/josh-alexander-alx
Websites: www.alxrealestate.com and www.silvertoncap.com

FELECIA FROE, MD

Wealth *B-Hers*
Helping Women Have Walk-Away Money

Felecia Froe, MD is a physician-turned-investor who broke free from the golden handcuffs of medicine to build lasting, values-driven wealth on her terms. Through her Wealth B-Hers International community, Felecia empowers women to convert income into autonomy by creating passive income streams that reflect their values, goals, and purpose.

Why?

There's a truth I've come to believe deeply: Every woman should have the financial ability to walk away from a job or relationship that is not in her best interest.

I thought about this in the waiting room with two of my sisters while my third sister was undergoing surgery for breast cancer. The majority of her surgical team were women, and as I looked around, I realized most of the people waiting were women too.

I thought, *Who are these women? Who are they waiting for? What's happening in their lives that got them here?*

My thoughts went to women I've spoken with—women who run households and manage family finances, yet still worry they won't have enough money. Well-educated women, working hard in demanding careers, with no option but to continue running the hamster wheel. Even while managing their household finances well, statistics show that most of them do not feel secure in their ability to invest for income and often abdicate this part of their finances to their spouse or a financial advisor.

Our Beginning

I am the oldest child. I was born in the Deep South—Tuskegee, Alabama—as were two of my sisters. The youngest was born in Indiana when I was 11. My parents were Black professionals. When I was born, my father was in veterinary school. My mother had graduated from college and worked as a secretary—it was the 1960s.

My mother and father's relationship was not harmonious. My sisters and I heard a lot of loud arguments and witnessed physical abuse. My mother stayed in this abusive situation until long after my last sister was born, trying to make it work. Her reasons for staying were complex, I'm sure. However, a significant consideration, I learned later, was wanting her children to have financial stability, something she was unsure she could provide.

All of my sisters and I were married and are now divorced. We're all doing our best—and, like many women, are juggling careers, children, and finances. We are all well-educated and have careers that support us. All of us, at some point, have felt we've had to stay in jobs we didn't want because we lacked the financial freedom to choose.

All I Thought I Had to Be

I guess I'm a typical oldest child, pretty driven and always trying to do the "right" thing. I got good grades through high school and was easily accepted into many universities. I attended college with the goal of attending medical school. College was not as "easy" as high school. All the freedom and distractions caused my first educational challenges. At the same time, I became insecure about my ability to be a doctor and have everything else I wanted in life—especially a husband and children.

Because of this fear, I quit pre-med after two years to attend pharmacy school. A couple of years later, I realized I did truly want to attend medical school. I applied once and got into the program at the University of Missouri School of Medicine.

In total, medical school and a residency in urology took 10 years and a lot of money to get it all done.

While in residency, I got married and had my first child. After she was born, I had six weeks of maternity leave. When that time was up, I REALLY wanted to stay at home. While we were fortunate that my husband's mother was able to care for her during the day, I felt I was missing out on so much. A day in the life of a resident can last anywhere from 12 to 24 hours. One day, I remember thinking, *I don't know what she ate or if she had a bowel movement. I'm her mother!*

It took me three or four months to decide that I would complete my residency. I know now that it was fear that kept me there. Fear that I would not be able to provide for my daughter or that I would not be able to pay off my school loans.

A Way Out

A year into my first practice in Minnesota, I had my second child. Again, I only had six weeks of maternity leave. Life was difficult. My husband was working, and the girls were in daycare. We barely saw each other. This wasn't the life I wanted! My children were being raised by someone else! I felt I was never seeing them or my husband, and when I did see them, they got the worst of me.

We ultimately decided my husband would stay home with the girls—at least we would be raising them. I felt I didn't have the choice to quit or work part-time. We had student loan debt, a new mortgage, a new car... we needed the money I was making.

I was struggling. About two years later, three years into that first practice, I knew I had to find something else. But what?

After five Minnesota winters, I'd had enough below zero for a lifetime. I found a new practice, and we moved back to Missouri.

In Kansas City, Missouri, I met a group of OB/GYNs looking to buy a building to practice from and joined in the endeavor. Working with these women was amazing.

I also met a businesswoman, Cheryl. We worked together to open a separate business, a women's wellness center. Cheryl also gave me *Rich Dad Poor Dad* by Robert Kiyosaki. This book introduced me to money in a completely new way. I was fascinated. I took it all in—reading nearly all of Kiyosaki's books and introducing *Rich Dad Poor Dad* and the game *Cashflow 101* to my family.

After a few months of study, we were ready to go. We bought our first rental property, a single-family house. We were so nervous but got the house rehabbed and rented without too much difficulty.

With proof of concept, we were ready to run. It was 2005, and mortgages were pretty easy to come by. We bought 18 properties in the next two years. At this rate, I knew I would be able to quit urology as soon as we had them all rehabbed and rented. Timing was good, so I closed my solo practice; but we still needed some W-2 income.

I started working a locum position—a temporary physician role—in El Paso, Texas. My husband stayed in Kansas City with the girls while working to get the properties ready to rent. For reasons I didn't understand at the time, turning the properties was taking a lot longer than I thought it should. It was hard living away from my family, and I traveled home as often as possible.

After two years, it became too much. I realized I needed to go back to full-time practice, and so we moved to Honolulu, Hawaii. If I had to stay in medicine, I was going to be someplace pretty and warm!

Unraveled

My husband stayed on the mainland for several months continuing work to get the properties rent-ready. In the end, most of them were never finished. Without renters, we needed more money to keep the mortgages afloat and continue rehabs. I was able to secure a loan for $50,000. We ran through that, and lender money dried up.

It was 2008. We did not have the money to continue, and we couldn't sell any of the properties. No one was buying. It was the hardest thing I've ever done: we walked away, stopped paying the mortgages.

It was a mess. Our fragile marriage fell apart. As we went through divorce, private mortgage insurance companies sued me and my credit score fell to the 500s. It sucked.

Forward – Stronger and Smarter

Somehow, I knew the problem was not real estate—it was me. Or rather, it was my lack of knowledge and strategy. I didn't know what I didn't know. I needed help. Still, I knew real estate was the way to get me out of medicine. I would start over, but for now, I had to stay in my career.

I started networking and met an accountant who introduced me to real estate networks. I paid for coaching and mentors. I attended real estate conferences. I started investing again, more slowly.

I learned syndication. I invested internationally. I learned about investing in projects that improved neighborhoods and families. Finally, I had found my place. This felt RIGHT!

It took over 20 years, lots of losses, and bouncing back to get to the place where I am now. Today, I know my investing knowledge and network will help me to live the life I envision.

And Then?

It is easy for us as women to put ourselves last financially, especially when caring for others. My sisters and I have each supported, or are supporting, our children to varying degrees financially. Often at our own expense. Did you know that a woman's probability of ending up living in poverty more than doubles after marital separation?

During her marriage, my mom worked at various jobs. Dad was the primary monetary provider for our family when my parents divorced in 1979. My mother, of course, continued to work. The story about women "making a killing" at divorce is not true.

Mom was able to buy a house where she lived until she could no longer take care of herself reliably. She didn't have long-term care insurance, and she didn't have a sizable nest egg put aside to help with her care. It was left to us children.

My sister, who lived in the same city as Mom, provided a lot of the care while Mom was still able to live in her home. In November 2019, at the age of 82, Mom got sick—really, scary sick. She was hospitalized in the intensive care unit for a week, and she was never the same. Her kidneys failed, so she started dialysis. My niece moved in with her to help, but after two years, my sister who was still providing care was exhausted.

In February 2021, I had finally quit my urology job and moved to Tulsa, Oklahoma to help finish a project: building and running a grocery store in North Tulsa—a food desert that hadn't had a full-service grocery store in over 10 years.

Mom agreed to move in with me in Tulsa—I think she finally said yes because I was willing to help with her peritoneal dialysis. She hated hemodialysis.

I have to tell you, caring for my mother, a fiercely independent woman who was now dependent on me, was one of the hardest things I have ever done. Caregiving is not for the faint of heart. Plus, I had not lived with another adult for over 10 years.

To anyone reading this and going through it, there is nothing wrong with you. This is more challenging than anyone who has never done it can EVER know. It is a struggle emotionally and financially.

Fortunately, we were able to sell Mom's house to help with the costs. Heartbreakingly, she fought the decision because she was sure she was going back home.

Mom died at my house on April 19, 2022, one day before her 85th birthday.

I don't know if I would do it again. I probably would, but the pain of that year is still very fresh, years later. What if I had not been in a financial position to stop practicing medicine and care for my mother? I never want my children to have to go through this. I want to be able to take care of myself, even when I am not able.

What Next?

I talk to women every day about financial wellness and investing. I host a podcast, share my story, and work to make these conversations real and accessible. But I've come to realize that information alone isn't enough. Many women nod along—but still hesitate to take the next step. That's what I'm focused on now: not just sharing knowledge, but finding new ways to inspire action. Because I know what's possible when we stop playing small and start building wealth on our own terms.

Most women know there is no Prince Charming coming to rescue them. Most are also confident that they can continue to work. But what happens if they can't? What if my sister, who recently had surgery for cancer, had to stop working for months or years due to treatments? Fortunately, this did not happen; she's good now. But, these are real issues being faced by women every day.

We live in a society where money is necessary for survival. We make all kinds of tradeoffs to have it because having it brings a sense of security.

Talking about money freely, especially as women, is not something we do. When we do, it's usually from a place of scarcity. I used to think having a high income meant I was set. Now, I know differently, and I know how to get out of that trap.

That's why I founded Wealth B-Hers—to create a space for women to talk about money openly. All things money: the concerns, the fears, and the wins. Because every woman should have the financial ability to walk away from any job or relationship that is not in her best interest. Every woman should be able to take care of herself and the people she loves if she wants to.

There's power in having options. Let's build them together.

Q&A WITH FELECIA

What is your favorite song?
"At This Point in My Life" by Tracy Chapman

Who is your favorite sports team?
The Kansas City Chiefs and the Arsenal Gunners

What is a guilty pleasure that you love but don't always admit to?
Watching *American Greed*. Seeing how people have been scammed—and having been scammed myself—makes me more careful in how I approach opportunities and more committed to being transparent with potential investors.

How do you recharge?
Travel!

What are a few of your favorite quotes?
- "What would you do if you weren't afraid to fail?" – Eleanor Roosevelt
- "Stop talking about the problem and start thinking about the solution." – Brian Tracy

What is a skill or quality you're currently working on improving?
I am always working on my patience.

What are some favorite places you've traveled to?
So far:
- Kigali, Rwanda
- Zanzibar
- Doha, Qatar
- And I loved living in Hawaii.

What would you tell your 18-year-old self?
Don't be afraid.

Think about what you want to do and who you want to be. Discover it for yourself and go for it.

Imagine a community of women you can trust, who remind you of your true power. With Wealth B-Hers, you are not alone. Felecia Froe, MD's experience can guide you through your money fears and help you feel confident that you can walk away from any job or relationship not in your best interest. Check out Wealth B-Hers at moneywithmission.com/wealth-buildhers
LinkedIn/Instagram: @moneywithmission

 Let's Talk!

PAUL HERCHMAN

Persistence, Lessons, and Faith

Paul Herchman is a serial entrepreneur, investor, consultant, and the co-founder and CEO of GetHairMD, a company that offers a multi-modality suite of hair loss and growth solutions. With over 30 years of experience in the medical/aesthetic industry, he has led several successful start-ups and raised capital from various sources. He is a visionary and strategic leader who can identify market needs, create new program concepts, and leverage emerging technologies and trends.

Early in my career, I developed an idea for a company that would market technologies to physicians allowing them to do more advanced procedures. I told a friend, Kevin O'Brien, about it, and he wanted to join the endeavor. He quit his job, came over, and we started to raise a little money.

We did very well. In 1992, we were ranked the seventh fastest-growing private company in Dallas, Texas. In 1994, we were written up in Inc. magazine. In 1996, we took the company public on the NASDAQ at a relatively young age. In 2000, we sold to a pharmaceutical company for $30 million.

I was on to my next venture. I started a new, fast-growing company. We won some awards. Soon, it became apparent that I was unequally yoked with my partner. When we started becoming successful, he changed. Where once we were on the same page, I realized that his actions and how he wanted to run the company were not in line with my core beliefs. I left the company, but not without entering a major legal battle. I had no income and was spending big money on the proceedings. Then the recession hit.

I began to try to make something happen and found I just couldn't. Up until this point in my life, if I was doing something, it just worked. It didn't work just a little bit, it worked really well. I kept trying to do different start-ups—various things. I was the same guy with the same work ethic, ethics, standards, and belief in God, but nothing was working.

We were struggling. Thankfully, we were able to sell our home in Southlake, Texas. We lost the kids' college fund, we lost all of our savings, we lost our automobiles, and we went to live with my brother and sister-in-law. My wife, Donna, and I slept in my nephew's bedroom, looking at his baseball trophies. My mother gave me her old car to drive, and I was lucky to have it. Donna drove her mom's old car. I was barely surviving.

I had a couple of individuals stand up. These were good friends who went above and beyond the call of duty, writing me personal checks. Tom Montgomery, my fraternity brother, who actually helped me set up my first, $30 million company, told me he was going to buy me a house. He would co-sign on the loan. He only asked that I did the best that I could do on the payments, and if I couldn't make it, let him know.

I started a new company with promising medical technology. I got some good friends to invest, but the company was just barely making it. I couldn't pick up a meal for the family. I bought the Christmas turkey on my American Express. I had gone from very successful to, you know, not. My wife and I were married 28 years. Donna spent her time primarily being a mom and taking care of our kids, and suddenly we needed help. She'd been out of the work force for 25 years. She tried to sell custom clothing; that was doing okay. On Saturdays, she would go and sell bread for a company at festivals. If we could get $150, we needed it.

Our mental health suffered. We questioned our marriage.

I remember now people basically saying, "You've had your time. You can't even support your family. You can't even support yourself. You really ought to give it up and just get a job. Go to sales." But I felt that there was something out there for me. I owed my friends who invested in me too much money. I could never pay them back if I wasn't an entrepreneur.

Donna noticed my elbow was swelling, and it was really hurting. We went to the emergency room and I was diagnosed with some unknown infection. We had no health insurance. I was getting sicker. With an infection like I had, you get real sick, and then you get better or you die. I didn't realize how sick I was.

I was in and out of the hospital for months. I started to think about Kevin O'Brien. We'd been competing in the same marketplace since he left in 1997. He's my business soulmate. We had built my most successful company to date together. We connected in many ways, especially on the spiritual side. We recalibrated our relationship. We were both prayerful. I wanted to work with Kevin but had no idea what we should do. Kevin came to visit me. He said he'd been praying and felt he was supposed to be working with me. I felt the same way.

He quit his job again and came over. He told me about this new tech, the most disruptive technology in plastic surgery. We felt like we could make something happen, and we needed capital. I didn't want to go back to my fraternity brother, Tom. We made efforts to raise funds, but met obstacle after obstacle. Tom was always there. When he saw that we were in danger of losing our company, he cosigned on a loan for $270,000. He was one of my most successful friends, and our friendship is one example of the huge importance of keeping relationships.

We were up and running. Our technology was established in the treatment of neck and back pain, using targeted heat to neutralize the problem nerve, but we knew it could completely disrupt the plastic surgery industry. When you're selling something medically, you can only market it for what the FDA clears you for. There's always a ton of off-label uses of drugs and medical technology, but FDA restrictions make expanding your business into those areas difficult.

Our tech was only approved for treating nerves for pain. We didn't have any money, but we had great relationships from both of our careers in this space. We determined we were going to stay lean. We would sell product directly to physicians. The way the medical market really moves is under the influence of community leaders. You need those influencers on your side to have success.

We decided that being strategic was our only chance of making money. Only a physician who saw what this could do would value our company at that time. We began to sell them the product at a discount and were raising money from physicians who were in this space. Our first year we brought in a million dollars.

I had this horrible feeling that, if I wasn't successful, I would be a 75-year-old guy selling something and die at a Holiday Inn Express at night. That thought drove me. I was haunted by how my life had changed. That's what I would have to do if this failed.

At a trade show, we couldn't market off-label. We began to sell and we were organizing a clinical advisory council. Organizing doctors who wanted to be a part of a new, disruptive opportunity. We were raising capital. When you're raising capital, you have to disclose all the relevant information, everything that you know. So, we didn't say we were selling technology, we said we were raising capital. We had them sign non-disclosure agreements and we were able to fully share with them all the things we thought it would do, how it could do it, and ultimately where we thought the company was going. Because they needed to know before they put their money in.

We ended up selling five million dollars in 2013. Five times last year's raise. The next year, we did 11 million. Then, we were awarded the 7th fastest private growing company in Dallas, the same Kevin and I had won in 1992. It was surreal to be back accepting the same award.

You have to compensate people for the contributions they make to your company. I've seen this so many times. If you have cash or options, share them with those who are doing something for you. Most people are unwilling to do that.

When I was younger, I was too aggressive, too greedy. We didn't want to ruin the company by trying to do too much. We shook hands and said the minute we can sell the company and get five million each, we sell.

We needed people to help us. We didn't have the cash to pay. We used our options as our currencies. We got some of the best talent. They didn't make as much at first. When we sold the company, we had 200 option holders that we distributed the money to.

When we got to a $24 million valuation, we had accomplished our goal. We felt even better about the ongoing sharing of options. And the cherry on top was when we sold our company for $80 million.

I repaid those who gave money to me with my personal stock. They ended up getting three to four times their money. None of these men ever made me feel beholden. We stayed in touch, but it was just an amazing thing. That says something about them. Selling the company and returning their money multiplied was amazing. I felt great taking care of them. My family, for generations now, is taken care of. The first investors made eight times their money. The last made two to three times.

We became very thankful. Things happened to us that were beyond our control. When the storms hit, I hit the rocks and whatever little boat I was building was crushed. When the storms hit, and they would hit, the wind would blow, and when it passed, we would look up and be heading in a new direction. And that new direction was always better.

We learned to be so thankful for everything coming to us just in time. Not ever early, but just in time. Over all those years, it was an amazing journey of faith. I've kept this Bible verse in my wallet since mid 2012.

> *Again I saw that under the sun the race is not to the swift, nor the battle to the strong, nor bread to the wise, nor riches to the intelligent, nor favor to those with knowledge, but time and chance happen to them all. – Ecclesiastes 9:11*

Through my failures, I learned a lot. There's 100 things that could have happened that would have been far worse. None of it happened to us. I don't know why we were blessed in this way, but we were. For generations, my family is going to be in good shape. To go through something like that, I don't want to do it again, but you come out with a different perspective. More compassion. We're all better off for that.

If you're not in the game, on the field, you're not going to score. If I would have said, I'm just going to go to work somewhere, get a job, I didn't feel like I could do that because I owed too much money. I had an obligation to pay it back. I learned so many of the cliches. But they hang around because they're true. If you stay in the game, you have a chance. Keep trying.

Q&A WITH PAUL

What is your favorite song?
"Don't Back Down" by Tom Petty

How do you recharge?
I've been an avid pickleball player for several years. I like to work out and also to hike when I'm in Colorado.

I also like to cook. I'll put some music on, get a glass of wine, chop a salad, and cook up something. I mostly make pretty, simple things to unwind and enjoy family and friends.

What is something most people don't know about you?

I was a physical education major at Texas Tech. And, it took me six years to get that. That's always a little surprising when people look at some of my business accomplishments.

What do you consider to be your superpower?

I just don't quit.

What is your greatest lesson?

I always believe the best in people. And… the stripes on a leopard won't change. That just means accept that you can't change everybody. Don't get hung up on trying to make someone be or do something they don't want to be.

Connect with Paul Herchman by emailing paul.h@gethairmd.com or finding him on LinkedIn: https://www.linkedin.com/in/paulherchman/ And to learn more about GetHairMD go to https://gethairmd.com/

LINDA GRIZELY

When the Shell Breaks
A Story of Transformation

Linda Grizely is a financial planner, educator, and motivational speaker who has empowered hundreds of individuals on their transformational journeys. She thrives on inspiring others and is widely recognized for her ability to connect deeply, create a safe space for personal growth, and cultivate an environment where people feel truly seen and heard.

The Year of Awakening

For a long time, I pushed myself to make everything perfect. I worked hard to create an image of a flawless life. I was trying to prove to others, and to myself, that I had made it.

That drive came from the challenges I faced growing up in a lower socioeconomic environment and being a single teenage mother. My drive was my way of proving to the world, and to myself, that where I started didn't define me and that I was accomplished, no matter the obstacles.

But sometimes, the hardest challenges are the ones we experience through the people we love.

In 2007, my young adult daughter was facing some hard battles. We sought the best support, resources, and guidance for her, but no matter how hard everyone tried, she couldn't be persuaded to choose a healthier path. It was heartbreaking. We had to let her walk on her own journey. It was one of the hardest things I've ever done. Tough love is tough on everyone. I'm very grateful we still have her in our lives today.

And then there was my brother, who was brilliant and Mensa-level smart but battling the demons of alcoholism and depression. He leaned on me as a confidant, and I did my best to support him. Though I didn't struggle with addiction or depression myself, in retrospect, I can see reflections of my own challenges in his. We both faced limitations in finances, education, social connections, opportunities, and big-picture thinking. In the end, his demons dragged him under. He took his own life at age 40, in September of 2007.

Looking back, I see that these challenges taught me lessons that I could only grasp by living through them. One of those lessons is that growth isn't always about personal victories—it's also about learning how to accept others as they are, even when it hurts.

I had spent so much time trying to control every detail of my life, believing that if I just worked hard enough, I could shape everything into perfection. But the truth hit me hard; I realized I couldn't control everything.

No matter how much I tried, I couldn't take away my daughter's struggles or ease my brother's pain. That was a bitter pill to swallow.

Both of their journeys came to a head that year, 2007, a year that changed everything. In the end, for me, it became more than a year of adversity—it was an awakening.

Embracing Imperfection

I had always been afraid of failure. But sometimes, what we see as failure isn't about personal shortcomings—it's about accepting the hard truth that some things are beyond our control. These experiences forced me to realize I couldn't control everything. And that truth, as painful as it was, cracked my shell of perfection and allowed me to start breaking free.

I saw this change in action in a small, fun way one night when I went out to karaoke. Previously, I would go out with others who sang, and I would have a great time, but I never joined in. I was terrified of what others would think, and I hated the idea of being imperfect. But one night in 2008, after everything I had been through, I stood up and sang, fully aware that it wouldn't be good, much less perfect. And you know what? I didn't care. It was freeing and gave me a much-needed outlet for my emotions. It was a small act, but it felt monumental. It was my first step toward vulnerability and letting go of the need to be perfect.

This shift in my mindset didn't happen overnight, but facing things I couldn't control forced me to stop hiding behind a facade of perfection. It taught me to be more open, more vulnerable, and to show myself more grace. To allow myself to have the same compassion I give to others. I was beginning to learn that growth doesn't happen in neat, picture-perfect moments—it happens in the mess and the rawness of the journey. And sometimes, it happens when we're learning to accept things we once fought so hard to change. I was emerging as a different person. I was stronger, more self-aware, and no longer afraid to embrace the messiness of life. I began to continually step outside of my comfort zone.

The Evolution of Mindset

Ten years later, in 2017, life looked a bit different. I was post-divorce, newly remarried, and focused on building my life through external achievements.

I was building my resume through education, gaining new skills, and once again proving to myself and others that I could succeed. I was constantly pushing forward, checking the boxes of accomplishments, and looking for the next thing to add to my list.

That year, 2017, I sat in my first mastermind event, listening to the ideas and insights being shared, when I had an epiphany: I had been so focused on external growth that I had neglected internal work that was equally, if not more, important. And, that success isn't just about what you accomplish, it's also about how you see the world and your place in it.

I began to understand that success wasn't just about achieving more or accumulating accolades. Success was about the way I thought and the beliefs I held about myself, about what was possible, and how I approached challenges. If I wanted to grow in a more meaningful way, I needed to stop seeking external proof of my worth and start focusing on my internal transformation. I needed to think bigger, and not just about what I could do, but about who I could become.

Thinking bigger didn't happen overnight; it took a lot of introspection. I had to ask myself tough questions like, "What limiting beliefs am I holding onto? What if I saw setbacks not as roadblocks, but as redirections to something better? How would my life change if I believed abundance was available to everyone, including me?" It was uncomfortable at times, but this internal journey became just as important as any external milestone I had ever reached.

As I shifted my mindset, I began to focus on my ability to take risks and on believing in what was possible for me. Thinking bigger meant embracing challenges as opportunities, seeing failures as stepping stones, and understanding that I didn't have to be perfect. I started trusting myself to take on new challenges, to invest in my internal and mindset growth, and to embrace uncertainty as part of the journey. No longer limited by small thinking, I began to see endless possibilities.

In 2018, I gave my first motivational talk, titled "What It Means to Be Resilient." Over the years, I've modified and refined it, and I still give this talk today, and a workshop version as well.

Who I've Become

Looking back in 2025, I can see how far I've come, not just in what I've accomplished, but in who I've become.

Becoming your best self isn't always about pushing through your challenges. Sometimes, it's about learning to accept the things you can't control and stepping aside from paths that aren't yours to walk. You can remain on the sidelines and cheer for people on their journeys—whatever they are. Other times, it is about discovering your most authentic self and unlocking your greatest capabilities from within. Now, I'm driven to be the resource to others that I never had, offering guidance and support that can make a difference in the lives of others.

As a financial planner, I have the privilege of listening to clients' unique stories and journeys, and together, we craft financial goals and plans that reflect their values and aspirations. One of the most rewarding parts is educating clients by breaking down complex financial concepts into clear, digestible pieces, helping to ensure they feel empowered and confident in making decisions about their future.

As a financial educator, I strive to make money feel less intimidating and more approachable. My goal is to meet people where they are and provide tools that foster financial clarity and confidence. I believe financial literacy is a powerful form of self-respect, and I'm passionate about equipping others with the knowledge to make informed, values-aligned decisions.

As a motivational speaker and workshop facilitator, I encourage people to broaden their perspectives, challenge their perceived limitations, and pursue a life of greater achievement and fulfillment. I aim to ignite a spark of inspiration and motivation that drives lasting, positive change in people's lives.

Still Becoming

Even now, the journey continues. I don't have all the answers about where the road leads, and I'm okay with that. Instead of striving for a perfect finish line, I'm learning to trust the unfolding. Life has taught me that growth doesn't stop when you reach a milestone; it deepens as you show up, stay open, and allow yourself to be shaped by new experiences.

I am still building, still dreaming, still becoming. And maybe that's the most important lesson of all: transformation isn't a one-time event, it's a lifelong invitation.

Q&A WITH LINDA

If you could have dinner with three people, living or deceased, who would they be and why?

Maya Angelou, because of her profound impact on personal growth, resilience, and empowerment. I would ask her what advice she has for those seeking to inspire others.

Mel Robbins, because of her experience in motivation, personal growth, and practical strategies for overcoming challenges. Mel always seems to send out the message that I need to hear right when I need it most.

Oprah Winfrey, because of her journey from adversity to becoming a global icon of empowerment and resilience. Her insights into storytelling, connection, and inspiring others through authenticity would make for an enriching conversation.

What is a motto or mantra you live by?

Progress over perfection. This reflects my belief in embracing growth, taking bold steps, and learning from every experience. It aligns with my mission to inspire others to think bigger, overcome challenges, and move forward with confidence, even when the path isn't perfect.

What are you passionate about?

I am passionate about inspiring personal growth, resilience, and empowerment in others. I believe that everyone has untapped potential and the ability to achieve their dreams. I hope to connect deeply with others, helping them think bigger and embrace meaningful change. I thrive on empowering people to align their values with their goals, turning challenges into opportunities for growth and fulfillment.

What is your guilty pleasure?

Without a doubt, Nestlé Toll House chocolate chip cookies are my guilty pleasure. I've had the recipe memorized since I was 12, though these days, I make them with gluten-free flour.

What are a few of your favorite quotes?

Hands down, my favorite quote is, "The ultimate measure of a man is not where he stands in moments of comfort and convenience, but where he stands at times of challenge and controversy," by Martin Luther King Jr. This powerful statement emphasizes the importance of character and resilience and has guided me through some difficult times.

Another great one by MLK, Jr. is, "Faith is taking the first step even when you don't see the whole staircase." This encourages taking bold, courageous actions toward your goals, even when the full path is unclear. It speaks to the power of trust and perseverance in the face of uncertainty and aligns with my life.

I also love this powerful quote from Maya Angelou: "We may encounter many defeats, but we must not be defeated." This speaks to resilience and the strength to rise above challenges, reminding us that setbacks are part of the journey, but they don't define us.

Have you had any past challenges that turned out to be blessings?

I can't think of a single challenge I've faced that didn't ultimately bring something positive. Often, I reflect on opportunities I lost, only to discover that an even better opportunity was just around the corner, and I wouldn't have been able to seize it if the first had worked out.

Linda Grizely has spent a lifetime thinking bigger, overcoming obstacles, and empowering others to do the same. If you're looking to gain clarity on your finances, would like Linda to speak at your event, or want to explore what she's up to next, visit LindaGriz.com/connect.

 Follow Linda on LinkedIn

TYLER VINSON

Becoming Your Best Self
The Person You Were Always Meant to Be

Tyler Vinson is a professional real estate investor with 23 years of experience and a real estate tokenization expert, author, and speaker. He is the Co-Founder and CEO of REtokens USA Inc. and the Founder of Extant Investment Real Estate Company. He is an Eastern Washington University alum with degrees in marketing and international business.

The Moment I Had to Decide

Just days before Christmas in 2008, I was sitting alone in my bedroom with my head in my hand. Everything had fallen apart. Several of the tenants in my rental houses couldn't pay or had just up and moved with no notice. My bank account was nearly drained, and my car had just been totaled in a snowstorm. I felt lost and broken—mentally and physically.

I couldn't make money as a Realtor because the banks were not making loans. I was out of money, and my real estate was now a negative monthly cash flow. My empty properties needed fixing since the tenants had vacated. I couldn't do it myself because I was injured and fighting with the insurance company for a replacement vehicle. With three small children, two of whom were twin preemies needing specialized formula and medical plans, I felt like my dreams of being a real estate entrepreneur had come to an end.

I remember standing there in the kitchen, looking at the ground, when my former wife said to me, "How are you going to pay the mortgage? You can't even support your family! You need to get a real job!" The weight of those comments was so heavy... I couldn't help but think she was right. In the bedroom, I cried as I finally printed out an updated résumé. I sat there and stared at it, knowing I was about to walk away from my professional dreams.

But what I didn't realize at the time was that this would be the beginning of my journey to become my best self.

Radical Ownership

The truth that has shaped my life more than any other is this: **We are each responsible for where we are in life.**

We may not be responsible for what happens to us—trauma, betrayal, a crashing market—but we are always responsible for how we respond.

That was a hard truth to swallow as a young father—with a collapsing real estate portfolio, no income, and the weight of my family's future on my shoulders.

I had every excuse to quit. To blame the economy. To point the finger at my tenants. To be a victim of the timing. But none of that would have changed anything.

So, I made a decision.

Not a grand, cinematic one. It was one of quiet desperation. I slid the printed resume into the nightstand drawer and sat in silence. At the moment, I didn't feel very smart. But I did know I needed to come at this with a mindset of abundance. I knew that thinking only in terms of how to make enough money to pay my bills was not going to direct me on the right path. So, I asked myself:

If I had $1 million in the bank—what would I be doing right now?

And that was the moment. That question required me to shift my mindset away from scarcity, and I started to imagine.

The Power of Visualization

I deeply believe that you have to **visualize and feel the life you want before you live it.**

Every single thing I have in my life today—from the car I drive, to the lake house where I spend summers with my family—I have seen, visualized, and even daydreamed about hundreds of times.

But, visualizing your best self isn't just about closing your eyes and daydreaming.

It's about crafting a vision with *clarity*. Seeing it so clearly, you can describe the smell of your office, the feel of the leather steering wheel, the sound of your children's laughter echoing off the dock. When I had that level of clarity in my mind, my decisions began to align with who, deep down, I really was. I made choices, sometimes unconsciously, and I began showing up as the person I visualized.

Identity Is Everything

Becoming your best self starts with understanding who you are and who God intends you to be.

The best version of you is not something outside of you. It's not someone you "achieve" or fabricate. The best version of you is already inside of you.

That version of you is being blocked—often by old programming: fear, doubt, laziness, shame, or a belief system handed to you by someone else or your environment. Becoming your best self requires letting that old version of you die so the next version of you can be born.

It requires you to consciously reprogram your mind.

It requires you to break up with mediocrity.

It requires you to be ruthless in your honesty and disciplined in your behavior.

I've lived both sides. I've tasted success and I've almost lost it all. Let me tell you, **success is one thing; sustaining it is a completely different beast.**

The Real Work is in the Routine

There's a myth that becoming your best self comes from one heroic act. One flash of brilliance. It doesn't.

If you want to become your best self, you need more than another motivational video. You need a routine and habits that create consistency. So that, little by little, you become who you are intended to be.

For me, that looks like waking up at 4:00 a.m.

From there, it's black coffee, scripture, meditation, and reading professional or personal development.

At 6:00 a.m., I dive into my most important creative or focus work for two to three hours, and then it's off to the gym. My mind is already tuned to the frequency of discipline, clarity, and abundance before most people have gotten out of the shower.

These aren't hacks. They're anchors.

Anchors that keep me from drifting when the winds of stress, uncertainty, and chaos start blowing.

Real transformation is found in the habits you commit to, not the performances you hope for.

Mission Matters

My personal mission is simple: Help people build wealth through real estate and achieve freedom through cash flow.

That mission has shaped my businesses, my investments, and my conversations. It's who I have always been becoming.

After the day that I slid my resume back into the drawer, I navigated multiple business models in search of the best way to serve this mission. Some failed. Some barely survived. Every iteration brought me closer to the model that I believe will allow me to help the most people. A real estate investment marketplace that evens the playing field—REtokens.

I co-founded REtokens with one purpose: to make real estate investing accessible—at amounts that work for everyday people. Not just the wealthy. Not just the insiders. Almost everyone.

We tokenize real estate so that ownership can be fractionalized, transparent, and accessible. I believe in a marketplace that democratizes access to one of the most proven wealth-building tools in history.

This isn't about hype. It's about impact.

It's about helping the everyday investor break through the walls that kept them out. It's about a path to real ownership and real cash flow.

And it's the legacy I plan to leave.

Faith, Vision, and the Long Game

My faith has always played a central role in my journey. I believe God has a purpose for each of us—a purpose unlocked through becoming the best version of yourself.

You are not defined by your past, your bank account, or your last mistake. You are defined by the person God created you to be—and your willingness to pursue becoming that person with everything you've got.

I'm a father. A husband. A real estate entrepreneur. A speaker. A creator. But above all else, I'm a man who decided not to quit.

Not after the crash.

Not after the divorce.

Not after the sleepless nights trying to make payroll.

And definitely not now.

Who You Are Becoming

You were not put here to live a life of doubt and limitation.

You were designed with a unique purpose and a unique potential. But unlocking that version of you requires action. Clarity. Discipline. Faith. Humility. And a relentless commitment to growth.

So who are you becoming?
Not who do you *want* to be.
Not who you were told to be.
But who are you truly becoming—in action, in thought, in spirit?

That is the question I ask myself every morning. And it's the question I leave with you now. Who are you truly becoming—and what does that person need to do today?

Because becoming your best self isn't something you achieve once. It's something you commit to *every single day*.

Q&A WITH TYLER

What is a habit or ritual that has significantly improved your life?
Having an evening routine. I often get asked about my morning routine, but it is a consistent evening routine that sets me up for morning success.

Who is your favorite sports team?
Seattle Seahawks

How do you recharge?
My recharge is to be by myself. Every quarter, I do an isolation session where I turn my phone and computer on airplane mode and go to my lake house by myself for a couple of days.

What is your favorite quote?
"All men dream: but not equally. Those who dream by night in the dusty recesses of their minds wake in the day to find that it was vanity; but the dreamers of the day are dangerous men, for they may act their dreams with open eyes, to make it possible." – T. E. Lawrence, *Seven Pillars of Wisdom*

Have you had any past challenges that turned out to be blessings?

I have found that my greatest challenges are my greatest blessings because life doesn't happen to us, it happens for us.

What makes you feel inspired or like your best self?

Momentum. When I am staying consistent with my designed habits and routine, it generates momentum and my most productive self.

How do you define success?

Success is showing up to become the best version of yourself. Loving relationships, wealth, and spiritual fulfillment are the results.

Tyler Vinson is the CEO and Co-Founder of REtokens USA Inc. Download the "Quickstart Guide to Real Estate Tokenization" at www.REtokens.com or reach out to Tyler about bringing your real estate investment company into the digital future: tylerv@REtokens.com.

LAUREN DONAHUE

The Cave That Changed Everything

Lauren Donahue is a health and wellness expert and creator of Unplugged, a 9-step process to help people reconnect with their true selves. A certified trainer and former fitness studio owner, her work has reached hundreds of thousands and been highlighted in national media from print to prime-time TV. She hosts global retreats, runs Retreat Launch Formula for aspiring leaders, and founded Laleigh Coffee, which supports the Parkinson's Foundation.

Ready, Go

I never planned on living in a cave for 60 days. In fact, if you had asked me a few years earlier what my life was about, I would have told you it was about *more*: more work, more connections, more noise, more doing. I was running fitness studios, modeling, traveling constantly, and building a career in health and wellness.

From the outside, it looked like I had it all figured out. My name had been featured in places like *USA Today Sports, Marie Claire Magazine, Mind Body Green*, and I'd appeared on **FOX, NBC, CBS, and E! Entertainment.** I had tens of thousands of people following me online, and I was leading workouts that reached hundreds of thousands worldwide.

But here's what no one could see: I was drowning in *always on* culture. My phone was my alarm clock. Notifications dictated my day. I said yes to every opportunity, every meeting, and every coffee chat because I didn't want to miss out. My mind never stopped racing, and my body was running on autopilot.

The life I had built was full of movement, but it lacked stillness. Full of connection, but often missing depth. I didn't know it yet, but I was desperately craving an interruption.

To my surprise, that interruption came in the form of a cave.

Life in the Cave

I was invited to be a part of a reality TV show where I spent 60 days in a cave. The cave wasn't glamorous. There was no electricity, no Wi-Fi, no hot showers. Just me, the natural elements, and an unrelenting silence that left nowhere to hide. For the first few days, I battled restlessness. My fingers reached for a phone that wasn't there. My body twitched with the energy of habits I had carried for years.

But then, after about seven days, something shifted.

I began to hear things I hadn't heard in years: the sound of my breath, the rhythm of my footsteps, the subtle hum of the Earth itself. I felt my nervous system soften. The pressure to perform, to respond, to "keep up," dissolved.

In the darkness of that cave, I started to see myself more clearly than ever before. Without distractions, I had to confront the truth of who I was, what I believed, what I feared, and who I wanted to become.

During those 60 days of radical disconnection, I began to imagine a different way of living. A way that wasn't about constant *doing*, but intentional *being*.

Lessons from the Cave

Several lessons from those 60 days became the foundation for everything I do now.

1. Silence is a teacher.

We are so used to filling silence with podcasts, music, conversations, and scrolling. But silence, I learned, has wisdom. It's in the quiet that your inner voice becomes audible. So many answers I had been seeking through external sources revealed themselves to me in the silence. I realized those answers had been within me waiting for me to get quiet and still.

2. Discomfort is growth.

The cave was uncomfortable, cold, dark, and unfamiliar. But that discomfort stripped away everything superficial and taught me resilience. When you can sit with discomfort, you unlock strength. I now seek and befriend discomfort because I know that is where I expand and grow the most!

3. Less is more.

Without technology, clothes, or comforts, I realized how little we need to survive and thrive. What I missed most wasn't stuff. It was connection, presence, and simplicity.

4. Presence is power.

The cave forced me into the present moment. There was no multitasking. No rushing. Just being. And from that presence came clarity. It taught me to be where my feet are because there is nowhere else to be other than where we are. People can really feel when you are present and not distracted. I believe that is how we connect deeply with others.

The Birth of *Unplugged*

When I returned from the cave, I knew I couldn't go back to life as usual. The experience had rewired something in me. I felt calmer, clearer, and more grounded than I had in years, or maybe ever.

And yet, the moment I stepped back into society, the notifications, the noise, and the busyness all came rushing back. That's when I realized: if I wanted to hold onto what I had learned, I needed practices, anchored habits, that would keep me aligned with what mattered most.

That's how *Unplugged* was born.

At first, it was just for me—a simple routine to help me carry the lessons of the cave into everyday life. But soon, I realized these steps weren't just for me. They were for anyone who felt overwhelmed, distracted, and disconnected. They were for the mom juggling a thousand things, the entrepreneur glued to their inbox, the student pulled in every direction.

The *Unplugged* 9-Step Framework

U – Union (with yourself)

"Within you, there is a stillness and a sanctuary to which you can retreat at any time and be yourself." – Hermann Hesse

Practice: Begin each morning in union with yourself. Place your hand on your heart, close your eyes, and take five intentional breaths. You may choose to pray, meditate, or simply sit in silence. Ask yourself: *What do I need today to feel whole?*

N – Nourish (mind, body, soul, relationships)

"Take care of your body. It's the only place you have to live." – Jim Rohn

Practice: Choose one way to nourish each area today: mind, body, soul, and relationships. Write it down. (Example: read 10 pages, drink more water, pray for someone, send a handwritten card to a friend or family member). Small daily nourishment compounds into long-term vitality.

P – Play

"Play is the highest form of research." – Albert Einstein

Practice: Write down one way you'll play today, something that makes you laugh, move, or feel lighthearted. It could be as simple as dancing to a song, playing catch, or doodling for five minutes.

L – Learn

"Once you stop learning, you start dying." – Albert Einstein

Practice: Learn something new today. Read a chapter, listen to a podcast, or ask someone you love a thoughtful question. Jot down the single biggest takeaway and how you can apply it immediately.

U – Unleash (let go)

"You can't start the next chapter of your life if you keep re-reading the last one." – Unknown

Practice: Write down one thought, belief, or resentment you're ready to let go of. Imagine yourself holding it in your hand, then visualize releasing it, blowing it away like a feather, or dropping it into water.

G – Gratitude

"Gratitude turns what we have into enough." – Melody Beattie

Practice: Instead of just listing things, try *feeling* gratitude. Write down five things you're grateful for and take a breath after each one, imagining your heart expanding as you acknowledge it.

G – Generosity

"The meaning of life is to find your gift. The purpose of life is to give it away." – Pablo Picasso

Practice: Identify one way you can give today, your time, encouragement, presence, or a small act of kindness. Write it down and commit to doing it.

E – Exercise

"If you don't take time for your wellness, you will be forced to take time for your illness." – Unknown

Practice: Move your body in a way that feels joyful. Instead of focusing on duration or calories, ask yourself: *How can I move in a way that feels good today?* Write down your chosen movement.

D – Declare (I AM)

"I AM are two of the most powerful words, for what you put after them shapes your reality." – Joel Osteen

Practice: Write down three "I AM" statements that reflect who you are becoming. Example: *I am strong. I am worthy of love. I am walking in purpose.* Say them out loud while looking in the mirror.

Life After the Cave

The cave was the catalyst. But what happened after is just as important.

I carried *Unplugged* into everything I did. When I climbed **Mount Kilimanjaro**, I leaned on the resilience and presence I had cultivated in silence. When I launched **worldwide retreats**, I built them around the idea of creating space. Space for people to breathe, reflect, and reconnect with themselves.

I launched my brand, **Unplugged**, and began teaching others the exact practices that had transformed my life in the cave. From online coaching to retreats along the **Camino de Santiago**, I've seen firsthand how powerful these steps are for people from every walk of life.

I've stood on stages across the country, spoken on news outlets, and sat with women at the mayor's house in Los Angeles, all to share one message: *you don't have to live in a cave for 60 days to experience this kind of transformation.* You just have to unplug daily, intentionally, and consistently.

Becoming Your Best Self

Here's the truth: becoming your best self isn't about adding more. It's not about more followers, more accolades, more hustle. It's about subtraction. Removing the noise, the distractions, and the false expectations, until what's left is the truest version of you.

For me, that discovery happened in a cave. For you, it might happen in your kitchen before the kids wake up, on a quiet walk without your phone, or in the 10 minutes you choose to breathe deeply before opening your laptop.

Resilience isn't built by avoiding discomfort. It's built by leaning into it. Attitude isn't about pretending everything is fine. It's about choosing how to respond when life strips everything away. And personal growth isn't about reaching some destination. It's about becoming more of who you already are when you remove all the noise.

That's what *Unplugged* is about. That's what the cave taught me. And that's the invitation I want to leave you with: to unplug, to return to presence, and to give yourself permission to simply be.

Q&A WITH LAUREN

If you could have dinner with three people, living or deceased, who would they be?

Jesus, Mother Teresa, and my grandfather, Raleigh. All three have profoundly influenced the way I live, and I would love to sit with them, learn from their wisdom, and hear their stories.

What is a motto or mantra you live by?

The mantra I live by is something my grandfather, Raleigh, repeated to me often: "The cream always rises to the top."

At first, it was just a phrase I heard over and over again as a child, but with time and experience, I came to understand the depth of what he meant. He taught me that while some people may climb to the top quickly, sometimes by cutting corners or taking advantage of others, that kind of success is rarely sustainable. True success, the kind that lasts, is built on integrity, patience, and doing the right thing even when it's hard.

This mantra has carried me through seasons of disappointment, moments when doors closed, or when I felt overlooked. It reminds me that if I stay kind, tell the truth, keep showing up for people, and do what I say I'm going to do, eventually the results will come.

How do you recharge?

For me, recharging happens when I unplug… fully, intentionally, and without apology.

I recharge best when I'm completely off-grid for a few days, tucked away in the mountains, sleeping in a cozy cabin or under the stars, with a creek nearby or the sound of a waterfall in the distance. I hike, move my body, breathe in fresh air, and let the rhythm of nature reset my nervous system. There's something sacred about waking up with the sun, journaling by a fire, and remembering who you are without the digital world dictating your every move.

Whether it's a few days away in nature or a few intentional moments of movement and stillness each day, recharging is less about escape and more about returning to yourself.

What is a habit or ritual that has significantly improved your life?

Two habits have profoundly shaped my life and supported me in becoming my best self: my Unplugged Mornings and my daily mile run.

Running one mile a day, no matter what, has been life-changing. The first time I committed to it, I ran for 444 days in a row. The second time, I made it 1,032 consecutive days. Those miles weren't just about fitness, they were healing. Some of the hardest chapters of my life were processed and released through those daily runs. And the beauty of the mile is that it removes the excuse of "I don't have time." In just 10 minutes, I could sweat, reset my mindset, and remind myself of my strength. That simple act of consistency became a powerful anchor.

Unplugging and running have taught me that small, daily choices shape our lives more than we realize. And they've helped me become more grounded, more resilient, and more me.

What do you consider your superpower?

My superpower is connection. My friends often call me "the human connector," because as soon as I meet someone, I instinctively know who I want to introduce them to.

For me, it's not just about networking, it's about weaving community. I believe we are all better when we're connected, and some of the greatest joys in my life have come from bringing people together in meaningful ways.

What are some favorite places you've traveled to?

Adventure travel is where I come alive, so some of my favorite places are the ones that pushed me outside my comfort zone and connected me more deeply to myself and the world.

One of the most memorable experiences of my life was hiking Mount Kilimanjaro in Africa, followed by a safari through the Serengeti and spending time helping out in local villages. The physical challenge of the climb, the awe of seeing wildlife in their natural habitat, and the grounding perspective of connecting with the communities there made it truly unforgettable.

Another favorite was traveling through Thailand and the surrounding regions, exploring the islands, experiencing the culture in Chiang Mai, standing in wonder at Angkor Wat in Cambodia, and even stopping in Singapore. That trip was full of adventure, beauty, and playfulness.

And perhaps the most transformative journey I've taken was walking the Camino de Santiago in Spain, a 500-mile pilgrimage that is as much about the inner journey as the outer one. Along that trail, I found so much healing, silence, and connection, not just with myself, but with fellow travelers from all around the world.

What books do you often recommend?

I love recommending books that have not only inspired me, but also given me practical tools to live with more clarity, purpose, and alignment. A few of my favorites are:

The One Thing by Gary Keller – A powerful reminder to simplify and focus on what truly matters most. It taught me how to cut through distractions and pour my energy into the things that actually move the needle forward in life and business.

Secrets of the Millionaire Mind by T. Harv Eker – This book shifted the way I think about money and abundance. It helps you identify and reprogram the beliefs that may be holding you back financially, which is essential for creating a life of freedom.

I Can See Clearly Now by Dr. Wayne Dyer – A beautiful reflection on the power of perspective and how everything in our lives is connected. It's a book that brings peace and trust in the journey.

The Surrender Experiment by Michael A. Singer – One of my all-time favorites, it reminds me of the power of letting go and trusting life's flow. It's a testament to how much beauty unfolds when we stop trying to control everything and instead allow life to guide us.

What makes you feel like your best self?

I feel like my best self when I'm prioritizing self-care, not just the surface level kind, but the deep, intentional rhythms that keep me grounded, energized, and connected to my purpose.

For me, that starts with sleep. When I've had eight solid hours, everything else flows. From there, my Unplugged Morning routine is essential.

Daily movement is another non-negotiable.

Adventure and connection light me up, and when those are part of my life, I feel fully aligned.

I'm at my best when I'm consistently choosing practices that honor my body, mind, and spirit and when I make time for the people and experiences that bring me joy.

Lauren Donahue is a global retreat leader, speaker, and founder of Unplugged, guiding thousands to step away from the noise and reconnect with what matters most. Connect with Lauren at laurenldonahue@gmail.com or www.laleigh.com.

 Connect With Lauren

ANTHONY CHARA

From Burned Out to Purpose
The Journey to Teaching Real Estate Investing and Building Wealth

Anthony Chara is a real estate investor with experience dating back to 1993. He turned to apartments full-time in 2004 and has since owned or syndicated over 2,100 apartment units, a hotel, and agriculture around the world. Today, he's managing partner of Apartment Mentors and founder of Success Classes, educating beginning and sophisticated investors.

Trapped

It was 1986, and my job was literally making me sick and tired.

I was flying from Denver, where I lived, to Las Vegas for the third week in a row. My mission: convince the company's technical support that the equipment failure they kept sending me to resolve was a software issue, not hardware.

My job was flying around the 11 western states to fix equipment problems on high-speed electronic mailing and sorting equipment—the problems that others couldn't figure out. I was very good at my job. Unfortunately, I was an electronic technician, not a software engineer.

Thirty minutes into the flight to Vegas, I felt a wave of nausea. I looked for the restroom, but the food cart was in the aisle behind me, and the beverage cart was in front of me. I was trapped and determined not to throw up in front of anyone, even in a little disposable bag.

I didn't realize it at the time, but the stress from my JOB was getting to me—in my gut, in my chest, in the trap of that cabin full of strangers at 30,000 feet.

From that point forward, every time I got on an airplane, I felt nauseated the entire flight. This in itself was stressful. I saw a gastroenterologist. After two years of appointments and my second endoscopy, I asked my doctor if this could be in my head. The only times I felt nauseated were when I was in a crowded plane, train, bus, church, or movie theater. All situations where I felt "trapped" and couldn't escape.

The doctor said, "Yes, it could be." Two years after that flight to Vegas, I realized that holding in all the stress from work had turned into claustrophobia.

Now that I knew the problem, the short fix was to stop doing things that put me in situations where I felt trapped—like flying. The answer: I quit my job and went into business with a friend creating video CliffsNotes for college courses. This was about the time VHS was becoming popular. Unfortunately, my friend's ego was larger than the business, and we crashed and burned within six months.

I had bills to pay and no income. Looking to return to the industry I had just left, I contacted the salesperson at my former employer and asked for our competitors' contact info. Unbeknownst to me, he contacted his boss in Los Angeles. His boss contacted my former boss's boss. They all agreed; there was no way they wanted me to go to their competitors. At 8:00 a.m. the next day, I got a call from my former employer offering me a job—a local technical position with almost no air travel. I accepted.

The Real Pivot Point

I worked my way back up the ladder, but this time on the management side. When my boss quit, I accepted the position of service manager.

A few years later, the company reorganized. There were 10 service managers in our Western division. The company laid off four of them. They told me I was one of the lucky ones because I got to keep my job! I went from having 13 technicians in four states and a one-million-dollar budget to 35 technicians in seven states and a three-million-dollar budget. My reward for being lucky? A whopping 10% pay increase. And, now I was back on airplanes flying from Colorado to New Mexico, Texas, and Oklahoma.

Four months later, and once again, my JOB was making me sick and tired.

The Courage to Leap

At that point, I had a conversation with my wife, Sue. Fortunately, she was understanding and had a good job herself. She knew I was unhappy and stressed. No one should stay in a job they hate.

I didn't know what I was going to do, but I knew what I didn't want to do. We'd find a way to survive even if her job wasn't enough to support us long-term. It was enough for now.

I quit. But I knew if I quit right away, all of my stress would end up on my former techs. I told my boss I'd stay on board for four more months, or until he found my replacement, whichever occurred sooner.

I think the most surprising reaction I received was from multiple techs. They didn't believe me when I told them I resigned and didn't have another job lined up. A few of them said, "There's no way I could quit without having something else lined up." I learned long ago from a mentor that you have to take your foot off of first base to get to second base. That was not the first time I quit a job without having something else lined up. In the back of my mind, I just knew I'd land on my feet.

It took three months to find my replacement. I took some time off to decompress and started looking for second base.

Around this same time, Sue and I learned several things that changed our lives forever. First, the tax code is written to benefit people who invest, especially if they invest in real estate and in creating businesses. Investing in real estate creates housing for people who can't afford to buy their own home. And, people who start businesses create jobs.

Second, if you follow the IRS playbook, you learn one reason why most people struggle to make ends meet. If you think about your paycheck, what's the first thing your employer retains from your earnings? Taxes! The more you make, the more the government keeps. You make money, pay taxes, and live off the remainder.

However, if you follow the rules for owning your own business, you pay all of your expenses first, then get taxed on the remainder. In essence, you have a lower tax rate because you're taxed last instead of first.

With this new revelation in mind, my wife and I attended a franchise/business show in Denver. We found a few options we were interested in, and the one that made the most sense was a restaurant delivery business, much like Uber Eats or DoorDash today. But this was back in 1997, when the internet was in its infancy.

We took the training and began signing up restaurants that would allow us to deliver their food. It started slowly but picked up quickly—almost too quickly. Finding good, reliable drivers was the crux of the business. Sometimes, I'd have to do deliveries. Sometimes, my wife would have to do deliveries after she worked an 8- or 9-hour day as a senior finance manager for a software developer. It was the nature of the beast.

Imagine ordering food and having someone deliver your order dressed in nice business attire. She got some looks!

After three years of busting our butts, my wife told me either the business went or she went. We were spending too much time working in the business instead of working on the business. I chose my wife.

Fortunately, around this same time, we heard about another company buying up small restaurant delivery businesses like ours to create one large, coast-to-coast operation. We sold to them for a nice profit, and it was onto the next adventure.

One thing I did learn was that, even though I was working a lot, I was much happier working for myself than I was working for someone else. It was much more satisfying.

Being so entrenched in the business, I didn't realize we had grown the company 40% year over year for three straight years. Wow! I was proud of what we had accomplished.

The Next Adventure

I heard a late-night infomercial about buying real estate notes or the accounts receivable of a cash-restricted business at a discount. The latter is called factoring. I gave this a shot for six months, but it wasn't working for me. However, Sue and I attended a national note convention in Dallas, Texas, to learn more, and that's where we met Robert Allen.

Robert Allen was a renowned real estate guru who taught people how to become real estate investors. We liked what we heard and signed up to become his protégés. We're glad we did, as his training started us on the path we lead today.

We learned about wholesaling (buying properties at a discount and flipping the contract to someone else), doing fix and flips (buying run-down properties at a discount, fixing them up ourselves, and selling them to end users), marketing, asset protection, and buying apartments.

I tried wholesaling and fixing and flipping a couple of times. It felt too much like a JOB, and I spent too much on the fixing, which reduced profit margins. I was fixing them as if I were going to live there.

Around this same time, I met my first real estate partner, George Antone, at a Robert Allen training on how to put together courses and sell from the stage. Real estate was hot in the early 2000s, so teaching seemed like the next logical step.

Learning to Teach

One of the things George taught me was to take what I learned and to do it. That way, I'd see if I liked it, and I'd see if the training was any good. George called me up and asked me to fly to San Jose, California, where he lived.

"Why," I asked?

He said, "To put into practice what we just learned."

"When do you want me to fly in?"

"This coming Tuesday."

"What are we going to teach?"

"I don't know. We'll figure it out when you get here."

"Where are we going to teach it?"

"I don't know. We'll figure it out when you get here."

"Who are we going to teach it to?"

"I don't know. I'll send out some emails and see who shows up."

I said, "Okay, I'm in!" Talk about a leap of faith.

I arrived on Tuesday, and within 24 hours, we figured out we both knew something about finding and buying properties from people in financial distress, put together a two-hour class that was nothing more than handwritten notes on yellow lined paper, found out the library would let us use a room for free to teach the class as long as we left the door open to the public, and sent out a few emails to find some willing participants.

We ended up with four attendees, three of whom George already knew, and one attendee's brother. I taught the first hour, and George taught the second. The whole experience felt natural to me, and after receiving great feedback from the attendees, I knew I was hooked.

To build this into something bigger, George and I had to figure out what we wanted to teach. There were quite a few people teaching courses on wholesaling and fixing and flipping, so George suggested we teach apartment investing. We only knew one other person at the time teaching that topic. But, as I told George, I had NO experience with apartment investing. George assured me he did have experience and he'd teach me as we went along. We were off and running.

In *Multiple Streams of Income*, Robert Allen and Mark Victor Hansen wrote that the idea of working for the same company your entire life was over, so you'd better concentrate on multiple streams of income to create the life you want.

One of our streams of income was our rental properties. Sue and I owned eight or nine single-family houses and condos at the time. But that alone wasn't enough to replace my income. Teaching others how to become real estate investors could be another stream.

This led me to my current path: teaching and investing around the world.

George created about 90% of our course content, starting with a one-day workshop that led into a three-day boot camp. I taught sections on locating properties and property management, since I knew those already. He and our third partner, David, taught the rest, including evaluating, making offers, financing, due diligence, negotiations, and closing. It was 2005, and I had yet to buy an apartment complex. I relied on George's experience and learned from him as he was teaching everyone else.

The Big Deals

My first deal with George was us riding on the coattails of a developer who had already purchased three large apartment complexes in Tucson, Arizona. He was converting them to condos and was raising five million dollars to complete the conversion. George, David, and I raised $1.35 million from our investors for the project. We were off and running.

Our next two or three deals were similar. Someone else had found the property, analyzed it, put it under contract, and secured financing, and they just needed more cash to close the deal. Joining others who had already been there, done that, enabled us to grow fast and helped me gain experience and credibility.

Ultimately, using Robert Allen's *Multiple Streams of Income* approach, we started honing our strategy. George and I both knew we wanted to create passive income with investing, but at the same time, we realized we couldn't make it on our own. The training was enjoyable, a source of income, and a way to meet potential investors.

We partnered with Real Estate Investment Associations (REIAs) around the country and started teaching our classes coast to coast.

After a few years, we had a falling-out with our third partner. Two years later, George decided he didn't want to travel as much, and he signed the company over to me. By this time, I was teaching the full class, and we had purchased 700-800 apartments.

I was a little scared to go out on my own, but I loved teaching others how to successfully invest in real estate. It also helps when people tell you you're a natural and that you can make a complicated subject like investing in million-dollar apartment complexes easily understandable.

The irony of my story is that I now travel more than I did with my technical job, and my claustrophobia hardly bothers me anymore. I think this is probably because, now, I travel because I want to.

Sue and I teach classes all over the world, which allows us to take "business trips!" One of our favorites is a week-long training on a catamaran in tropical destinations.

Q&A WITH ANTHONY

Who is your favorite musical artist?
Led Zeppelin

If you could have dinner with three people, living or deceased, who would they be?
Benjamin Franklin. He's a great statesman and inventor.

George Washington. He was a reluctant leader who begrudgingly became our first president.

Thomas Jefferson. As one of the founding fathers, he had a huge role in many of our country's historical documents.

How do you recharge?
I camp at Lake McConaughey in western Nebraska with my wife and dogs or travel to some far-off, exotic locale.

What is a habit or ritual that has significantly improved your life?
Working out every morning.

What hobbies do you enjoy?
Golf and watching movies.

What do you consider your superpower?
My wife says my superhero name should be The Instigator! I tend to ask provocative questions to get a reaction out of people.

What philanthropic causes do you support?
Military (Soldiers' Angels, Tunnels to Towers)
American Red Cross
Salvation Army
Denver Rescue Mission
Make a Wish

What are some favorite places you've traveled to?
Fiji, Italy, France, Germany, Alaska, most of the islands in the Caribbean, and Belize.

What books do you often recommend?
Think and Grow Rich by Napoleon Hill
Rich Dad Poor Dad by Robert Kiyosaki

What is one thing you hope people remember about you?
That I made them laugh.

What would you tell your 18-year-old self?
Invest in real estate sooner.

What makes you feel inspired?
My students calling or emailing me about their successes.

If you'd like to connect with educator, entrepreneur, investor, and mentor Anthony Chara or learn more about his Apartment/Commercial properties investing workshops, boot camps, and catamaran training events, you can email him at anthony@successclasses.com or use the QR code.

 Scan for Apartment Mentors educational events.

AMBER DISKIN

The Story Behind the Smile
Resilience, Real Estate, and a Life Built in Vegas

Las Vegas native Amber Diskin is a real estate professional who helps first-time buyers gain confidence and build lasting security through homeownership. A proud mom of two, Amber built her business from the ground up and now works alongside one of her sons. She's known for her honesty, heart, and commitment to helping others take control of their future.

In Contrast

Growing up, you don't know what you don't know. You rely on your parents or guardians to teach you, and you learn from what you see—your family, your friends, and the world around you.

I would consider my upbringing to be middle to lower class. That became clear to me in junior high when some of my friends came from families with more money—and they made sure we knew it. My mom's side of the family were lifelong renters, while my dad's side all owned homes. I remember my mom speaking negatively about people who had more than we did, but even then, I thought, "They worked hard for those things. I want to have nice things too when I grow up." I guess I was lucky to have seen both sides.

On my mom's side, addiction and instability were common. Her siblings struggled with drugs, and her brother was in and out of jail. My dad's side lived very differently. We were much closer to my mom's side, though. My maternal grandparents lived around the corner, and whenever I got mad at my mom, I'd say I was running away—to Grandma's house.

Even though we were close to my mom's side, I always felt like I was treated differently by some of them. My parents were married and took care of me, which wasn't the case for many of my cousins. They'd call me a spoiled brat, but it wasn't my fault my parents weren't on drugs. It hurt being treated differently, but it was just the way it was.

I never liked getting in trouble. If I made a mistake and got punished, I wouldn't do it again. I took responsibility for my actions and understood that I was in control of the decisions I made—and the consequences if I made the wrong ones.

As I got older, I realized that you can't keep blaming your circumstances. I knew I didn't want to end up stuck, struggling, or dependent. I wanted better, and I chose to create a different path.

Wanting Control

I know my parents loved me, but my mom had a very different upbringing than I did. She was controlling, and it took me many years to find my own voice. It wasn't until my mid-20s that I started standing up for myself. We clashed often after that—even about things as simple as car preferences.

When I got pregnant with my first son, Allen, and then my second son, Cole, my relationship with my mom grew more and more strained. My mom was very possessive of Allen, as if he were her child. It was incredibly hard—trying to become my own person while not wanting to upset her. When I had my second son, Cole, she treated him differently. That hurt because I wanted to treat my children equally.

Eventually, my sons' father and I divorced. I waited a few days to tell my mom he wanted a divorce, and her first words were "He's always treated us like crap,"—us as in her and my dad. That was not helpful. I felt like my world was crumbling.

I didn't know then that this painful time would be the beginning of something better.

The divorce felt like a weight lifting off my shoulders. He's a good man and the father of my kids, but we were very young when we got together, and just weren't meant to be.

Finding a Voice

At the time, I didn't have many friends. I had done everything for my ex and our family. While I'm grateful I got to be home with my kids, at 24, I didn't have a voice or know who I really was. After the divorce, I moved back home for three months while I got back on my feet, and I made new friends who helped me realize I could be whoever I wanted to be. I began finding my happy. I was still young, still learning, still growing.

In my business, I'm a strong communicator because what I do is important. But in my personal life, I struggle. Having a controlling parent made it hard for me to communicate effectively as an adult. I was silenced for so long that now, if I feel challenged, I sometimes shut down.

If my mom were still here, I think I'd ask her to go to therapy with me just to speak my truth. She passed away when I was 30 and she was 54. When I get upset about the past, I remind myself: she did the best she could with the tools she had.

True Terror

We all experience trauma—some big, some small. It's not a competition. Trauma can be growing up in an abusive home, having a controlling parent, being in a toxic relationship, or going through a traumatic event.

For me, one of those traumatic events happened on October 1, 2017 at home in Las Vegas.

It was supposed to be a fun weekend at a country music festival with friends. Jason Aldean was just a few songs into his set when we heard the popping sounds. At first, I thought it was something happening on the Strip. Then came the rapid fire. People dropped to the ground. The lights came on. Chaos.

We hit the ground, tried to make phone calls out—nothing. I told my friends, "We have to get the f*** of here." During the breaks in gunfire, we ran.

There were 30,000 people there that weekend. It was like I had tunnel vision. I saw my two friends in front of me, my two friends behind me, and nothing else. I don't remember going back down to the ground again, but they said that we did. We were going through food trucks when I realized there were more people around us. Then I saw the medic tent I had visited on Friday night to get a Band-Aid. I knew right next to that tent was an opening to get out. I told my friends to go that way.

As we were flooding through the gate, I somehow lost them. I stopped and I looked back, and there were so many people there was no way I was going to find them. I remember seeing a girl whose face was bloody. I still wasn't comprehending what was going on. The shooting just kept going and going. I had no idea where it was coming from. I remember seeing officers lined up and going in as we were all running out. When I realized there was no way I was going to find my friends, I just kept running. I knew they had their arms locked two and two, so I knew at least they were together.

I ran into the Hooters parking lot, saw this couple jump in their truck, and asked if I could go with them. They let me in and two other girls. When we were leaving the parking lot, there were so many people coming up to the truck. The driver said, "I'm sorry, we're full," and drove down Tropicana towards Henderson.

That couple drove us to their house in Henderson. I finally got a call through to my husband and told him to meet me there. When he arrived, I cried and said I wasn't going back for my car. He said, "You don't have to. We're going home."

Fifty-Eight

Those eight minutes—from the first shots to getting in that truck—were the longest, most terrifying minutes of my life. I felt like a child who just wanted to teleport home. All I could think about were my boys.

Fifty-eight people lost their lives that night. I wasn't physically hurt, but my scars are emotional.

The community response was incredible. People lifted each other up. Two veterans in my life opened up to me, sharing what to expect when your body reacts to that kind of experience. That helped tremendously. When something happened that caused me to start to go into a panic, at least I knew somewhere in my mind that it was normal to feel that way. Almost eight years after the shooting, my body sometimes still reacts. On July 4th, I went into a state of anxiety. My mind knew I was safe, but my body would not calm down. I put on headphones, cried a little, squeezed my husband Mark's arms all night, and reminded myself that I would feel better in the morning. Thankfully, when I woke up on July 5th, my body was calm, and I felt so much better.

You can let an experience like that destroy you—or you can grow from it. I chose the latter. I still go to concerts. I still love live music. It wasn't easy, but I won't let someone else steal my joy. I'm stubborn like that.

That night changed me. It made me stronger. It gave me clarity. I stopped letting toxic people ruin my peace. I blocked my husband's ex and her mom, and I'm so glad I did. I told my husband, Mark, "I'm done. I can't do this anymore." He completely understood and supported my decision.

It's wild to say, but almost being murdered gave me the courage to finally stand up for myself. People tell me I seem strong and confident. I wish I could always see what they see. Deep down, I often don't feel that way. I've always been a people pleaser. I take on too much. But now, I try to make each day count. You never know when your time will run out.

A Career of Confidence

I met Mark a year after my divorce. He was also divorced with two boys. We took things slow, not wanting to introduce our kids until we knew it was real. I respected that about him. Mark is kind, confident, and never pushes. He encourages. He listens. He's been my rock since 2010.

It was Mark who encouraged me to go solo in real estate. I didn't have the confidence then, but with his support, I took the leap—and it was one of the best decisions I've ever made.

Real estate has treated us well. I've been able to tailor my schedule around my kids. Today, one of our boys works alongside me. We've built something strong.

When I bought my first home, my mom tried to talk me out of it. She didn't want me to leave home. Coming from a family of renters, the idea of homeownership seemed distant or unrealistic. But I knew better.

Helping first-time buyers is one of my favorite parts of this job. Watching young adults achieve the American Dream—and knowing I had a part in it—is a feeling I can't describe.

When it comes to real estate, I'm a great communicator, and I want to educate people on how powerful homeownership can be. Because it's not just about buying a house—it's about choosing your future.

I've walked through some dark valleys, but I've also stood on the other side with clarity and purpose. I don't have it all figured out, and there are still days when self-doubt creeps in—but I've learned that strength doesn't mean never breaking. It means choosing to rebuild—again and again—into someone you're proud of.

Here's to healing. Here's to growth. And here's to building a life you love—one day, one choice at a time.

Q&A WITH AMBER

Do you have a favorite movie?

A Million Ways to Die in the West. It's the stupidest funny movie ever—and I love it! I'm all about laughing and keeping things light. Life's too short to be unhappy.

What is your favorite song or musical artist?

That's tough because it always changes. I really believe music reflects different seasons of life. If I had to pick a top three:
- Linkin Park (We're even going to see the new version of the band this year!)
- Britney Spears
- Carrie Underwood

I love all kinds of music—heavy metal, R&B, pop, even classical—but my go-to is definitely country.

Who is your favorite sports team?

The Golden Knights! I'm a Vegas native, and growing up, we never had a pro team. When the Knights came to town, they became our first, real pro team. I never thought I'd be a hockey fan in the desert—but here I am!

Also… I have this pink flamingo costume I wear to games. It's our thing—when they win, fans throw plastic flamingos on the ice. It's wild and fun!

What is a motto or mantra you live by?

"Everything always works out."

Maybe not the way you expect, but in the end, things do work out. I have to remind myself of that when I'm stressed.

What are you passionate about—and why?

Real estate. It's more than a job—I'm truly passionate about it.

My favorite part is handing over the keys to a first-time buyer. They're usually the most excited and grateful.

Real estate can be stressful, but I do my best to shield clients from the chaos. Most of them end up saying, "You were so calm through the whole thing." I take on a lot of stress behind the scenes so their experience is as smooth as possible.

How do you recharge?

I'm pretty good with self-care. That might be booking a trip, buying concert tickets, getting a massage, or hitting the gym, which is my personal "me time."

Who are your mentors or biggest influences?

My husband, Mark, has been a huge influence in different ways throughout our 15 years together. We've both helped shape each other.

I also have clients who became close friends—they're like adopted parents now. They've been an incredible support system, and I know I can talk to them about anything.

As for real estate, I've had different coaches at different stages. I'm learning when it's time to change voices and evolve—and how to communicate that better.

What is your superpower?

Staying calm in chaos. I can focus and push through even the worst situations. That's also why I always try to get the exit row on a plane:
- I know I'll stay calm and get us out.
- I don't trust strangers with my life.
- No kids!

What causes are close to your heart?

Animals, especially senior dogs. It breaks my heart when people dump their dogs just because they're old and need care. One day, I'd love to open a senior dog rescue where they can live out their final years in peace and comfort. If I donate or volunteer, it's usually with The Animal Foundation.

What are some of the favorite places you've traveled?

Tahiti. Hands down. We stayed in an overwater bungalow in Bora Bora, then visited another small island. It was like something out of a magazine—so calm and peaceful.

What hobbies do you enjoy?

Building Legos! I have several kits on display in my living and dining room—Disney castles, the Snow White cottage, Beauty and the Beast… and a few waiting to be built. It's such a relaxing creative outlet for me.

What advice would you give your 18-year-old self?

It's okay to have your own voice and opinions. You don't have to follow the crowd. Don't let others dim your light, and always trust your gut.

What makes you feel inspired or like your best self?

Conferences. Especially Brian Buffini events. I love that they focus on all areas of life—not just business, but also spiritual, financial, family, and personal growth.

It's not just about selling more homes—it's about becoming a better version of yourself. I leave feeling energized and motivated.

How do you define success?

Balance and freedom. Success isn't just money—it's having the freedom to enjoy life. Spending time with family, having personal space, doing meaningful work, and still being able to have fun—that's what success looks like to me.

Amber Diskin, a proud Southern Nevada native, has been serving her hometown with care and expertise since 2003. Whether you're buying, selling, or just have questions about real estate in the Las Vegas Valley, reach out at AmberSellsVegas@gmail.com or connect on social:
Facebook facebook.com/RealestateGoddess702
Instagram @702realestategoddess

TEON SINGLETARY

SEEDS of EXCELLENCE

With over 25 years of leadership experience in the Army National Guard and the civilian sector, Coach Teon Singletary embodies a remarkable blend of military skills, executive prowess, and inspiration. Through his TSLE Weekly Live Inspiration *podcast, he shares insights on transitioning from a poverty mindset to a growth mindset, empowering listeners to unlock their full potential.*

Story Time

When I talk to young men about making hard choices, I always start with a story. It's about a kid I used to know....

It was the first week of school for this young man. During lunch break, he wandered across the school grounds with a friend. The sun was blazing, and the air was thick with the buzz of new beginnings. The young students approached the athletic field when something caught the young man's eye. In the middle of the field were a group of cadets performing their craft. Rifles spun through the air like helicopter blades, flying from one hand to the next with precision and power. One cadet launched his rifle behind his back, caught it effortlessly, and snapped into a perfect salute.

The student stopped in his tracks, mesmerized. "I want to do that," he said.

Beside him, his friend laughed. "That's JROTC. They treat them like the Army, and they're just cadets."

But something sparked in that student, something deeper than curiosity. That moment planted a seed. It was a calling.

Three years later, that student was no longer a bystander. He became the first sergeant of the C. E. Murray High School Junior Reserve Officers' Training Corps (JROTC) War Eagle Battalion in Greeleyville, South Carolina, and the proud commander of the drill team. Some said he was the best drill master on the team.

The student's pride didn't come from the trophies or the titles. It didn't even come from the reputation that made other schools pack up and leave competitions early. His pride came from the sacrifice. While others spent their breaks hanging out or their evenings playing games, he stayed late drilling, perfecting, and sweating. Rehearsing the craft he once watched from the sidelines with wide eyes, he wasn't just practicing. He was becoming.

Growing into a Leader

The War Eagle Battalion lived by a simple but powerful motto: *"To Motivate Young People to be Better Citizens."* To the student, it wasn't just a motto. It was a mission.

JROTC became more than a program. It became his compass. His foundation. His training ground not just for the field, but for life. It taught him *discipline, character, commitment,* and most of all, **LDRSHIP**: loyalty, duty, respect, service, honor, integrity, and personal courage. These values shaped the young man and guided him toward his future.

In his senior year, this student earned the highest achievement a cadet could, the position of battalion commander. That same year, he enlisted in the Army National Guard.

In the summer of 2005, he became a full soldier. By 2009, he was a commissioned officer through the South Carolina State University ROTC "Mighty" Bulldog Battalion.

Over the years, he deployed, led, succeeded, failed, and learned. And through every challenge, he discovered what leadership was and what it wasn't. Those moments forged him into the leader he is today.

If you're wondering who that student was… **It was me.**

And yes, I stand by this: I'm one of the greatest Drill Masters to ever come through the JROTC War Eagle Battalion and the National Society of Pershing Rifles Kilo-4 Company at South Carolina State University (SCSU). I still take pride in the seeds of excellence within me, and I'll never turn down a friendly rifle drill challenge!

A New Mission

Living that story inspired my journey to become a coach.

I've seen so many young people, and adults, who lack the support they need to foster their seeds of excellence. I want to be that guiding light and help them realize their potential.

This passion led me to partner with the Maxwell Leadership Certified Team and the Neuroencoding Institute, equipping me with valuable tools and insights to support personal growth. I especially enjoy working with individuals who have a vision close to the heart and a strong desire to achieve. Together, we can make a meaningful impact.

I've always lived with the mantra of striving for excellence in everything that I do. Did I hit the mark every single time? No! I made plenty of mistakes and failed a lot. However, I execute what John C. Maxwell teaches, *"Sometimes You Win, Sometimes You Learn."* With that thought process, I began to create a new mindset for myself.

On my *TSLE WLI* podcast, I like to call myself the Motivator of Excellence. This mindset has also supported me within my military career. There were times I was lost and had to fall back on my foundations and what excellence means to me. Striving for excellence is not just words to me, striving for excellence is a lifestyle.

Leadership in Action

During the summer of 2025, I was honored with the opportunity to volunteer as a lead mentor of 30 energetic teenagers during the South Carolina Army National Guard Youth Summer Camp.

The first thing I did was share my expectation of them, which was, of course, we will strive for excellence in everything that we do. Let me tell you, the growth we witnessed in these teenagers was priceless.

What does it mean to strive for excellence? For me, what it doesn't mean is performing average. Average begets average. In other words, average action equals average results. If you don't want average results, then it's time to go beyond average. You need to excel above average. You've got to have that champion mindset. You must create within yourself the thing I call the competitive edge, not to compete with others, but to compete with yourself. Am I a better person today than I was yesterday? This is something I do daily to ensure that I strive for excellence.

What if you made striving for excellence part of your lifestyle? What seeds of excellence would this produce for you?

While you ponder that, I ask that you continue to be great in who God has created you to be. If you do this, I will see you at your peak on the mountain.

Q&A WITH COACH TEON

If you could have dinner with three people, living or deceased, who would they be?
Abraham, David, and King Solomon so that I may witness the true essence of their leadership.

What is a motto or mantra you live by?
You don't know what you don't know, and to go up, you must grow up.

What are you passionate about?
Adding value to others. It feels good to help others and add value to them. It's fulfilling for me. It makes me happy.

How do you celebrate your wins—big or small?
To celebrate a victory, I will treat myself to a round of golf or a few hours of video gaming (my guilty pleasures). I believe celebrating is a strong part of reframing the mind to understand what actions are required for greater success. Celebrating has improved my productivity. It works for me.

How do you recharge?
When I need to recharge, I do something to get away into my own world. That could be going for a drive to the beach or putting in earbuds and listening to some good tunes.

What are a few of your favorite quotes?
- "Be the change you wish to see in the world." – Mahatma Gandhi
- "Be before you Do, Do before you Have." – Zig Ziglar
- "Let go of yesterday so you can reach for tomorrow." – John C. Maxwell
- "If you can look up, you can get up. You got comeback power!" – Les Brown

Who are your mentors and greatest influences?

Undoubtedly, my father, Leon Singletary, stands as the most profound influence in my life. He has shaped the positive aspects of my character. From him, I learned the essence of being a strong, African American man grounded in morals and values. The most enduring lesson he imparted to me is the importance of taking ownership of my decisions and accepting their consequences with maturity.

Also, I owe a debt of gratitude to several teachers from my school days. During my early education, I struggled to grasp many of the lessons presented to me. Through their dedication to education and patience, they provided me with the necessary skills to thrive. They fostered the development of my character, guiding me along the path to becoming the person of integrity I am today.

What is some of the best advice you've received?

Learn a little, do a little. Fall and grow your wings as you fall. Sometimes you win, sometimes you learn. Everything worthwhile is uphill.

What is something most people don't know about you?

I am a gamer. My current system is PS5 and my current game is *Call of Duty*.

What philanthropic causes do you support?

Helping Hands of Georgetown: I worked for them for four years because of the support they offer local citizens.

American Red Cross: I volunteered by providing speaking training for military service members while deployed in Africa. The Red Cross serves service members all around the world.

Friends of Africa: I volunteered over 454 hours. The hope that they offer community members is priceless. I found a new sense of compassion just by being there.

What books do you often recommend?

- *The Slight Edge* by Jeff Olson
- *I Declare* by Joel Osteen
- *Intentional Living* by John C. Maxwell

What are some favorite places you've traveled to?

Barcelona in Spain, Italy, Africa, Germany, and Norway, just to name a few.

What is one thing you hope people remember about you?

He was always happy and willing to add value to others. He lived life with love and compassion.

What would you tell your 18-year-old self?

Do it afraid. While you are young, seize your opportunities.

What has been your greatest lesson?

I had a mentor tell me straight up that I was not a good leader. It forced me to look internally and decide what type of leader I wanted to be in my life. It made me ask myself, "Why am I not a good leader?" This question changed me and changed how I lead.

What makes you feel inspired?

When one of my clients shares with me that I made an impact in their life.

What makes you feel like your best self?

Living life in my giftedness.

How do you define success?

Am I healthy, happy, and financially free? Am I better today than what I was yesterday?

Investing in yourself is crucial, so feel free to connect with Coach Teon Singletary for support. He's excited to provide you with further resources to enhance your life. Download complimentary gifts like his *Reflection Time & Goal Setting* ebook and a lesson taught by Dr. John C. Maxwell.

 Growth comes with dedication and commitment. Commit to your personal growth today.

KATIE KILISZEWSKI

Courage to Endure

Katie Kiliszewski is a wife, mom of three, runner, and mentor to women in eating disorder recovery. She believes if you have faith, you have hope, and if you have hope, you have everything. Katie's is a story of resilience and grit in overcoming anorexia and addiction. Her passion is sharing her story to inspire.

The Perfect Storm

I didn't choose this storm. It chose me.

I've tried to make sense of it all and understand why. I don't know if it was one thing, a series of small things, something I was born with, or a mix of my makeup and environment that created the perfect storm.

When I was 14, I was diagnosed with anorexia. I lived with an eating disorder for close to half of my life. After fighting my way through this storm, I am proud to say I have found freedom. I have reclaimed my life and am proud of where I am today.

There were many small moments in my early years that seemed insignificant, but looking back, were warning signs. First grade brought knots in my stomach. Second grade brought perfection. And in third grade, I'll never forget the first time I felt uncomfortable in my skin, a discomfort that made me want to disappear. Some neighborhood kids singled me out, and, just because I was "bigger" than my friends, they made fun of me. Remembering the name they called me still breaks my heart. I remember thinking, *Is there something wrong with me?* I could see, I wasn't as thin as my friends were. *Does that mean I am not pretty?* And just like that, the weeds of insecurity, judgment, self-criticism, and comparison crept into my childhood.

When I was 10, my pediatrician commented on my weight and told me what foods I should not eat for lunch anymore. From there, my focus on food started to grow. I swapped my sandwiches for salads and was complimented for making "healthy" choices. These compliments only fueled the storm that was brewing within.

It wasn't that anyone told me there was something wrong with me or that I needed to change, but I could feel it in the pit of my stomach. I could hear little whispers telling me that I was not good enough. I was not fast enough. I was not pretty enough. I needed to be this and not that. With every passing year, this unease grew.

Running on Empty

Once running entered the picture, everything changed. I did not know what I was doing when I started restricting and overexercising. I thought I was being healthy by getting in shape. My coaches praised me for my newfound endurance. I had a soccer coach who congratulated me for starting to run and started making me race slower girls on the team. I started thinking that if being a little disciplined made people notice, more would make everyone proud of me.

Fun runs turned into punishment, to shrink, to burn off calories. With every mile, I felt like I was winning. In reality, I was running from the pain, anxiety, fear, and every other uncomfortable feeling I had. I ran alone because that's how I felt, alone.

At 14, I remember going to a new doctor and being told I needed to start logging my food. I was incredibly detailed—exact number of almonds consumed, dated and time-stamped. I lost weight. A win, I thought. I was then referred to an eating disorder psychologist, and I was diagnosed with anorexia.

I don't think I really understood what an eating disorder was when I was first diagnosed. I was a child. I didn't know what I was doing other than trying to be what I thought was healthy. But my struggle with weight and perfection started long before. Those insecurities that had once been small whispers were now a constant scream, and I quickly lost control of the wheel. The Katie everyone knew and loved was just a passenger to her eating disorder.

My need for control and discipline grew. Anxieties around fear of weight gain and loss of control became obsessive. The obsession was a never-ending loop of calculations and restrictions on top of comparisons and competition with peers in my head.

I withdrew from many of my friends. I only had time for my eating disorder. It was all calories in, calories out, run faster, push harder, thinner is the winner. It was never enough. I was never enough. I was placed in my first inpatient facility when I was 15. I felt so alone.

A Mirror of Lies

An eating disorder isn't just about food. An eating disorder is a mental and physical addiction. It brainwashes you into believing rules and rituals you make up for yourself, no matter how insane they may sound. It's about control. Developing a routine so rigid that I did not have to *feel* was a coping mechanism to silence the chaos.

Looking back, I can see how deeply I was trapped. But in the moment, every restriction, every mile, every pound lost felt like progress—like I was finally in control. I felt powerful and worthy.

The power and increased self-esteem were illusions. I was losing myself, piece by piece, until I was nothing more than a shadow of the girl I had once been. A forced smile and a fake "I'm fine" was all that I had become.

By my late teenage years, my eating disorder took over my mind and ran my life until I couldn't take it anymore. When the pain of starvation became too much, I turned to alcohol to turn my brain off.

Drinking was the only thing I found that allowed me to silence the obsessive thoughts. It numbed the hunger and made me forget—temporarily—until the effect wore off and the sick merry-go-round started again. Just like my eating disorder, drinking became a prison of my own making.

I believe in miracles—because it's a miracle that I am still here. Alive. Looking back, I can say with certainty that I am lucky to be alive. It wasn't until recently that I realized how much pain I was actually in. I was drowning in pain. Drinking brought out the worst parts of me. I was unrecognizable and cared about very little, including myself. I settled for abusive relationships. I felt worthless and put myself in dangerous situations. The police were called as a result of my drinking more times than I would like to admit.

Finding Strength in the Struggle

In my late 20s, after years of inpatient hospitalizations, intensive outpatient programs, therapy, heartache, and rock bottom after rock bottom, I broke. I couldn't do it anymore. It took me a long time to get to this point. Sometimes I think too long. But I also don't think I would be the person I am today if I didn't have such a strong determination and a bit of a stubborn heart.

I had just been released from another hospital stay and went to see my therapist. She said, "Katie, you have one of the worst eating disorders I have ever seen. If you don't start changing, you will never change." She gave me an ultimatum: she wanted me to see more doctors and increase my therapy, or she would not see me. I realized I was no longer in control—and I have always hated when I felt controlled. I didn't have the energy in me to keep it up. Every time I hit a new bottom, I lost more and more. I didn't have it in me to keep picking the pieces back up and putting myself back together.

Getting in the car with my dad after that session, I just cried. I said, "Dad, I am done. I can't do it anymore. I don't want to go to therapy anymore. I'm done."

My dad, who has always believed in me, said, "Okay, Kate. We can figure it out together."

I decided to take a break from therapy. This was not a decision I took lightly. I believe in the power of therapy for healing. I'm still in therapy today with someone I look up to and trust, but at that time, taking a break was the right decision for me.

Living with an eating disorder takes tremendous determination, grit, and strength. I am living proof that when that energy is used to fight back against the eating disorder, extraordinary things happen.

This was the first time, after years of fighting against change, that I fought back against my eating disorder so that I could take my power back.

I wasn't just fighting for myself. I was fighting for my future and the life I always wanted. I was fighting for real happiness. I was fighting for the people who had never given up on me, the lights in my life who led me through the darkness until I could see the light.

Healing wasn't easy, but nothing worth fighting for is easy. I had to relearn everything I thought I knew. Years of rules I made for myself were like poison to my brain. I had to "unscribble" my mind and become friends with my uncomfortable feelings.

My eating disorder was like the world's worst boyfriend. Healing can feel like going through a terrible breakup. To this day, every sad love song and angry breakup song reminds me of a time when I was so afraid to let go of what felt comfortable to me. But when I was finally brave enough to break up with my eating disorder, the skies began to clear—and I was able to change.

Things didn't change all at once. I had a lot of hard days, but the more I continued to put one foot in front of the other, the more good days I was able to stack. During this time, I learned I am excellent at getting up every time I fall. Recovery from anything is not perfect, but if you can learn to just keep going, you'll make it to your finish line.

I began to embrace my vulnerability and leaned on my support team: the ones who motivated and never gave up on me, even when I was ready to give up on myself. I am so thankful that my parents always answered their phone. When I felt like I wanted to give up, I would call on my parents, sometimes in the middle of the night. I remember my dad telling me he would do the exact opposite of everything I wanted to do. In a way, I did that. I've learned that mood follows action. With help, I became so focused on a routine that was energy-boosting for me that, eventually, I unscribbled my brain. I still tell myself, if my day is full of energy-boosting activities, it makes sense that I will feel good.

On paper, it all sounds easier said than done. Overcoming an eating disorder is the most challenging thing I've ever had to do. The thoughts are loud and constant at first, but small steps build momentum. In less than a year, I got engaged to my now husband, graduated from college with my degree in psychology, started working full-time at my dad's insurance agency, and bought my first house. I always felt so behind in life, and in a matter of months, I was able to say that this is exactly how I imagined the end of the story would turn out.

I've spent the last 12 years of my life focusing on my recovery, and I am proud of what I have overcome. I feel incredibly grateful to live the life I do today. I have accomplished many things in recovery, but my greatest accomplishment is becoming a mom. I'm a blessed mom of three amazing children who continue to teach and inspire me to grow every day.

I always say my story starts and ends with running. Running, once again, has become my salvation, but not in the way that it once was. It's been a gift to be able to run again, like a bird set free. Runs are no longer about punishment or shrinking myself. To me, running is about freedom and celebrating what my beautiful body can do. Instead of running away from feelings, I choose to run towards the things that bring me the most joy—reclaiming my body, mind, and life with every mile.

Another gift recovery has given me is the bonds it strengthened within my family, especially with my dad. Running has brought us even closer. We've trained together for many races. In 2023, we trained for our first half marathon together, Hell on the Hill, the hilliest half marathon in the world. Pushing ourselves up the endless incline, I learned it wasn't about the race at all. It was about resilience and proving to myself that I can still do hard things. May 18, 2023, will forever be one of my favorite days.

That weekend was also the first time I shared my comeback story in front of a group, 200 people. It was an emotional and freeing experience for me. As soon as I took the mic, I said, "Hi, I am Katie, and I know I am going to cry."

I cried as I shared my story and dedicated each of the 60 hills I climbed to the warriors in eating disorder recovery. Afterwards, people who had gone through their own storms surrounded me. For the rest of the weekend, I felt something I hadn't felt in a very long time. I felt at home. I felt seen. These were my people, people who knew what it meant to fall down and get up again and again.

I didn't know it that day, but that 13.1-mile finish line was a launching pad. That year, I went on to run my first marathon, and placed first in my first ultramarathon.

Never Give Up

I've learned that everything that happens to me happens for me. I believe my pain is for a purpose. I always say that God did not give me an easy life, but he gave me the power to weather any storm.

If I had tried to fight this storm alone, I would have easily drowned in my pain or been completely brainwashed by my eating disorder. But I had people who cared and never gave up on me. They are my lights who refused to let me get lost in the darkness. They helped me up time and time again until I was strong enough to stand on my own.

To anyone who is struggling in the midst of their own storm, keep going. It will get better, and one day you will look back on this time of darkness and realize that your pain was for a purpose. If you are ever low on hope, you can borrow some of mine.

I never chose this storm. It chose me.

I never chose this fight, but I chose to beat it.

Q&A WITH KATIE

What is your favorite movie?
Forrest Gump

What is your favorite song?
"Bird Set Free" by Sia

What are you passionate about and why?
Being a mom and spending as much time as I can with my kids. Time is the one thing we don't get back.

Sharing my story. Hopeful stories matter, especially when you are stuck in the struggle—keep going.

Who are your mentors and greatest influences?
I have a lot of mentors: my parents, my grandmother, Dr. Robert Cohen, Kelsey Lensman, Rich Roll, Ken Rideout, Jesse Itzler, David Goggins, Alexi Pappas, Chadd Wright, and Chris Hauth. Each of these people will always hold a special place in my heart. They have inspired me and challenged me to share my story, to think differently, to live a life outside of my comfort zone, to never give up, to build my life resume, to expand my limits and inspire others to do the same.

What is some of the best advice you've received?
Every day, you get a chance to write the next chapter of your story. Don't waste time.

What is a habit or ritual that has significantly improved your life?
Gratitude – My foundation is built on gratitude. Yoga and meditation both improved my life significantly. It's important to slow down and just be.

What do you consider your superpower?
I am the best at getting up when I fall. I'm a great cheerleader—very encouraging.

What philanthropic causes do you support?

The Release Recovery Foundation provides scholarships for people seeking treatment for substance use and mental health challenges. This year, I'm running the New York City Marathon to support their mission.

What books do you often recommend?

Bravey by Alexi Pappas, *Can't Hurt Me* by David Goggins, and *Greenlights* by Matthew McConaughey.

What would you tell your 18-year-old self?

One day you will turn pain into purpose, to let go of things, to stop holding everything in. Your vulnerability, sensitivity, and kind heart will be your superpower.

How do you define success?

Always trying your best and being as good as you can be in the areas of your life that matter most to you. If you always try your best, you cannot fail.

To connect with Katie about her story or to book her to speak, you can reach her at katiewolf22@comcast.net or on social @katiekili

NEWY SCRUGGS

Home Runs, Heartbreaks, and Pivots
Resilience Beyond the Broadcast

Eighteen-time Emmy winner Newy Scruggs has been the sports director at KXAS-TV (NBC) in Dallas-Fort Worth, Texas, since 2000. Stops along the way have included gigs in Myrtle Beach, South Carolina; Austin, Texas; Cleveland, Ohio; and Los Angeles, California. Newy combines his media expertise with a commitment to personal growth and lifelong learning.

The Fall and Rise of Josh Hamilton

The first time I saw Josh Hamilton swing a bat, it was clear he was something special. He was the kind of athlete baseball scouts dream about: a five-tool player with power, speed, and an effortless swing that seemed born for October lights. Drafted No. 1 overall in 1999, he was destined to be a superstar. But destiny doesn't always run straight.

What followed wasn't the standard highlight reel of a phenom ascending to glory. Addiction gripped him, and Hamilton's career fell into darkness. His name became a cautionary tale. The talent was still there, but the discipline, the focus, and the clarity to use it vanished. For years, he disappeared from the game entirely.

Most people wrote him off. In sports, opportunities don't wait around forever. New names rise, new stars fill the headlines, and yesterday's prodigy becomes an afterthought. Yet, Hamilton wasn't finished. He fought his way back step by grueling step. He got clean. He rebuilt his body, his swing, and his trust with the game.

In 2007, he returned to the majors. And in 2008, during Yankee Stadium's Home Run Derby, Josh Hamilton gave the world a glimpse of redemption. He launched baseballs into the New York night—28 in one round, a record-shattering display. The crowd rose to its feet, chanting his name. For that moment, the fall was forgotten, and resilience was on full display.

Hamilton didn't win that Derby—Justin Morneau did—but that hardly mattered. The real victory was Hamilton's return, his refusal to let the worst chapters define his story. He went on to become the

American League MVP in 2010 and helped lead the Texas Rangers to back-to-back pennants.

In Game 6 of the 2011 World Series, Hamilton provided one of the most unforgettable moments of his career. In the top of the 10th inning, he launched a two-run home run to give Texas a 9–7 lead over St. Louis—a swing that felt, in that instant, like it would clinch the franchise's first championship. But baseball can be cruel. The Rangers couldn't hold the lead. They lost Game 6 in devastating fashion, and the Cardinals went on to take the series in seven games.

His journey wasn't without relapse or regret. But Hamilton's life reminds us that resilience isn't about perfection. It's about persistence. You don't erase the past, and sometimes even your greatest moments don't end the way you dream—but you refuse to let them be the period at the end of your story. Resilience doesn't erase the past. It refuses to let the worst chapters be the final word.

"100% of Your 70%"

Hamilton's story wasn't only about grand comebacks and headline-grabbing moments. Sometimes resilience is quieter. It's not about lighting up Yankee Stadium or nearly sealing a World Series—it's about showing up on days when you feel like you've got nothing left.

There was a day when Hamilton arrived at the ballpark feeling less than himself. Maybe it was fatigue, nagging soreness, or the emotional grind of the season. He told his manager, Ron Washington, that he was only at about 70 percent that day.

Washington didn't hesitate. He looked at his star player and said: "That's fine. I just need 100 percent of your 70 percent."

It was a simple statement, but it carried weight. Washington wasn't demanding perfection. He wasn't telling Hamilton to be a superhero. He was asking for commitment. Give all you've got from where you are. Don't dwell on what's missing. Pour everything into what you do have.

That's a lesson for all of us. There are days we feel like we're operating at 70 percent—maybe less. Life wears us down. But giving 100 percent of whatever we've got left, that's where resilience lives. And often, it's enough.

Hamilton took that message to heart, and it became part of how he played the game. And it's part of why his teammates and coaches respected him. He wasn't perfect, but he was willing to give all of what he had.

The Pivot from Los Angeles to Dallas

Not every test of resilience happens in the public eye. Some happen quietly, away from headlines, when life hands you a plot twist you didn't expect.

For me, that moment came in Los Angeles. I was there, living in one of the greatest sports markets in the world. I had covered the rise of Kobe Bryant, the dominance of Shaquille O'Neal, and the start of Phil Jackson's dynasty with the Lakers. Los Angeles wasn't just a job—it was the dream. I loved it.

But television is a business, and contracts don't always go the way you expect. I found myself in a contract battle that I ultimately lost. The door to stay in LA closed, and suddenly, I had a decision to make. That decision led me to Dallas.

I accepted the deal in Texas, but I never wanted to leave Los Angeles. I missed it from the moment I left. Dallas was a city I respected, but in my heart, I wanted to stay where my career felt most alive. To make it harder, Los Angeles kept winning championships while Dallas went through a long drought. Every highlight reel from the West Coast was a reminder of what I thought I'd lost.

Resilience isn't just about bouncing back from addiction or injury. Sometimes it's about reframing disappointment. I learned that Dallas wasn't a punishment. It was a pivot. Over time, I built a career that has spanned decades, earned me 18 Emmy Awards, and culminated in my induction into the Silver Circle of the Lone Star Emmy Chapter. Dallas became the foundation of my professional life in ways I could never have scripted.

What I thought was the end of a dream turned out to be the beginning of something bigger. That's the thing about attitude: it changes how you see the map. The road you resist today may become the path that defines your legacy.

Wooden's Wisdom

If Hamilton's story is about resilience and my pivot is about attitude, John Wooden's life ties them both to the larger journey of personal growth. Wooden is remembered as one of the greatest coaches in history—10 national championships at UCLA, a standard of excellence still unmatched. But what made him remarkable wasn't just the winning. It was how he defined success.

Wooden didn't measure his players by the scoreboard. He measured them by their preparation. In his eyes, victory wasn't the number on the scoreboard at the buzzer; it was knowing you had done your absolute best to prepare, to give everything you had, and to never cheat the process.

He often reminded players: "Don't make a second mistake because you're thinking about the first." In other words, let go of failure quickly and focus on the next possession. Another of his core truths was: "Only you know the score that really matters." Success wasn't beating an opponent. It was measuring against your own standard of effort and discipline.

I used to see him often in Los Angeles—at games, Wooden Awards, Wooden Classic events. Even in his later years, his presence was magnetic. He had a way of making you believe that excellence wasn't about talent alone. It was about character. About the daily decision to show up, prepare, and grow.

Wooden's philosophy connects the threads of Hamilton's resilience and my pivot to Dallas. Both journeys weren't about chasing a perfect outcome—they were about refusing to let setbacks define the finish line. Wooden would say that Hamilton succeeded the moment he chose to get clean and swing again. He'd say I succeeded, not when a contract fell apart, but when I leaned into the opportunity in front of me instead of pining for the one behind me.

Becoming Your Best Self

Resilience, attitude, and growth are not abstract concepts. They are choices we make when life throws us off balance. Josh Hamilton showed that you can fall to the bottom and still climb back to the top. His manager, Ron Washington, showed that even on the days you're not at your best, you can still give all of what you've got. My own career path revealed that what feels like a setback can be the foundation of something greater. And John Wooden proved that success is less about winning and more about living by your principles, day in and day out.

Becoming your best self isn't about never falling. It isn't about always getting what you want. It's about how you respond when the lights go out, the contract crumbles, or the scoreboard reads the wrong number. It's about refusing to quit, reframing disappointment, and committing to growth no matter where the road leads.

If Hamilton's swing at Yankee Stadium and his heartbreaking World Series home run, Washington's call to give '100 percent of your 70 percent,' my pivot to Dallas, and Wooden's steady wisdom share anything, it's this: life will test you. The question isn't whether you'll be tested, but how you'll respond. And in that response—in that resilience, in that attitude, in that pursuit of growth—you become something greater than the circumstances around you.

That's what becoming your best self is all about.

Q&A WITH NEWY

What is your favorite movie?

Days of Thunder with Tom Cruise. I first started covering NASCAR around the time it came out, and everybody who covered NASCAR loved or hated it. "Oh, it's Hollywood! It's not real." But it was my introduction to the sport. I love Tom Cruise, the dynamic between him and Robert Duval, and the way Tom Cruise as Cole Trickle fought to become a race car driver.

Who is your favorite musical artist?

If I have to pick, Stevie Wonder is fantastic. Being discovered in the '60s, breaking out and becoming the artist he was in the '70s with *Songs of the Key of Life*, and to be able to keep making music for so long, and to be so good for so long, is unmatched. There's really not an occasion where you can't pull out a Stevie Wonder song, whether it's a wedding, a funeral, or a party.

Who is your favorite sports team?

I grew up a Cowboys fan. I was the kid who had the Cowboys lunchbox, pencils, raincoat, pajamas, curtains, and leather jacket. I was the person who wore the royal blue Cowboy jersey when they couldn't win in them and it was considered a curse. I had the blue Tony Dorsett, number 33. I also loved Roger Staubach, Drew Pearson, Harvey Martin, and "Too Tall" Ed Jones.

That was one of the reasons I wanted to get into the business, and luckily enough, I got to cover my favorite team. I've spent 30 years covering the Cowboys, and am grateful to say that these guys know me.

I also grew up a fan of Jackie Robinson, and covering the Dodgers was special, as was being around Tommy Lasorda when he managed the team.

Plus, I'll never forget covering the Lakers—watching them on TV, seeing Magic Johnson in his final season at the Forum in Los Angeles, and being there at the start of Kobe and Shaq's era.

What are a few of your favorite quotes?

Ralph Waldo Emerson wrote, "What I must do, is all that concerns me, not what the people think." In 1988, I learned about this in Mr. Stanton's English class at Westover High School, and those words carried me, challenged me, and helped me understand who I was.

Pat Riley's book *Showtime: Inside the Lakers Breakthrough Season*, Chapter 13: Motivation, says, "Be so good at what you do that they can't think about replacing you."

Pat Riley also says, "What do you get when you squeeze an orange? Orange juice. Put anything under pressure and you'll bring out what's inside."

Bill Parcells: "I don't have to be fair, I have to be right."

What do you consider your superpower?

My ability and desire to learn and read books. Therein lies the power to do whatever you want to.

What would you tell your 18-year-old self?

Read The Book of Proverbs and then reread it, highlight it, and journal about it.

Follow eighteen-time Emmy-winning sportscaster and sports director at KXAS-TV (NBC) in Dallas-Fort Worth, Texas.
X: @newyscruggs
Facebook: NewyScruggsSports

JENN SHULL

The Courage to Fly

Jenn Shull is an Air Force veteran and a commercial pilot for a major US airline who left the comfort of corporate behind to build a second career in the skies. When she's not flying, she enjoys volunteering, horseback riding, and Krav Maga.

Heavy

Under the low hum of the overhead fluorescent lights made harsher by the dark and dreary winter sky, I stared blank and bored into an iris-searing computer screen. While a different document, it was really the same document that I'd seen over, and over, and over.

As a corporate business systems analyst, my life had become a series of same. Same schedule, same commute, same people, same everything. Up to this point, that sameness was okay. But now, I was ready for a change.

Taste of Freedom

I'd hit a point in my business career where the only way up was to go into management, and that was not a path I was interested in. While I enjoyed leading and inspiring, I did not want to babysit adults, give reprimands, or have to deal with remediation plans. It appeared I'd reached the peak of my career and was staring down the barrel of 40 more years of same.

For a while, same had been actually more than okay. It served me well. My corporate career allowed me the opportunity to explore things I enjoyed in my free time, most captivating of all, learning to fly!

A few years earlier, I had started flight training to shake off the monotony. I'm grateful I was in a position to fund such a fun hobby!

That's right, hobby. I'd only anticipated being a weekend warrior, but the flying bug bit me!

Aviation gave me an immense feeling of freedom and, at the same time, great responsibility. I thrived in it. I decided to become a professional pilot. I put myself through flight training to get my ratings, left my corporate job, and never looked back!

The Leap and the Cost

Leaping into aviation was a process that took years... even after I made the decision to go pro. It's a very windy, expensive road with a lot of ups and downs.

Pilots couldn't get student loans (there are some programs now, but few), so I self-funded my flight training. This meant I'd fly, learn skills, sometimes have to take a break to replenish my coffers, then start back up.

Once I decided to become an airline pilot, it took about two years to obtain the certificates and hours I needed to get a job. Not a job as an airline pilot, a starter job.

The reality is that there's a huge gap between getting your commercial license and the hours and experience you need to get an Airline Transport Pilot (ATP) certificate, required to fly with any major airline. (There's a lot of minutia between different airlines, so having gone through it, I'm always happy to help others navigate the ins and outs.) This gap is so massive that most can't bridge the gap financially. For the responsibility and skill level, starter jobs are very low pay for a long time. In my first year flying people full-time, I made $16,000.

That number felt surreal. I was a fully trained pilot with lives in my hands, and I could qualify for government assistance. It was humbling. But it was also proof that I was all in.

My second and third year at that company were not much better. By the fourth year, I'd logged barely enough time to qualify for a job where I'd get jet time at $150 per day, approximately 14 days a month...for three more years.

When I'd hit the magic number to qualify to get my Airline Transport Pilot (ATP) and go to the majors... COVID-19 hit. The world stopped, and seemingly, so did my career. This part of my story is not unique to me. Many other aspiring airline pilots were thwarted by this massive setback. I was fortunate enough to find a charter gig, and it moved me out to Dallas, Texas.

Once the world opened back up and aviation was moving again, I applied to my target airline and GOT THE JOB!

Cleared for Take Off

In my current career, I've been so much happier and more fulfilled. I'm grateful I had the courage to leave a cushy, well-paying job to start at the bottom all over again. It took sacrifice, setbacks, and starting over, but I wouldn't trade it for anything. Sometimes, the scariest leap leads you exactly where you were meant to land.

Q&A WITH JENN

What is your favorite movie?
The Fifth Element – it highlights the law that where your attention goes, grows, in a fun and creative way. Multipass.

What is your favorite song?
"Landslide" by Fleetwood Mac

How do you celebrate your wins—big or small?
I don't, something I need to work on.

How do you recharge?
Hunkering down at home.

What are a few of your favorite quotes?
"Consistency is key. LFG."
"And the day came when the risk to remain tight in a bud became more painful than the risk it took to blossom." – Anais Nin

What is some of the best advice you've received?
Keep going.

What is a habit or ritual that has significantly improved your life?
I create a "flight plan" for my day: preflight, gratitude, flight plan (top three priorities), and nightly debrief (what went well, what I need to accomplish the next day, etc.).

What philanthropic causes do you support?
Equine therapy for veterans with PTSD (and other military affairs), Women in Aviation International, and animal welfare.

What books do you often recommend?
- *The Compound Effect* by Darren Hardy
- *As a Man Thinketh* by James Allen
- *The Let Them Theory* by Mel Robbins
- *When Violence is the Answer: Learning How to Do What It Takes When Your Life Is At Stake* by Tim Larkin

What would you tell your 18-year-old self?
Buckle up!

What has been your greatest lesson?
Not to wrap your worth in someone's opinion of you.

What makes you feel inspired or like your best self?
When I'm learning and executing on a plan.

How do you define success?
The freedom to spend my time growing, learning, and working on things that bring me joy.

Follow along with Jenn Shull's adventures in aviation.
Instagram: @skyhighjenn
TikTok: @skyhighjenn
Website: www.skyhighjenn.com

DR. EDDIE POOLE

The Reunion I Never Expected... The Lesson I'll Never Forget

Eddie Poole is a business leader, Realtor, and follower of Jesus who believes faith and work go hand in hand. He is passionate about helping business leaders "take Sunday to Monday" in their home and work lives.

Blast from the Past

It started with a phone call from my high school football teammate, Freddie. He said, "Eddie, do you remember Lee Merritt?"

Lee and I played football together in our early years before he dropped out of school. Freddie said, "Lee is at Walmart, and he's homeless. Go help him, Eddie."

I have to admit that my first thought was, *Why don't YOU go help him, Freddie?* But once I thought about it, I knew God wanted me to help Lee.

Didn't See that Coming

Lee had been living in his car in the Walmart parking lot. I called him and met him for breakfast with another former teammate, Tim Bryant.

It was obvious that the years had been tough on Lee. Still, even though he was limping and we later learned that he was in constant pain, his smile told us how happy he was to see us. We paid for his breakfast, and he asked us to keep in touch.

After that morning, whenever I had a business meeting and we had food left over, I would take it to Lee. He usually parked his car in the same general area and seemed to appreciate the gesture.

After about a month into our new relationship, Lee called me. It was about 10:00 p.m. Lee said, "Eddie, can you help me? I don't have anyone else to call."

He explained that he had been arrested and had just gotten out of jail. He was in downtown Nashville and needed me to pick him up.

When I asked why he was arrested, he said, "I didn't do anything," and I just knew he was lying to me.

But then, Lee explained that he had been living in California for the past five years. Before he left, he got a ticket that he didn't pay. When police pulled him over for a tail light that wasn't working, they saw the old warrant. That's why they took him to jail.

He needed a ride because they had impounded his car. He was still living in his car, so he didn't have anywhere to sleep. I asked him where he wanted to go, and he said, "I guess just take me to Walmart."

Letting him out in the Walmart parking lot, I felt a bit hollow inside. It didn't seem right, but I wasn't sure what else to do.

The next morning, Lee called early. He said, "Can you take me to get my car?"

"Sure," I said.

Lee hesitated. "Eddie, it will cost me $300 to get my car out of the impound lot. Can I borrow that from you? I'll pay you back."

I remember thinking, *Here we go!* I KNEW he would be asking me for money! Since he needed his car to live in, I decided to give it to him.

When I handed him the bills, I KNEW I'd never see that money again. I also knew that I would have a guilty conscience if I didn't help him.

Lee took the money, got his car, and I didn't hear from him for a week.

Then he called. "Eddie, where are you right now?" When I told him, he said, "I'll be there in a few minutes with the money I owe you."

Sure enough, Lee showed up 15 minutes later and handed me $300 cash. I didn't know what to say except "Thank you." Lee didn't just give me $300 that day. He gave me the ability to trust him.

Beginning of Trust

Lee and I started communicating more frequently. Every once in a while, I'd notice that he was extra fatigued. On several of those occasions, I would get him a hotel room to give him some good rest, at least for a night.

Lee's health was not good. One day, Lee called and asked me to take him to the emergency room. He had lung issues, among other things, and they decided to admit him to the hospital.

Because of his issues, they felt it was best to remove part of his lung. Lee was in the hospital for almost two weeks. When they were set to release him, he was going from the hospital bed to his car in the dead of winter. I knew he would freeze to death in the backseat in his condition.

I called my friend, the police chief, and asked him to check Lee's arrest record. The chief told me that Lee had a prison record, but it wasn't something he thought I should worry about, as far as my family goes.

I knew what God wanted me to do. While it was the last thing I wanted to do, I had to take him into my home.

I told Lee that he was invited to stay, but he could only be there while I was home. I still wasn't trusting him enough to leave him there alone with my young son, Adam, who was old enough to stay home by himself at times.

Lee stayed on my couch until an apartment in government housing became available about six weeks later. Both Lee and I knew that government housing doesn't come up that quickly. We both had been praying and knew that God had intervened.

A few years before, when Lee was living in California, he asked Christ to come into his life and make a difference, and God honored that prayer. That's when Lee gave up drunkenness and drugs. As a result, Lee's attitude began to change. He still looked like the same person on the outside, and because of his constant pain from an accident in his youth, he often came across as a bit grumpy. But I knew that he had a relationship with God. We talked about God often, and even before Lee stayed with my family for those six weeks, he had started going to church with my family every week.

Beginning to Soften

I found out that Lee's birthday was coming up. We got on the subject of birthday parties, and Lee told me that he had never had a party.

I couldn't believe it. The man was 60 years old and had never had a birthday party.

I called each of my five kids, my mother, and my wife, Marla, and we planned a party. We ate lots of food and cake, and everyone brought a gift.

After the cake, I leaned over and asked Lee if he'd like to open his gifts. He whispered to me, "Eddie, I can't. If I open the gifts, I'll cry."

My family ended up giving Lee the first, second, and third birthday parties of his life. Lee was also with my family during those three years for our Thanksgiving and Christmas celebrations.

Lee loved watching NASCAR, and he told me that one of his bucket list items was to go to a stock car race. I took note of that and got us tickets. Honestly, it was a spur-of-the-moment decision, but I was so glad I did it. Lee was like a kid in a candy store.

Somewhere along the line, Lee started borrowing money from me on a regular basis. Usually, it was $20 or $40. He would always pay me back, but it became an almost weekly occurrence.

Finally, I said, "Lee, why don't you come and clean my office once a week on Tuesdays? Then, I'll just pay you the money each week, and you don't have to pay me back." Lee took me up on that offer, and he became more particular about how my office looked than I was.

I discovered this disheveled homeless guy was actually a neat freak. Sometimes, he would even get on me about keeping things a certain way, and I had to remind him that he was working for me, not the other way around.

Lee went from being someone that I helped out of obligation and guilt to someone that I counted on.

Brothers Again

When he got his government apartment, Lee gave me a key. He said, "Eddie, if you ever call to check on me and I don't answer the door, you can use this key to get in."

On one occasion, Lee didn't answer my calls to check on him. I drove over to his place, and he was there. He didn't hear the phone ringing because he was sick and didn't have his hearing aids in. I was glad he was okay. Lee often called me his best friend and said he was glad that someone cared enough to check on him.

Lee's Early Life

As I mentioned, I was first friends with Lee from the time when we were in the sixth grade through the ninth grade. He was adopted, and I remember that his dad would drink a lot.

I'll never forget one football practice in the ninth grade. Lee's dad came to football practice and started yelling from the sidelines for Lee to get to the truck. This was in the middle of practice.

The coach went to the sideline to try to reason with him. But, there was no reasoning with him, so the coach went back to the field and said, "Lee, I guess you'd better go." I also remember a lot of yelling at his house from his dad.

His mom, on the other hand, seemed to love Lee dearly. Lee loved her very much and was lost after she passed away. He often spoke of her and how much he missed her. Lee was doing his best at living life, but he told me often that he couldn't wait to get to heaven, see Jesus, and see his mom again.

I've always believed that the drug and alcohol abuse that ruined much of Lee's life was rooted in the verbal abuse that he got from his dad. His dad told him that he wasn't worth anything, and Lee believed him.

When I was writing my first book, *Speaking Life in a Messed Up World*, I told the story of how Lee's dad spoke so unkindly to him. I also wrote about how proud I was that Lee had turned his life around and turned to Christ.

Before the book was published, I asked Lee to read the chapter about him. I was worried he wouldn't approve of me telling his story, or maybe it would hurt his feelings.

The opposite happened. Lee was so proud! He couldn't wait until the book came out. When it was available, Lee asked if he could buy five copies to give to a few people. I told him he couldn't buy them, but I would give them to him.

Meeting Jesus

One day, about six months after getting into his apartment, Lee called me. He was sick again and asked if I could take him to the hospital. They admitted him for about a week.

When it was time for him to be released, I picked him up, took him to his apartment, and picked up five of the six prescriptions that the doctor had called in for him.

The drugstore said the sixth prescription would be ready the next day. I was going out of town, but my mother agreed to pick up his last prescription for him, so I told Lee to call her.

When I got back home, my mother said that she had never gotten that call.

I started calling Lee. After several calls, I drove to his apartment. When he didn't answer the door, I used the key that he had given me to let myself in. When I walked into the bedroom, I found Lee lying absolutely still on the floor.

When I walked over, I could see that Lee was dead. The medical complications were just too much.

I called the police and waited until they took Lee away.

Lee had always told me that he wanted to be cremated and for his ashes to be spread upon his mother's grave. Don't tell anyone, because it's illegal, but I may or may not have honored his request.

Thankful for My Friend

God changed me through my relationship with Lee.

What started as obedience because of guilt or obligation ended with me having a softer heart and a new friend. What surprised me most after Lee's death was how much I missed the guy.

I'm so thankful that God chose me to be the one to reach out to Lee. I'm thankful for God's grace when He sent me a blessing that I was resentful of at first.

I'm thankful for God's patience, love, and the second chances that He gave to Lee… and to me.

Q&A WITH EDDIE

Who is your favorite musical artist?

My favorite artist is probably Skillet. As a Christian, I relate to their lyrics, and as a guy who likes a heavy sound, they fill that space, too. I've seen them live through the years, and I like them more every time.

Who is your favorite sports team?

I LOVE the Tennessee Vols football team. I've stuck with them through winning and losing.

What is a motto or mantra you live by?

I wrote my "Manifesto" a few years ago, and it reminds me of who I am. When I remember who I am, it usually clears up many of the decisions that I need to make. (I put it in my previous book, *Speaking Life in a Messed Up World*.)

What are you passionate about and why?

I'm most passionate about my faith. I believe everything I am flows from my relationship with God.

If you could have dinner with three people, living or deceased, who would they be?

I'm assuming Jesus is a common answer. The next three would be my parents, grandmother, and grandfather. They all helped to support and encourage me as I grew up.

How do you recharge?

I usually start my day with prayer and reading Scripture. It helps me focus on what's important.

The other thing that I do four to five times a week is spin class. I'm usually the oldest person there, but I keep up pretty well! I also work out regularly with a trainer.

Who are your mentors and greatest influences? How have they impacted your life?

Craig Groeschel is the pastor of LifeChurch (the largest church in the US) and also leads the *Craig Groeschel Leadership Podcast*. I've met him a few times. Craig speaks to my spiritual side, as well as my business side, and he always does it in a common-sense, easy-to-understand way.

Brian Buffini owns Buffini and Company, the real estate coaching company that I've worked with for 20 years. He helped shape the way I do business every day.

What are a few of your favorite quotes?

- "If you know who you are, you'll know what to do." – Craig Groeschel
- "Discipline is choosing what you want most over what you want now." – Craig Groeschel
- "Small disciplines, done consistently, lead to big results over time." – Craig Groeschel

If you're interested in getting *Speaking Life in a Messed Up World*, Eddie Poole's website is www.EddiePoole.com. If you know someone moving to the Nashville area and they want a realtor who knows Nashville, Tennessee, Eddie would love to help! You can reach Eddie at Eddie@EddiePoole.com or 615-973-4663

NATALIE CONTRERAZ

Make AI Your Co-CEO

Natalie Contreraz left college at 19 with no backup plan, built six figures in real estate, and went on to found Leads & Revenue. Blending marketing, AI, and systems, she helps entrepreneurs design businesses that create freedom instead of burnout. She is also a speaker and consultant.

Drop Out

Most people wait years to quit the wrong path. I quit with an email and no backup plan.

"Wait... you actually dropped out?"

That's what my soon-to-be business partner said when I walked into the coffee shop that morning. Less than 24 hours earlier, he'd told me he would help train me in sales and marketing... *if* I was serious. He didn't ask me to quit college, but in my 19-year-old brain, commitment meant going all in. So the next day, I handed in my withdrawal papers, grabbed a matcha latte, and showed up ready to work. He looked at me like I had two heads.

That decision—the one most people would call reckless—was the start of everything. Not because I loved real estate (I didn't), or because I closed a HUGE deal (I did, but it meant nothing to me). It was because I realized something that would shape the rest of my journey: freedom, not money, was what I was really chasing.

Since then, I've built and torn down businesses, learned the difference between strategy and tactics, and discovered the not-so-secret weapon that now runs my business alongside me: AI. But at the core, it all comes back to this: your business should serve your creativity and life force energy, not drain it.

At 19, I couldn't have put it into a neat sentence, but I felt it in my gut. Freedom meant not being trapped in a classroom, not being told how to think, not living a life that felt pre-scripted by someone else's expectations. I wanted to own my time, my energy, my choices. I couldn't breathe in the life I was living, and I knew if I kept going down that path, I'd suffocate.

Of course, freedom sounds glamorous in theory. In reality, my first taste of "freedom" came with chaos. The day after I dropped out, I had no idea what the future looked like. I only knew that I couldn't go back. That's when I started connecting the dots: freedom isn't handed to you... it's designed, piece by piece, decision by decision. But life had other plans that would test everything I thought I knew about freedom.

Redefining Freedom

Most people define freedom by subtraction.
- Freedom from debt.
- Freedom from a job they hate.
- Freedom from someone else's schedule.

And while that's part of it, I've learned that real freedom is defined by addition.
- Adding creativity back into your life.
- Adding energy into your day.
- Adding experiences, hobbies, and travel that make you feel alive.

Freedom is when your business fuels your life force instead of draining it. That became my north star...even if I didn't know how to articulate it in those early years.

The Turning Point

When my family's life got turned upside down, it changed the way I looked at freedom. Up until then, I thought freedom was about running away from responsibilities. But real freedom? It's about stepping into responsibilities on your own terms.

I dropped out for selfish reasons. I wasn't thinking about helping my family. I was thinking about getting out, getting space, breathing. And yet, through that decision, I stumbled onto a deeper truth: when you choose freedom, you also choose responsibility. If you want to direct your life, you have to carry the weight of it too.

The Energy Trap

Here's where freedom gets tricky. For years, I was caught in the energy cycle: the big high, the inevitable crash, the slow crawl back, and repeat. Freedom without structure is just chaos. I'd push myself into overdrive whenever there was a deadline or a crisis, then crash into brain fog and guilt, and then drift until the next fire came along.

What I realized is this: freedom isn't about doing whatever you want whenever you feel like it. It's about building systems that protect your energy, so you can keep creating without constantly breaking down. That's why I'm obsessed with the idea of life force energy. When it's high, you're magnetic. When it's low, you're invisible. And if you don't learn to manage it, you'll burn out long before you ever taste real freedom.

Freedom as a Business Strategy

Freedom isn't just a lifestyle goal… It's the most strategic business decision you can make. Why? Because a business that consumes your entire life isn't sustainable.

If you want growth, you have to design a business that runs without draining you. You have to protect your energy the way you protect your profits. You have to stop equating "busyness" with success and start asking: *Does this serve my freedom or take it away?*

That question has become my internal compass. I learned to measure opportunities, partnerships, and even day-to-day decisions against it. And here's the thing: the more I protect my freedom, the more my business grows. Because when you're operating from high energy, creativity, and clarity, everything compounds.

A lot of people talk about freedom like it's the endgame (retire early, live on a beach, sip cocktails all day). But that's not it. Freedom isn't passive. Freedom is active. It's having the space to try new hobbies, to travel, to build something bold, to spend an afternoon marinating in the sun because you feel like it.

The real flex isn't the revenue number. It's waking up and asking yourself, "What do I feel like creating today?" and actually having the space to do it.

But here's the thing about creating that space—you can't just wish it into existence. You have to engineer it. And that's where the most unexpected partnership of my entrepreneurial journey comes in.

AI as Your Co-CEO

When people hear me say "AI is my co-CEO," they usually laugh. Some assume I'm joking, others think I've handed over my business to robots. The truth? It's neither. I still make the calls, but I've stopped trying to do it all alone. AI isn't my replacement—it's my thought partner. My second brain. The teammate who never sleeps, never asks for vacation, and somehow knows more about my business than I do on my tired days.

At first, I used it like most entrepreneurs do (like a glorified assistant). Draft this email. Summarize this call. Spit out ten blog post ideas. Sure, it saved me a little time, but it wasn't game-changing. The shift came when I stopped treating AI like a worker and started treating it like a board member.

Instead of asking for answers, I let it ask me better questions. I'd prompt it to interview me about my strategy, poke holes in my assumptions, and surface blind spots I hadn't considered. Suddenly, it wasn't just doing tasks—it was sharpening my thinking. That's when I realized AI could help me lead, not just manage.

Here's how AI serves my freedom:

- **Pressure-testing strategy (protecting my freedom from costly mistakes)** – Before making big moves, I run scenarios with AI. "If we double down on this market, what risks am I not seeing?" It doesn't replace my judgment, but it forces me to think through angles I might ignore.
- **Acting as a 24/7 consultant (freeing me from dependency on others' schedules)** – I don't need to wait for a mastermind call or hire a $30k coach to get perspective. I can ask AI to roleplay as Warren Buffett, Myron Golden, or a composite of world-class strategists. The answers aren't perfect, but they sharpen my own thinking.
- **Designing smarter systems (creating the structure that sustains freedom)** – Remember the cycle I talked about that keeps entrepreneurs stuck between overdrive and burnout? AI helps me break it by building systems: project trackers, optimized schedules, even scripts for delegating tasks. It's like hiring an operations wizard without payroll.
- **Freeing up my creativity (returning me to the work only I can do)** – Instead of drowning in the weeds, I get to spend more time on the things only I can do: vision, storytelling, building relationships, and actually living the freedom I started this business for.

The irony is that technology, when misused, can make us feel trapped (endless notifications, constant busywork, the illusion of productivity).

But when you flip the script, AI becomes the exact opposite. It becomes the tool that creates margin in your life. It becomes the teammate that holds up the mirror and asks, "Is this really serving your freedom?"

Most people use AI for tactics: faster emails, better copy, prettier spreadsheets. That's fine. But if you're serious about freedom, you need to think bigger. The real leverage comes when you use AI for strategy. Strategy is timeless. It's about making the right choices, protecting your energy, and focusing on the 20% of actions that create 80% of results.

I used to be obsessed with tactics. The latest funnel hack. The newest social media trend. The "one weird trick" to get more clients. And sure, they worked (for about five minutes). But here's the thing about tactics: they're like caffeine shots. They spike your energy, give you a quick win, and then leave you crashing.

Strategy, on the other hand, is like compound interest. It doesn't just solve today's problem... it sets you up so tomorrow's problem is easier, and the next day's is easier still.

What Strategy Actually Is

People overcomplicate strategy. They think it's this grand 50-page plan in a binder somewhere. In reality, strategy is just the clarity to know what matters and the discipline to focus on it.

Tactics are about activity. Did you post today? Did you run the ad? Did you follow the script?

Strategy is about direction. Are you moving toward your vision? Are you protecting your energy? Are you building something that serves your freedom, not just your ego?

That's why I don't chase tactics anymore. I ask, "What game am I playing, and what's the simplest way to win it?"

Closing Thought

Most people treat freedom as the prize at the end of the race. I treat it as the starting line. Every decision, every strategy, every use of AI in my business is filtered through that one question: *Will this make me freer?*

Tactics change. Algorithms change. Tools change. But the leaders who win are the ones who anchor their business in timeless strategy and use every resource (especially AI) to protect and expand their freedom.

Because, at the end of the day, freedom isn't about doing less. It's about doing the right things, in the right direction, with the right energy. That's how you stop just surviving your business and start actually living your life.

Q&A WITH NATALIE

What is your favorite movie?
La La Land. I've always loved stories about people who take big swings for their dreams, even when the ending isn't tied up in a perfect bow. It's about chasing something bigger than yourself, knowing it might cost you, and still deciding it's worth it. That resonates with me because my own life has been about choosing vision over comfort.

What is your favorite song?
"Far Away Place" by Xinobi. There's something about the vibe—it feels like freedom, like being in motion toward something new. I play it when I'm deep in creative work or on long drives thinking about what's next for my business and life.

Who is your favorite sport?
UFC. I love the discipline and strategy that goes into it. It's not just physical—it's mental resilience, preparation, and being willing to show up under pressure. That's the same energy I bring to entrepreneurship.

If you could have dinner with three people, living or deceased, who would they be?
Myron Golden, God, and Steve Jobs. Myron because of how he integrates faith and business in a way that's powerful and unapologetic. God, because… well, I have so many questions. And Steve Jobs to ask questions about HOW he navigated being a trailblazer in tech.

What is a motto or mantra you live by?
Everything works out for me. It's not blind optimism—it's choosing to trust that even when things feel uncertain, they're moving in my favor. That belief has carried me through pivots in business, setbacks, and life changes.

What are you passionate about?

Trying new hobbies. For me, it's not just about adding skills—it's about proving to myself that I can always evolve. Whether it's aerial hammock classes, learning a new AI tool, or exploring a new creative outlet, every hobby challenges me to think differently and brings new energy into my work.

How do you recharge?

Working out and marinating in the sun. Movement clears my head and resets my energy, and being outdoors—especially near water—reminds me that there's a bigger world outside my laptop screen.

What is some of the best advice you've received?

Done is better than perfect. Perfectionism is just fear in disguise, and taking action always opens more doors than waiting for the "right time."

What is something most people don't know about you?

I like to cook. I'm usually seen as the "systems and business" person, so people are surprised to find me making recipes from scratch in my kitchen.

What is a habit or ritual that has significantly improved your life?

Working out. It's not just about fitness—it's the mental discipline and clarity that comes from showing up for myself every day.

What is a skill or quality you're currently working on improving?

Communication and speaking at events. I want my message to land with clarity and impact, whether I'm in a room of ten or a thousand.

What do you consider your superpower?

I learn things quickly. It's why I can adapt fast to new industries, master tools, and help others implement systems without the years of trial and error.

What are some favorite places you've traveled to?

Colombia—specifically Guatapé. The colors, the culture, and the people make it unforgettable.

BECOMING YOUR BEST SELF

What hobbies do you enjoy? Do you have any passion projects?

Aerial (the one with silks) and building apps with AI. One feeds my creative side and challenges my body, the other challenges my brain and opens new business possibilities.

What is one thing you hope people remember about you?

That I made them believe they could do more than they thought possible. Whether it's in business, faith, or life, I want people to feel like I left them better than I found them—with more clarity, confidence, and belief in themselves.

What would you tell your 18-year-old self?

Stop waiting for permission. You don't need someone else to tell you you're ready. You're going to learn faster by doing, and the mistakes you're afraid of will end up being your best teachers.

What has been your greatest lesson?

You can't outsource belief. People can mentor you, coach you, or give you the tools, but if you don't believe you're capable, you'll never take the actions that create results.

What makes you feel like your best self?

When I'm creating, leading, and physically active. The combination of mental challenge, leadership, and movement is when I feel fully in alignment.

Find @nataliemeaagan on all platforms. If you want to see how AI could become your Co-CEO and buy your freedom back, email Natalie at natalie@leadsandrevenue.com or send her a DM. She'll send you a free AI audit and help you see what's possible when your business starts running itself.

 Access Your Client Magnet AI Toolkit

CLARE MCKEE

Creating Conditions to Thrive
Lessons on Self Love and Transforming Pain into Power and Purpose

Clare McKee, known online as @Clare.Vibes, is a life coach who helps women design lives anchored in unapologetic authenticity and deep alignment. A seasoned interviewer and host across TV, radio, and digital platforms, Clare brings warmth and insight to every conversation. Clare lives in Arizona with her husband and their beloved pets: a chow chow and two cats.

The Alchemist's Origin

"Bloom where you are planted." Frankly, I have never.

I grew up in Northeast Ohio in the '90s in a middle-class family where my maternal grandparents lived next door and my paternal grandma just five minutes down the road. My days were spent with family, playing outside with the neighborhood kids from sunrise to sunset, and indulging a fascination with my grandmother's collection of geographic encyclopedias.

I am an only child to parents who married at 21 years old and decided not to have me until they were 38. I was the third adult in the equation since day one. I believe my soul came in with a specific plan because I chose two generous and supportive souls as parents who truly want the best for me. Even when I was moving across the country to San Diego at 22 with a dream but no job and in a relationship that had already reached its expiration, my parents have always been unwaveringly supportive.

No Rain, No Flowers

From kindergarten, I attended private school. I excelled in school, played sports, and had several friends. But in seventh grade, my best friend suddenly began bullying me. The same girl who had been my best friend for years, the girl I would go rock climbing with at the local YMCA every Friday, apparently rose out of bed one day and started acting as though she despised everything about my existence.

She also happened to be the popular girl at school—the one who all the boys liked and who the girls wanted to be. Within a matter of days, everyone in my class took a cue from her and stopped speaking to me.

Feeling like no one was in my corner was isolating and confusing. I had gone to school with these kids for nearly eight years, and overnight, everything changed.

I am grateful for one boy, Vince, my best friend since kindergarten, who ate lunch with me and hung out with me at recess. Without him, I would have been totally alone, but his support didn't outweigh the sadness.

Later that week, I was standing with Vince on the playground during recess when I felt something small hit my back. I flinched. Then I felt it again. I turned around to discover my now ex-best friend was throwing gravel at me from across the parking lot. I remember feeling stunned and overwhelmed. I was thinking, How could this be happening to me? Why? What had I done to deserve such treatment from someone I was so close with?

I was reaching my breaking point. As a teenager, you can't help but look at yourself and wonder if you are the problem, if you are unworthy, or incapable of fitting in. I couldn't comprehend what prompted such a dramatic shift so quickly. I'll never know what happened, but looking back, I wonder if other things were going on in her life that had nothing to do with me—maybe things too big for her to process in a healthy way at our young age. At the time, I had no awareness of any of this, and I felt devastated and betrayed.

Reclaiming My Power

My mom picked me up from school that day and noticed I was upset. The second she asked me what was wrong, I began sobbing and shared what had been transpiring that week.

My mother, a fierce mama bear, called to inform the school and advocated for my well-being and safety. Although my teachers and principals argued for me to stay, my parents and I decided it would be best for me to leave the school. I would instead go to the other private school in my hometown, where another best friend, Molly, and all the girls I played travel softball with attended.

It felt like an overwhelming decision. The thought of leaving the only school I'd known for eight years to be the new kid halfway through seventh grade was terrifying. I wasn't moving to a new town where no one knew me, and I was going to run into old classmates somewhere. Despite my doubts, I had this gut feeling that I must switch schools and that it was all going to be okay. Going back to the only school I had known just simply wasn't an option. I decided to trust that feeling, even if it meant I may face judgment from classmates.

Wounds Become Wisdom

This decision unlocked a new version of me—a version that gained confidence as I proved to myself that difficult situations could be incredible blessings in disguise. Not accepting mistreatment and having the courage to walk away was an important lesson in self-love.

That year and a half before high school still holds great memories with Molly, my best friend (more like sister), that induce belly laughs when she and I reminisce together over two decades later. What started as an embarrassing and uncomfortable fear of being "the new girl," not being accepted, or being mocked by past classmates, turned into riding my bike to and from school every day with my best friend, playing sports together, turning every group project into a performance, pranking each other, and more. It was not without challenges, but it was the exact realignment I needed. Also, our class dominated in sports, which was the cherry on top for my athletic, competitive spirit.

From Ecstatic Entrepreneur to Unemployed and Depressed

As I moved through competing in varsity high school sports, graduating college with honors, moving to California at 22, working multiple jobs, leaving behind a few failed relationships, and eventually making a career for myself in media and marketing in my mid-20s, I had faced many challenges—none of which would prepare me for the transformation 2020 would bring.

Between summer 2019 and March 2020, I courageously quit a stable job and, with my business partner, found investors, and launched a media business—Modern Media Network. We obtained clients and successfully ran the business for seven months until a pandemic changed the world.

I went from feeling a deep sense of satisfaction, determination, and purpose to being blindsided with heartbreak, as we quickly discovered that our in-person business model was no longer feasible and were forced to close the doors for good.

This experience sent me into a spiral of depressive thoughts and mental chaos. *Who am I now, if not a business owner? Great, I finally took the risk, and now I look like a complete failure. I'm about to turn 30, and for the first time in my life, I'm unemployed... with zero backup plan. How did I get here? Why is this happening to me? What am I going to do?!*

I became crippled with fear, self-doubt, and limiting beliefs. I felt like I had no control over what was happening in my life, despite the self-development and self-concept work I had been doing since 2015. I had tools to assist me in difficult times—such as my initiation into Transcendental Meditation (TM), Reiki II certification, self-development masterminds, and mindset work—but this time felt different.

I began to ruminate, *What is the point of starting something new if it is only going to be abruptly taken away again by circumstances beyond my control?*

I was giving up. I was giving my power away.

From Ruminating on the Past to Responsibility for the Future

In all the other transformational circumstances, I left on my terms. I was the one deciding when enough was enough and removing myself from what was no longer aligned. This time, the circumstances were not in my control, and I was forced to surrender and replant myself elsewhere just the same.

It took me three years to grieve and accept the loss of my business. For a while, I was doing my best to ignore not only what I had been through and the dramatic uncertainty of the state of the world but also what my soul was whispering for me to do—to start sharing the philosophical and spiritual wisdom I had been pouring my heart and soul into behind the scenes.

Before I knew it, years had passed, and all I had successfully done was run from myself and repeat the same disempowered narrative about how my business was taken from me. My lack of forward progress in any direction left me feeling more and more insecure, incompetent, and uncertain about myself and my professional future. The pressure to figure it out and "do it right this time" felt suffocating.

I had intended to start the self-development coaching business on the side, at my own pace, while running my other successful media business that would pay my bills. *It wasn't supposed to happen like this.* Except it was happening like this.

I was exhausted and suffering bouts of depression as I clung to the past with a victim mentality. Ruminating kept me in fear and void of action. I had to call myself on my own B.S. It was time to move beyond fear and put myself out there again in a new way. It was time to get over it.

Transformation is a process of destruction first and then rebuilding. It isn't linear—it's messy and takes time and effort and often looks like a few steps back and then several more forward. I had to learn to be patient and kind with myself during my expansion and focus on small progression over perfection. I had to remember who I am.

Becoming the Person I Needed

I was ready to tell new stories—rooted in inspiration and positivity. I started an Instagram and began sharing wisdom from my experiences in hopes of helping others seeking clarity, alignment, and the courage to start over. I created a free energy reset guide, and now, I offer personal development coaching for women who are tired of suffering through limiting beliefs and self-sabotage and know they are the only ones who can create their path forward.

When I was going through my rebirth, instead of spiraling, paralyzed in fear and self-blame, I needed to reclaim my fire and take bold, aligned action. I needed someone to remind me of *who I am*—someone who could offer solutions and reflect my magic back to me with honesty and intention. Someone who could see my pain, but more importantly, call me forward in my power.

Earning My Flowers

I know what it's like to start over when maintaining the same circumstances that created the suffering becomes unbearable. I know how it feels to be insecure, broken, and betrayed by people you care about. These experiences helped me realize that every challenge faced and every door closed directly precedes massive expansion and realignment for my highest good. *It isn't happening to me, it's happening for me.*

These difficult experiences taught me that it is my responsibility to my higher self to create the conditions for my expansion, so I could not just "bloom where I was planted," but rather, bloom in conditions suitable for me to thrive. I wasn't flawed, bad, or incapable of fitting in. I wasn't being punished. I was just in the wrong environment; I was being redirected.

I learned to be unwavering when it comes to leaving situations where being me is not enough. Rather than giving up when life becomes challenging or falling victim to circumstance, I learned to know myself, love myself, and follow my intuition unapologetically above all else.

Each time I choose alignment, authenticity, and integrity over what's easy, familiar, or comfortable, I amplify my self-concept and receive blessings abundantly as a result of my expanded embodiment.

Yes, bloom where you are planted, but take care not to create your own cage. We came to Earth to expand continuously. It is our responsibility to know when we have garnered all the nutrients from the soil, and it becomes time to grow and bloom in a new place.

Q&A WITH CLARE

What is a motto or mantra you live by?

I am highly favored. Everything works out better than I imagine.

What is a guilty pleasure that you love but don't always admit to?

I am a reality TV junkie. *Real Housewives*? I've watched every franchise. Competition shows? Check. Dating shows? Obsessed. The messier, the better. Watching the chaos play out is so entertaining to me and equivalent to watching a psychological and sociological experiment. I love to analyze human behavior—it's the coach and guide in me. I'm like, *Ooh let's dive deep and unpack this self-sabotaging behavior, boo!*

What are you passionate about?

I am crazy passionate about people understanding their true power as creators of their reality through knowing themselves, improving self-concept, and managing mindset. We are all powerfully creating all the time. But, without creating consciously, we often manifest what we don't want because, subconsciously, we are looping in limiting beliefs. It is my passion and purpose to remind people that they are so powerful they can create their own suffering OR create the life of their dreams—once they become aware of their power.

What are a few of your favorite quotes?

"Life will present you with people and circumstances to reveal where you are not free." – Peter Crone

"Until you make the unconscious conscious, it will direct your life and you will call it fate." – C.G. Jung

What do you consider your superpower?

My perspective. My intuition, combined with numerous transformational life experiences, allows me to see a 20,000-foot, bigger picture perspective, which makes me an excellent guide. I can easily see how other people are limiting themselves or how they can overcome challenges and patterns. But in my own life, I tend to overthink things and be too zoomed in... very 3/5 Mental Projector-esque of me (in Human Design).

What is one thing you hope people remember about you?

I hope that people feel that I reflect to them their unique power, magic, and beauty, and that they can then know that they are enough. That me being my biggest self empowers them to shine unapologetically and authentically.

To connect with Clare McKee for coaching, speaking engagements, and collaborations, please email helloclare.vibes@gmail.com, visit her website www.ClareAF.com, and for instant access to free content related to self-concept, shadow work, and soul alignment, follow her on Instagram and YouTube @clare.vibes and @clare_vibes on TikTok.

ROBERT COMMODARI

CHISELED

A Journey of Perseverance, Resilience, and Becoming My Best Self

Robert Commodari is a passionate speaker, #1 bestselling author of Better Than You Think *and* Next Level Your Life, *and host of the podcast* Chiseled. *He's inspired thousands of people to develop awareness to live a more fulfilling life. Rob has sold over 2,000 homes in his 23-year real estate career and now leads a top real estate team.*

Growing Up with Grit

Every one of us has faced moments when quitting seemed like an option, when the road ahead looked too daunting to walk. Those who choose to press forward—who dig deep when life is tough—come out shaped, refined, *chiseled* into something stronger.

I come from a large family—seven kids, two parents, and a dog—all crammed into first a two-bedroom, 745-square-foot house and then later a three-bedroom house in Northeast Baltimore. My three brothers and I shared a 10x10 bedroom with bunk beds. We were stacked double-high. Privacy? Never heard of it. We were poor. But here's the thing: we didn't even know it.

My dad worked three jobs to keep our heads above water. He was a grocery store clerk at A&P/Super Fresh for over 55 years. On the side, he parked cars at a funeral parlor and ushered at Memorial Stadium, where the Baltimore Colts played. My mom, a devout Catholic, stayed home to raise us. We had love, laughter, discipline, and faith that held our family together. But we also had need.

One day, when I was around eight years old, I went shopping with my mom at G.C. Murphy, a local discount store. I remember standing in the checkout line, where, instead of bills, she handed the cashier a booklet of stamps—food stamps. It hit me like a punch in the gut: *we're poor.*

That realization carved something into me. A quiet ache. A silent vow. I swore at that moment that I would work hard enough to never have to hand my kids food stamps. I didn't judge my parents—they did everything they could. In fact, I respected my parents for all they endured to provide for us. But I knew I wanted more for my future.

Even though my father worked himself to the bone, we still qualified for government subsidy. I remember the anticipation of seeing my dad coming around the corner from the bus stop on Friday nights, carrying a five-pound block of cheese. He'd take it to work to have it sliced for us. That may sound simple, but when you don't know you're poor, a block of sliced cheese makes you feel rich.

Despite the financial hardship, my mother insisted we go to Catholic school. She wouldn't budge. Public school was free, but in her eyes, faith and discipline were priceless. I'm sure my dad protested, but my mother persevered in her faith alone. That example of unwavering conviction still echoes in my life today.

I understood early that if I wanted to attend a Catholic high school, I would need to pay my own way. And I did. I delivered newspapers in the morning and evening. I hustled. I worked hard so I could walk through those doors with my head held high, knowing I earned my place. That resilience and determination were the building blocks of everything I would do later in life.

Looking back, those early jobs taught me far more than responsibility. They taught me to show up even when I didn't feel like it. They taught me how to talk to adults, how to be dependable, and how to deliver value. Those paper routes weren't just about getting by—they were training grounds for entrepreneurship, leadership, and personal ownership. They gave me confidence and purpose, even when life felt overwhelming.

The Hustle Years

By the time I was a teenager, I didn't hesitate to work. My siblings had paper routes too. That work ethic became my identity. In the winter, I'd go door-to-door with a shovel, offering to clear sidewalks for two to five bucks a job. I had one goal: make $100 in a day. It didn't matter how cold it was or how frozen my fingers and toes got. I was staying out until I hit that number.

Sometimes I think about those snowy mornings—gloves soaked through, my boots barely keeping the slush out, my stomach rumbling from skipping breakfast to get a head start. But I also remember the appreciation in a neighbor's eyes, the cash handed over with a thank you, and the pride I felt knowing I had earned it. That is the power of perseverance—doing what others won't so you can live how others can't.

That's what perseverance looks like when you have a goal. You can endure pain, fatigue, and discomfort when you know what you're working toward. Too many people want to go from A to Z without walking through B to Y. But the *dash*—the space between where you start and where you end up—is where the growth happens. It's where the chisel meets the stone.

Whether it's a baseball player taking hundreds of ground balls or a dancer practicing until their muscles scream, it's the repetition, the grind, the commitment that creates excellence. That principle would carry me through life again and again.

Success... and the Fall

I graduated from Florida Atlantic University in 1990, partially on a baseball scholarship, the rest paid out of my own pocket. I started investing in the early '90s—small stocks here and there. I was frugal, committed to personal development, and reading hundreds of books on growth and success. By the year 2000, I had amassed close to $750,000 in net worth. At 33 years old, I was almost a millionaire.

I remember driving with my wife, Deb, feeling proud. I told her we could sell everything and probably coast for the next 10 years. Life was good. I felt untouchable.

Then it all collapsed.

I was playing the leverage game in the stock market—writing naked puts, borrowing against equity, chasing the upside. When the market took a dip, I held on, assuming it would bounce back. It didn't. Each day brought another margin call. One by one, my positions crumbled. And finally, in March 2000, I sat in my car and sold the last of my holdings—my shares of T. Rowe Price stock. I had lost over $450,000. Nearly everything I had worked for.

It was like the end of a relationship you don't want to let go of. You know it's over, but you hold out hope anyway. Then, one day, reality slaps you across the face, and you have to let go.

I walked inside, head down, heart heavy, and told my wife, "Deb, we lost everything."

What she said next changed everything.

She looked me in the eye, put her hand on my shoulder, and said, "Don't worry about it, honey. We'll be okay. I believe in you."

That was the moment that chiseled me. It wasn't just the loss—it was the love in the midst of loss. Her faith in me when I had failed reminded me of the power of grace, of humility, of being believed in when you don't believe in yourself. That, my friends, is priceless. I had two choices: stick my head in the sand like an ostrich or come out fighting. My decision was made. I would come out fighting.

Rebuilding and Reflecting

It took about seven years to fully recover financially. But what I gained in those years was worth far more than money. I became more cautious, humble, and grateful. I no longer believed I was invincible. I knew I couldn't do it alone. God had allowed me to rise—and allowed me to fall—to teach me what real success looks like. It wasn't what He did *to* me; it was what He did *for* me!

That humility would serve me again and again, especially in business. Not long after this epic collapse, I decided to get my real estate license. In real estate, there are days you get the deal and days you get the call: "Rob, we're moving in another direction." It stings. But you have a choice—play the victim or grow from it. I've chosen growth. Every setback is a lesson in character. Every failure is a chance to be shaped. When failure hits, instead of sobbing or playing the victim, I look for something to be grateful for in that moment.

I've also learned that resilience doesn't always roar. Sometimes it whispers, "Try again tomorrow." There were mornings I didn't want to face the day, but I got up anyway. There were doors slammed in my face, but I knocked on the next one. And slowly, consistently, I rebuilt not just my finances, but my faith in myself, in others, and in God's plan.

Perseverance, Resilience, and Purpose

These stories—from food stamps to fortune, from shame to grace—are all part of my chisel marks. They've formed the person I am today: a man of resilience, faith, humility, and hope. But I share them not to boast, not to seek pity, but to *inspire*.

There are moments when the weight feels unbearable—standing in a checkout line, realizing life hasn't turned out as hoped, or sitting alone in a car, watching something hard-earned begin to slip away.

Even then, there is hope. Recovery is possible. What's broken can be rebuilt. And in that rebuilding, something stronger and more purposeful can take shape.

Resilience isn't the absence of failure—it's the will to rise again. Perseverance is the quiet refusal to quit. Humility becomes the anchor, steadying us in the storm.

The scars, the uncertainty, and the beauty of this journey transform us. They chisel us not towards a destination but into the person we were meant to become.

Hardship has a way of asking deeper questions: What's shaping us? Are we growing harder or more grounded? Are we being refined?

In the end, what matters most isn't perfection—it's authenticity. The world needs those willing to show their scars, to share real stories that carry real hope.

There's a quiet truth that emerges after being knocked down and lifted back up: the greatest challenges often become the greatest gifts. And what we find isn't what was lost, but who we've become through it all.

I'll finish with one of my favorite quotes from *Rocky Balboa*:

> *Let me tell you something you already know. The world ain't all sunshine and rainbows. It's a very mean and nasty place, and I don't care how tough you are, it will beat you to your knees and keep you there permanently if you let it. You, me, or nobody is gonna hit as hard as life. But it ain't about how hard you hit. It's about how hard you can get hit and keep moving forward; how much you can take and keep moving forward. That's how winning is done!*

Keep pressing forward. Let life chisel you. Let life come to you. Your best self is on the other side of the struggle.

Q&A WITH ROBERT

What is your favorite movie?

Shawshank Redemption: With hope and persistence, all things are possible.

Field of Dreams: This is personal to me. My dad was a soccer guy, and I was the only one of the siblings who had a love for baseball. I never played a game of catch with my dad until I was 34 years old. This movie brings it all together for me.

If you could have dinner with three people, living or deceased, who would they be?

Jesus Christ: To be in His presence and to ask him all the questions that come to mind about what He went through and how He managed to keep His faith in the Father would be incredible.

Og Mandino: Og was the first personal growth and development guru that I followed. I consider him my first mentor. His book, *The Greatest Salesman* in the World, took my life in another direction and was the beginning of my desire to read, grow, and become a great speaker.

The Pope: I'd want to talk about all the dynamics and philosophies of the Catholic Church. His philosophy and why He chose his path.

What is a motto or mantra you live by?

I'm a work in progress. It is what it is. Never give up, never give in.

What are you passionate about?

I'm passionate about reaching as much of my potential as possible and living a fulfilling life. I want to be what God created me to be. To serve His purpose. I believe I do that through my speaking. I want to speak to millions of people about developing awareness to live a more fulfilling life.

What are a few of your favorite quotes?
- "Fear for me, would be standing at the gates of heaven and God showing me all I could have done in my life, if I would have just had a little more faith in Him." – Robert Schuller
- "This too shall pass."
- "I can do all things in Christ who strengthens me."

Who are your mentors and greatest influences? How have they impacted your life?

Jesus Christ, Mom and Dad, my wife and children, Og Mandino, Matthew Kelly, Brian Buffini, Jim Rohn, and Zig Ziglar. All of these people, in one way or another, have inspired me to be the best person I can be. They have inspired me to grow, learn, and love myself and others.

What is some of the best advice you've received?

If you want something bad enough, you'll figure out a way to get it. Never give up. Do your best and trust God for the rest.

What is a habit or ritual that has significantly improved your life?

Reading, meditating, and working out.

What do you consider your superpower?

My ability to connect with people and storytelling.

What philanthropic causes do you support?

Alzheimer's Association—my mom has dementia.

The homeless—it pains me to see homeless people on the streets. I know some of it is self-inflicted, but I hate to see it.

What are some favorite places you've traveled to?

Grand Canyon, the Grand Tetons, Yosemite Park, Zion Canyon.

What makes you feel inspired?

A good book, good music, or an inspiring, motivational movie.

What hobbies do you enjoy? Do you have any passion projects?

I love reading, hiking, and exercising. I have a "Chiseled Project" I'm working on.

What books do you often recommend?

The Bible, *The Greatest Salesman* in the World by Og Mandino, *The War of Art* by Steven Pressfield, *The Slight Edge* by Jeff Olson

What is one thing you hope people remember about you?

My ability to make people feel that they matter and that I was a person who didn't quit and desired to live life to the fullest.

What would you tell your 18-year-old self?

You're going to face trials and tribulations in life. But this is how you grow. Don't see failure as failure. Failure is only a perceived failure. When you can take the lesson from that perceived failure and learn and grow from that, was it a failure? You will find yourself growing at an exponential rate when you can find the discipline to do this. Find the silver lining in everything. When you experience a setback, find something to be grateful for. It will change your perspective.

Don't judge others. Learn to understand who someone is. Learn to love and accept others for who they are and where they are on this journey in life. Love unconditionally.

What makes you feel like your best self?

When I use the awareness that God gives me and I share that with others to help them along their journey in life. When I'm feeling healthy and working out. When I am helping others achieve their goals and discover their purpose.

How do you define success?

Taking the unique gifts and abilities God gave me and using them to reach my fullest potential while fulfilling God's purpose for me.

To connect with Robert Commodari regarding real estate, visit www.talktorob.com. To learn more about his books, *Better Than You Think* & *Next Level Your Life*, and to book speaking engagements, email rob@talktorob.com or visit www.robcommodariauthor.com. To learn more about his Chiseled podcast, go to www.robcommodariauthor.com
Follow Rob on FB @RobertCommodari

RON WHITE

Two-Time US Memory Champion and Creator of The Afghanistan Memory Wall

Two-time US Memory Champion Ron White is a speaker, author, and trainer. He has been featured on Stan Lee's **Superhumans**, *National Geographic's* **Brain Games**, *CBS'* **The Morning Show**, *and more. Ron is the creator of the Afghanistan Memory Wall, his tribute to fallen soldiers in Afghanistan where he served in the US Navy.*

Paper Boy of the Year

My first job was a paper route at age 14. While the typical kid would sign up one household for the paper per day, I signed up eight to 10. It was the first time I felt good at something. If you got eight sign-ups in three months, you won a season pass to Six Flags. In a weekend, I was getting me, my parents, and my sister a season pass. I was Mid-Cities Daily News' carrier of the year. It was a fun time, and it taught me lessons that carry me to this day.

At 18, I worked as a telemarketer for a chimney cleaning service. It was brutal. One day, the man who picked up interrupted my script to say, "Ron, we don't want our chimney cleaned. We're trying to sell our house."

Then I said the words that changed my life: "Sir, don't hang up the phone. If you're trying to sell your house, you're going to need a clean chimney." I was only 18, but I knew how to overcome objections.

Laughing, he asked me, "Do you want a job?" He offered to pay me more than I was making, which was pretty easy to do, and I took the offer.

How My Speaking Career Began

It was July 1991, and I was beyond eager to start my new position. At the time, there was a popular infomercial on TV for Kevin Trudeau's Mega Memory. It seemed like magic to me. Now, I had the chance to work with them.

When I started telemarketing for them, I observed their speakers going out to give presentations and sell, and I knew that's what I wanted to do. The company wasn't interested. I was 18, and they didn't have a speaker under 28. Most of them were closer to 40, and all were established in business.

So, I joined Toastmasters and invited my sales manager to go with me. I wanted him to see me speak. Once he did, he said, "Ron, you need to get a tent and do revivals. You can speak!"

I said, "I don't know if I want to do revivals, but maybe…memory training?"

That's when a speaker, who was bringing in a remarkable $30,000 a month, quit the company. There were two choices—cancel all his speeches or get a new speaker. They had no speakers in training, but they had me. Even if I didn't make any money, they wouldn't come out any worse with me than if they had canceled.

The first year, I was terrible, the worst in the company by far, according to the numbers. With the generous coaching from the president of the company, it took me a year to achieve the company average. Now, I do much more than that. I just had to take that time to learn.

Memory Expert, But No Special Ability

People always want to know when I realized I had special memory ability. The truth is, I don't have a special ability. I learned a system that anybody can learn. People will say, "I remember the face, but I don't remember the name." That's because they look at the face but never see the name.

The mind remembers what it sees, so you have to visualize what you want to remember, whether it's a deck of cards, phone number, poem, quote, or speech. The first step is to turn what you want to remember into a picture. The next step is to place that picture somewhere. This step is a technique called the mind palace, which has been around for 2,500 years. Put simply, in the mind palace technique, you use your house to memorize things.

The majority of people can say with confidence that they can memorize three words. The magic of the memory palace is that you can use this system to memorize three items one hundred items or 7,000 items once you understand how it's done. The trick is to apply the technique to what interests you—a speech, your classmates' names, or knowledge to help you in your job.

Naval Service, Two-Time US Memory Champion

When September 11th happened, I joined the Military as a Navy Reservist at 28 years old.

I served in the United States Navy from 2002 to 2010. In 2007, I was deployed to Afghanistan. I was an Intelligence Specialist. IS1, Petty Officer 1st class.

I did 51 convoys, but I saw no combat action. There is nothing extraordinary about my service or deployment. It was just a regular deployment like many others. But countless men and women were in extraordinary circumstances. Combat veterans and too many others paid the ultimate sacrifice.

When I got back, I decided I wanted to compete in the US Memory Championships. I hired a coach, United States Navy SEAL TC Cummings. He taught me a lot about mindset and discipline. He had me memorizing cards underwater. He had me memorizing cards in noisy bars. He had me changing my diet, getting up early, and training like a Navy SEAL would train for war so that I would be a well-trained brain athlete for the memory tournament.

I won back-to-back years, becoming a two-time USA Memory Champion, and set the record for the fastest to memorize a deck of cards in the United States. That record held until 2011.

The Afghanistan Memory Wall

After winning, I wanted to do something more special with my memory, something I was passionate about. As a Veteran of Afghanistan, I decided to create a tribute for everyone who died there, so they would not be forgotten.

More than 2,400 US Military died in the War in Afghanistan. As a Veteran and an American, this deeply affects me. I've memorized the rank, first name, and last name of each of the fallen. Those 2,400 names were made of over 7,000 words, and I memorized each of them using the mind palace. I travel the USA rewriting each name entirely from memory on an expansive traveling wall to honor their memory and service.

When I was memorizing the wall, for a year, I lived in solitude. I took a book filled with each soldier's name with me everywhere I went. When I was sick, I was memorizing. When I was tired, I was memorizing.

I'm humbled by all who have come to witness this across the country and at major events like NFL games, NASCAR races, MLB games, Independence Day at the National Mall in Washington, DC, and on Veteran's Day. I have countless stories of how The Afghanistan Memory

Wall has made an impact on friends and family of fallen soldiers that shake me to my core.

Every time I set up the wall, I brief my helpers beforehand, because I know what is coming. "I don't know when it will happen today, but it will. Someone is going to walk by this wall and ask what it is. In an instant, their eyes are going to fill with tears, and they will be barely able to contain themselves. Then they will give us a name and ask us if it's on the wall. I will take them to that name, and they will stand in silence with tears running down their face."

When I began the process, I didn't know any of them personally. Now I feel like I know all of them. Not just their names, I feel like I know them. Honoring and giving respect to others has given me purpose and a mission that I would not trade.

My Day Job

Since 1992, I've been a full-time speaker and trainer on the topic of memory. Companies and organizations have me come and speak at their conventions and to their teams.

I make memory entertaining. It is something I love doing. I also have multiple courses on memory, including Black Belt Memory.

I love what I do because it impacts others, adults and children alike! I do not have a special memory, and anyone can learn to do what I have done, whether it's setting the world record for the fastest to memorize a deck of cards, winning and defending the US Memory Championship, or memorizing the names of 2,400 fallen soldiers. That is what I love to teach.

Following Your Passion

I've learned that when I'm training for something, whether it is a memory tournament or The Afghanistan Memory Wall, that's when I'm at my best. There are times I think I need to focus more on my business, but the truth is, when I follow my passion and I have a big project or goal that will serve others, that is the very thing that helps grow me and my business. To paraphrase Jim Rohn, the true reward is the journey and what you become in the process.

Q&A WITH RON

What is your favorite movie?
My all-time favorite movies that have impacted my life are *The Adventures of Indiana Jones* trilogy. He always was standing up for something that was right, and I love the adventure of it. He was an adventurous guy and traveled, and that's something that has been part of my life. He loved history. I've always been a collector of historic things, especially old presidential autographs and memorabilia.

Who is your favorite sports team?
The Texas Rangers. I'm a long-time season ticket holder. I went to my first game as a kid and just fell in love with the team However, I'd say that for five to 10 years, I've become more of a UFC fan, and honestly, just a fan of working out and exercising myself. The nights I used to spend watching the Rangers I now spend doing jiu jitsu or watching fights.

How do you recharge?
Two ways help slow my mind down. I like to go for walks. I enjoy doing that out in nature. I also do jujitsu because, when you're there, if you are thinking about anything but jujitsu, you will lose or even get hurt.

Who are your mentors and greatest influences?
There are two great influences on my life. The first was my mom, and I didn't exactly realize how much she influenced me until she died. I know now she did, and the impact she had on my life was tremendous. I admired her strength. She lived her life under tremendous grief for decades, and she handled it with such grace. That is such an inspiration to me. I wish I could have five seconds with her just to tell her that.

The second is Kyle Wilson. I met him 20 years ago, and he believed in me and my product. When I was in a tough situation, getting ready to get kicked out of the Navy for $40,000 in debt to the IRS, he gave me a loan and started selling my memory course. Within six months, I had repaid him through the sales proceeds. He wasn't just a mentor of mine, because he has been a tremendous friend, and a mentor in how to market myself.

What would you tell your 18-year-old self?
Get a good CPA. It would have saved me 10 years of mistakes.

Have you had any past challenges that turned out to be blessings?

I think some of my biggest disappointments have blessings. I won the 2009 and 2010 USA Memory Championship, and in 2011 I was defeated. It was crushing. When you win the championship, the media surrounds you. You're on *Good Morning America*, *The Martha Stewart Show*, and *The Dr. Oz Show*. The next day, your phone is ringing off the hook. But when I lost in 2011, I found myself walking around New York City. My phone wasn't ringing, and I thought to myself, How do I stay relevant?

If I had won, I would have had to start training to defend my title. Losing was the greatest gift to me because it freed me up to no longer focus on the USA Memory Championship. I shifted to The Afghanistan Memory Wall, which became 1,000 times more important, more grand, more everything.

What is some of the best advice you've received?

My mom would say to just be kind. Be kind to people regardless of how they treat you. If they're treating you bad, you don't have to stay there in the situation and let them treat you bad. Just walk away.

What is something most people don't know about you?

I'm an introvert and need solitude and alone time.

Also, I'm a student of stoicism. Marcus Aurelius said, "You have control over your mind—not outside events. Realize this, and you will find strength." A lot of stoicism has to do with not trying to control the uncontrollable. Just try to control your mind. That quote sums that up for me. I aim to just worry about myself, my mind, and my thoughts.

How do you define success?

Success is contentment.

The two-time US Memory Champion and professional speaker Ron White can be found at www.blackbeltmemory.com, YouTube, Facebook, and Instagram. Email: ron@ronwhitetraining.com
Podcast: www.americasmemory.com

M. A. MAC CURFMAN

It's a Process

M. A. Mac Curfman is a transformative business trainer, speaker, and coach with a straightforward style. An entrepreneur and an iconoclast thinker, he is the founder and chief learning evangelist of M.A.Curfman Learning, a global training and coaching firm. Mac is a traveler, coffee roaster (and drinker), outdoorsman, and bibliophile.

Hard Stop

I was blessed by spending the first 47 years of my life without a stay in a hospital, other than the day I was born. But these next two weeks were shaping up to be very different, and in many ways.

I have a strong Christian heritage. My parents were strong Christians. My brother and my two sisters are strong Christians as well. My maternal grandfather was a preacher. I have two uncles and four first cousins who were pastors (two of whom have taught at theological seminaries). There has never been a time when I didn't know Christ as my Lord and redeemer. I am cognizant and appreciative of that rich heritage. That doesn't mean, however, that the pathway of my own faith journey hasn't been rocky at times.

It was Thursday, and I was at my weekly Rotary Club meeting when I started feeling poorly. My son, who was seven at the time, had been sick all week, and I remember feeling annoyed that I had picked up the same bug.

At the time, I was working three jobs. I was working a nine-to-five job selling leadership training programs, trying to build a consulting business on the side, and delivering newspapers at night to make some extra money. It was a lot. There wasn't much time for anything else, including sleep. I typically slept two or three hours a day. I did that seven days a week—for three years. Then, my body said, "No more."

I felt horrible that weekend and thought I was fighting the flu. My wife finally convinced me to go to the doctor the following Tuesday. The physician's assistant examined me in the office, swabbed me for the flu, and discovered that I did not have the flu. She drew blood from me, did a quick analysis, and discovered that I had some unidentified virus. She told me to continue treating it like the flu, and it should run its course in about a week. I recall thinking I was so glad I had just spent $100 on that generic and, as it turned out, terrible advice.

On Wednesday and Thursday, I felt even worse. On Friday evening, my wife came home from work and tried to convince me to go to the emergency room at the hospital. I don't like going to the doctor and despise the ER. However, she did convince me to go to the urgent care clinic.

When I walked into the urgent care, with a great deal of assistance from my wife and my son, the doctors in the clinic did two things that saved my life. First, they slapped oxygen on me and tested the oxygen in my blood by putting a pulse oximeter on my finger. Blood oxygen usually reads high 90s, almost 100. That day the meter read 82. The doctors in the urgent care said that number meant I was in trouble. I later learned that if the percentage of oxygen in the blood falls to 79 or lower for a prolonged period, there could be brain damage.

The second thing they did was call 911. The ambulance came and took me to the ER. After examining me thoroughly, the ER doctors said, "You're not in trouble… you're in big trouble. You waited far too long to come to the hospital."

They later diagnosed me with double opaque pneumonia. I knew what double pneumonia was because my father had that when I was growing up, but opaque was a word I didn't recognize with that diagnosis. The doctors showed my wife the X-rays of my lungs, and they were completely white, which meant that they were full of fluid, and I had no more room in my lungs for oxygen.

They admitted me to the hospital right away. That was Friday night. Early Saturday morning, they told me that the numbers were not improving and rushed me to the intensive care unit (ICU). I remember being hooked up to all the wires, probes, and IV bags in the ICU, and I remember being frightened. I was connected to a BiPAP (bilevel positive airway pressure) machine that literally forced air into my lungs, and I remember feeling like I was drowning in air.

I was in the ICU for six days and spent a total of 10 days in the hospital. While I was there, the doctors sat down with my wife twice to prepare her because they did not think I was going to live.

The 2x4

On Sunday, the doctors had transferred me to the larger downtown hospital, where, on Monday, they were planning to drain my lungs in a procedure called thoracentesis. I remember lying awake Sunday night, wondering if this was it for me.

That's when I heard a voice close to me. I looked around, but no one was there. The voice was distinctly a man, and I believe—I know—that it was God speaking to me. It has been the only time in my life that I have heard an audible voice from God.

In the middle of the night in that ICU, God asked me a question. He asked, "Do you trust me?"

I paused and said, "Yes, Lord, I have faith in you."

"No. That's not the question that I asked you," He said. He asked again. "Do you trust me?"

Truthfully, I was a bit annoyed that the question was being asked again. I answered back curtly, "Yeah, I trust you."

Once again, He said, "No."

He asked a third time—this time in my ear, a whisper yet emphatic. "Do. You. Trust. Me?

It was like a 2x4 on the side of my head, and I finally understood the question and why He was asking it.

I paused, and after a while, I answered, "Yes, Lord. I do trust you with all my heart and with all my mind."

Then, He simply said, "Let go," and the voice fell silent.

It would be another two months before I was fully recovered from the pneumonia, but God used that night to get my attention. You see, even though I have been a Christian all my life, there were areas of my life that I had ceded control over to God, and there were other areas that were still under my control. In that ICU bed that night, God asked me that question because He wanted it all.

The Struggle Is What's Important

Former Dutch Prime Minister and founder of the Dutch Reformed Church, Abraham Kuyper (1837-1920), said it this way: "There is not one square inch in the whole domain of human existence over which Christ, who is Sovereign over all, does not cry, 'Mine!'"

I wish I could report that I fully and completely gave over everything to Christ and His Lordship starting that night in my ICU bed. I have not. Truthfully, it's an ongoing struggle! It's a day-by-day, hour-by-hour, and moment-by-moment battle. What I have discovered, however, is that the struggle is what's important.

Our struggles with the Lordship over our lives are, at least in part, what Jesus' younger brother, James, meant when he wrote in James 1:2–4 (ESV), "Count it all joy, my brothers, when you meet trials of various kinds, for you know that the testing of your faith produces steadfastness. And let steadfastness have its full effect, that you may be perfect and complete, lacking in nothing."

James says the struggles are necessary to produce a steadfastness or perseverance in us. The struggles, though annoying or even heartbreaking in the moment, produce changes in our lives. When enough time has passed and we can detach ourselves from the emotions of the struggles, we see that the results are either fruit or chaff.

The chaff is useless and is swept away by the wind. For me, that looks like superficial relationships, money, and possessions. Chaff does not survive.

We want our lives to produce fruit. For me, that means I have deep and meaningful relationships with my family and friends. It also means that my vocation has a positive and lasting impact on others and society. Finally, and most importantly for me, that means I have an intimate relationship with my God on a forever basis. Those are the things I need to pursue. Those are the things that the struggles produce.

Don't run away from the struggles in your lives. Welcome them. Learn from them. Allow them to produce fruit in your lives.

Q&A WITH MAC

Who is your favorite sports team?

I am a rabid Pittsburgh Steelers fan and have been so all my life! I grew up in Western Pennsylvania in the 1960s and 1970s when the Steelers were the dominant team in the NFL. Players like Terry Bradshaw, Franco Harris, Rocky Blier, Mean Joe Greene, Donnie Shell, Lynn Swann, and Jack Lambert all made the game an absolute blast to watch!

For me, the Steelers of that era represent winning in a time of losing. By the mid-1970s, the steel industry in Western Pennsylvania and Eastern Ohio was in a deep depression. Many plants were closing, and many people were losing their jobs.

My dad owned a service station and an auto mechanic's garage. Many of my dad's customers lost their jobs as the Lordstown, Ohio, General Motors auto plant, the Cooper-Bessemer engine plant, and the Saxonburg US Steel plant closed their doors.

The Steelers represented great victory in a time of great defeat in Western Pennsylvania.

What are you passionate about and why?

I am passionate about learning and growing and about instilling that in everyone I can influence.

When I was young, I was very shy and had no self-confidence. There were several people, including teachers, who said to me or made me feel that I would never amount to anything. My second-grade teacher punished me by making me stand in the corner for not reading fast enough. My fifth-grade music teacher said I should never attempt music. Bullies in junior high school made me feel I was worthless.

Others, however, poured into me and built me up. My parents were constantly building me up and encouraging me. I remember another music teacher, Miss Pool, encouraged me to practice making the sound of a siren. She would tell me, "Your voice needs to be heard!" I still practice a form of that today. My voice is heard today because of her.

My English teacher in 10th grade nearly forced me to audition for the drama club. No one was more surprised than I was when I landed a leading role in the play. In fact, I earned significant roles in every play we did in high school.

There were still others, like my high school band director, Mr. Calvert, my 9th-grade civics teacher, Mr. Kline, an upperclassman, Bob Morgenstern, and my high school principal, Mr. Hartman, who coaxed me to learn and who pushed and pulled me along the way.

I am passionate about building others up. I want to be the person others think of when looking back on their lives and point to where they grew and changed positively.

What are some favorite places you've traveled to?

I have traveled to 47 US states and territories and to about a dozen countries on five continents. What I hold dear are not the places so

much, but the people. I love traveling, meeting new people, and building relationships with them.
- Utqiaġvik (formerly called Barrow), Alaska (one of the northernmost towns in the world). I was there twice (2013 and 2015) to conduct training for members of the North Slope Borough government. The second trip was during the third week of January in 2015. It was dark 24 hours a day and 40 degrees below zero (F). My client picked me up at the one-gate airport and drove me to the dormitory of Iḷisaġvik College, where I was to be staying. On the way to the dorm, he explained to me that all the outside doors to the dorm were unlocked. I thanked him for the information and asked why that was important. He said to me, "When (not if) you see a polar bear, you can duck in one of the doors quickly."
- Dakar, Senegal (the westernmost point on continental Africa). For over a decade, I have spent anywhere from two to 12 weeks a year speaking to, training, and building relationships with Senegalese businesspeople.
- Guangzhou, China, where I spoke to members of a "shop church" in a factory on marketing. One little, old woman in the back of the room asked me how I could be a Christian and market my services because marketing is all about lying about your products and services. That led to a beautiful hour-long discussion on how to be a Christian and a businessperson and marketer.

What hobbies do you enjoy?

I have loved the taste of coffee ever since my dad gave me my first cup when I was 12. I was constantly on the hunt for the perfect cup of coffee. Then, one Christmas, about 25 years ago, my wife got me a home coffee roaster. It was life-changing! When I tasted the coffee made from the beans I had just roasted, I knew I was never going back to anything else. The taste was that different!

I also enjoy the alchemy. In the roast, we control time and temperature. The bean, which is one lobe of the seed inside the cherry of a tree from the genus *Coffea*, has approximately 300 chemical compounds and tastes terrible raw. As the internal temperature of the bean rises toward 450 degrees Fahrenheit, it releases moisture and cracks. It almost sounds like popcorn. At the end of the roast, the bean has over 600 chemical compounds and tastes lovely when ground and brewed with hot water.

What are a few of your favorite quotes?

- "Make no little plans; they have no magic to stir men's blood and probably themselves will not be realized. Make big plans; aim high in hope and work…" – Daniel Hudson Burnham, American Architect/Urban Designer
- "Jut the jaw." – Dave Rhodes, Scout Master, Boy Scout Troop Number 71, French Creek Council
- "Fixed the newel post." – Clark W. Griswold in *National Lampoon's Christmas Vacation*

How do you recharge?

I recharge alone.

I go deep into the woods to hunt and to self-reflect. My wife calls it "taking my gun for a walk." I love stepping into a stream to fly fish. It's just me and the fish.

I love going to my garage to roast coffee beans. As the beans are changed in form in the alchemy process, so am I.

What is a motto or mantra you live by?

My mom would push my brother, my two sisters, and me out the door every morning towards the bus stop, and the last thing she would say to us was, "**A day without learning is like a day without sunshine.**" That one phrase instilled in me a want—a need—to learn every day! It does so to this day! I start every one of my training sessions with that story.

What books do you often recommend?

I'm a reader and a book collector. I have about 4,000 books in my library, and I am constantly giving book recommendations. Here are my top three:

1. *How to Win Friends and Influence People* by Dale Carnegie
2. *The 7 Habits of Highly Effective People* by Stephen Covey
3. *Re-imagine* by Tom Peters

What is one thing you hope people remember about you?

He was a faithful servant to the end.

M. A. Mac Curfman is the chief learning evangelist at M.A.Curfman Learning, with nearly 20 years of experience in helping people advance their success. Reach him at mac@macurfman.com or +1 (803) 904-8855. Go to www.MACurfman.com to sign up for his weekly email with more ways to grow and learn.

 Scan to schedule a discovery call with Mac.

TAKARA SIGHTS

Perfect

Pulled by a love of stories and a desire to keep growing, Takara Sights has spent nearly a decade surrounded by words as a book editor, writing coach, and author. As a writer, she explores big ideas with language that's deliberate and clear. As an editor and coach, she values being the support that helps an author's voice be heard.

Finding My Voice

I had walked to the park for a change in scenery. While I had taken writing seriously all through school, this time, it felt different. This was personal. This was hard.

I had graduated from college a couple of years before, and it was hard for me to admit that I was still finding myself. This opportunity to be an author was cool and new. Writing was always something I wanted to do more of, and this being a project put on by Kyle Wilson, there was a lot of pressure. Saying yes put me in proximity to people who had made something of themselves, and I wanted to make something of myself too.

The wind was blowing more than I expected. At a picnic table with my notebook pages half-tamed beneath my elbow, I scrawled page after page, working through versions of my story. I had already lived it, but the process surprised me. Before long, I found myself wiping away tears. Next thing I knew, my legs had fallen asleep from sitting.

Days passed before I was ready to look at what I'd written. With the deadline creeping up, I took my notebook back to the park and propped it up next to my laptop. In those lines, I could see myself—a young woman with big emotions and dreams pushing herself to be honest on the page.

For a first draft, it cleaned up well enough. And yet, my gut clenched at the thought of sending it to Kyle and my editor—that meant someone was going to *read* it! A few days later, holding my breath, I emailed it anyway.

When feedback came, it was helpful and complimentary. Still, I worked and reworked each line—looking for just the right words to capture the experiences I wanted to describe. With every pass, I saw another paragraph that could be more tightly phrased or closer to the truth.

No matter how much I polished, my gut still clenched at the thought of publishing. It was vulnerable. But, I wanted to try this. So, I did it anyway.

Hello, Opportunity

Months later, I was scrolling Facebook when I saw a post from Kyle about wanting help with editing projects. I had first met Kyle at a real estate conference with my mom. After that, I attended a couple of his Inner Circle Masterminds, and I was impressed. Kyle seemed like a good man to know. So, I sent him a message offering my help.

When Kyle called me, I told him the truth: I had edited before—my own work mostly—but others' too as part of my education. I admitted that my bachelor's degree in environmental studies with a minor in architecture and sustainability was unrelated, but I was a good writer, and I liked editing. Selecting a word based on its layers of meaning and surgically removing words that weren't pulling their weight was like a puzzle for me. Storytelling was harder, but having grown up an avid reader and movie-watcher, I had an instinct for it that was ready to be developed.

We decided I'd help him with one project, then another. When those went well, I became editor and project manager of the very book I had been writing for in the park, *Passionistas*. Later that year, we began two more books.

Before I met Kyle and signed up for *Passionistas*, I had dipped my toe into entrepreneurship and started a private label drop-shipping company on Amazon.com. After a few years of editing, I put the business on pause, but the experience I gained with Amazon's backend was valuable when it came to publishing and promoting each book Kyle and I worked on over the next decade.

Perfectionism

With every book, I learned a ton.

When I first started as a professional editor, I was eager to prove myself. With each draft, ideas jumped out at me: *If we delete this paragraph, tighten that sentence, swap in a more formal synonym, and mellow out the tone, this would sound much more polished and professional!* I'd color-code each suggestion in detail as I read.

Then, when I'd show all of the edits to Kyle, he'd sometimes say something like, "That's great, and I see why you'd recommend that. But, it's not actually better than what the author originally wrote. Let's defer to the author."

While I accepted Kyle's feedback, I didn't fully understand it. I thought if an author didn't want to sound their best, that was their choice, but if I could share my ideas, at least they'd have all the options. I believed there was a best way to structure a sentence and a best word for each situation, and I believed I knew what they were.

In reality, when I was telling an author what I thought sounded best, I was editing them to sound like a "picture-perfect" professional that I imagined—not who they told me they wanted to be or who they really were.

I realized that in my need to prove myself, I lost the plot. I so wanted the books to be excellent, but in many situations, just by sharing my ideas, I was over-editing. I was gripping my work with both hands. To be better, I needed to practice letting go.

I've come to understand that my work as an editor isn't about reshaping writing to reflect a perfect form I come up with. It's about honoring someone and what they trust me to help them say. I'm grateful that people have been willing to share their stories with me. I want to be curious, to listen, and to understand.

Even 10 years later, sometimes it's still hard not to overstep. No matter how curious I am, I will always see through my own lens. That's why I focus on empathy. I really believe in listening to one another, even when we're different. I'm glad to help people share and to help them be seen. And I'm honored to bring their stories to readers who learn not just how-tos but also empathy and wisdom.

It's not easy to tell your story. But each time we do, we celebrate it—who we've been, who we are, and who we hope to become. That's meaningful work.

Seeing Beauty

As an editor, discernment is part of the job. Sentences without clarity, words without punch, and stories without soul make me itch. But outside of editing, my critical eye has often skewed from discernment into judgment.

Over the years, I've spent more time than I'd care to admit playing the role of a critic. To different degrees, I've torn down comedy specials, restaurant food, my home, my loved ones, and myself. I've thought and said things that the world would have been better off without.

Focusing on what could be better can inspire actual improvements, but too much hurts others and can make you feel hopeless. I'd rather look around in awe and gratitude, replacing hours spent dwelling with moments spent admiring.

My work as an editor became a mirror for this self-work.

At my keyboard, the more I practiced letting go of my idea of "better," the more I could embrace what was beautiful, good, and worthy of celebration in each story. It felt good, and I started to wonder if I could look at the rest of the world this way.

It's not about getting it right. It's about being a curious witness and enjoying all there is to see—even what's crooked or a little left of center.

They say "writing is never finished." I think it's true because we're never finished. We're always improving, always learning, and always becoming.

Q&A WITH TAKARA

What are some favorite places you've traveled to?

The Amazon Basin in Peru – I pet a bat on a riverboat, slept under a mosquito net dotted with spiders, danced with a green anaconda, and swam with piranhas.

Honolulu, Hawaii – On sun-washed Saturdays I would paddle an outrigger canoe with my team out over deep ocean. I lived in Hawaii during high school, and it was incredible.

South Africa – We woke to full sun at 4:00 a.m. and walked long days through the townships, calling out *izinja*—"dogs" in Xhosa—so families could bring their pets to us for flea baths in the plastic tubs of water we carried. We practiced field sutures, vaccinated goats and trimmed their hooves, joined humane nyala captures and relocations, and spent weekends on game drives watching giraffes, lions, elephants, and more.

I've been lucky. There's been so much more, like floating Missouri's rivers with my dad, eating cocoa fruit right off the tree in Belize, Puerto Rico's downpours, sharing hot chips with chicken salt seaside under the Sydney Opera House, San Francisco's magic, and NYC's power—too many amazing memories to list.

What is a guilty pleasure that you love but don't always admit to?

Buffy the Vampire Slayer. I was introduced to this show in college, well after it aired, and got hooked. For starters, the heroine triumphs over a new monster each week—it's hard to get better than that. Then, the writing is fun, campy, and way darker and more grounded than I expected. Willow is my favorite—awkward, brilliant, powerful, open-hearted, and so gay. What happened behind the scenes puts this pleasure in the guilty category, but I still keep coming back.

What is something you love to learn about?

I love research in general. For me, it's fun following the rabbit trail of learning something new and digging in. I especially enjoy biodiversity; it's amazing how plants, animals, and other forms of life persist within their complex environments—from the chemical scale to the cosmic. Whether it's reading science articles, growing my balcony garden, or studying veterinary medicine, I can lose hours.

What are a few of your favorite quotes?

"Don't Panic." – *The Hitchhiker's Guide to the Galaxy* by Douglas Adams

Connect with editor, writing coach, and writer Takara Sights by email at tsights@gmail.com, on Instagram @takarasights, and on LinkedIn.

ZACH

Message

What follows is a message Zach received during meditation and felt compelled to share. He invites you to read with an open mind and see what resonates.

Allowing the natural unfolding is the next step in human evolution.

What is our message and who are we? We are the collective consciousness that is tied into all creatures and things. We are the intelligence that all past teachers have tapped into. We are the thing that millions have pushed away. Pushed away as did the person who is currently writing this message.

Yes, there is a person behind these words, receiving this message. Receiving this message though a relaxed process of allowing. This process of allowing is something that we teach.

Most self-help books talk about doing and goal setting. Striving, struggle, and hard work: While we acknowledge these are all part of the process of being and doing as a human being, this is not the only way. In fact, we wish for you a life of ease and flow. This flow is right inside you. It is allowable by simply turning on a switch.

As the author explained, he finds himself drifting off and receiving this flow. This is a trained response to meditation and being in a state of allowance. We believe that all are capable of doing this. You simply must relax and allow it to be.

This may be a challenge for many people. It was for this author, before a spiritual awakening and divorce in 2016. It may take a major change in your life to allow an unfolding and awakening of your mind. We hope that you are able to tune into us before the world pushes you, but this is the story for many great teachers. We believe that all are capable of tuning into this message and flow that we are here to offer.

Some people learn to turn this switch on by using drugs, through a traumatic loss, or by some other gateway. We call this a gateway because this is a bridge into the unknown, what most humans have yet to experience. We tease this experience, **because you do not believe your fellow man unless you experience it yourself**, which in the world in which you currently live, can be understandable. Feeling and understanding this through your own eyes is a human desire. The beings that already are awakened and enlightened do not need to see proof. They can feel it. And we are convinced that all are capable of this here and now. Not all will, but they can. To become your highest self is to be fully engaged and to flow with life.

This force of nature that we wish to unfold and present to you is not without challenges. The person sharing these words has chosen to remain pseudonymous, in order to serve up these words for your own judgement, without providing a label or persona. He wishes for you the same experiences that he has, but without the same resistance.

This author has resisted his calling for many years now, due to feeling isolated, but we tell you and we tell him, that heaven on Earth (a peace and unfolding) is completely possible when all men and women learn that they are a part of something so great—unfolding and growing—that this is simply the best time to be.

We bring you this message in order to facilitate this unfolding to the next step in human evolution. This is what we ask of you:

- Go quiet—be with yourself and allow messages to come through. We are confident that if you are able to quiet your mind, through meditation, yoga, or relaxation, you will receive these same messages as the author here. We invite you to do this now. Do not try to make it happen. Relax and see what happens. There is nothing more frustrating than to strive to achieve a state of relaxation and be frustrated. Try with no expectations. See what happens. You might be surprised. It all started with a 15-minute meditation for this author in 2016. What if you are only a meditation away from accessing the full power and consciousness of the ever-unfolding universe?
- We also ask that you share in your abundance by giving to your fellow man through time, kindness, laughter, and play. You do not have to give money to get to heaven—giving kindness will pay more dividends than any tithe or charity. Your kindness and acceptance of others is the currency of humanity, not the made-up currencies that you create and worship. Be kind and allow the world to unfold. Jesus gave of Himself through presence and seeing people as healed and complete. What if you were able to tap in and see your fellow man as complete and unfolding beings,

rather than through judgement and fear? Imagine the universe and system we could build.

- Building on this, we ask that you next allow the natural unfolding of the universe by being present. You have heard this in many other messages, but being present and grounded in the moment we are in now allows for the universe to align and send you the building blocks you need to build that life you desire. By looking here and now, rather than in the past or future, you allow the blocks to come to you, rather than struggle and striving. There is nothing wrong with doing things the hard way, but you will find that if you do things our way—the way of the present—you will allow this universe to come into play.
- Next, we ask that you be with others more than you are alone. The author himself has often found himself alone. Alone with thoughts and alone with purpose leads to a misguided approach to life and being. You can be alone in order to reset and find answers you seek through solitude, but you must allow the universe to be—by going forth and engaging with others. Yes, you live in separate houses in a modern world and that is perhaps the downside to your current way of life, but this is no excuse to not engage with the world. Go forth and be with others, wherever you may find them. If you find yourself in a funk and you cannot seem to get out, this is likely the cause. Go forth and do this. Be with others.
- Lastly, we ask that you share this message with others. Do not be afraid to speak words that you receive. If you are afraid, do as this author has done and simply share these words as they come through any medium that can be shared. You do not have to identify or author these words as your own. Simply share and allow others the chance to decide for themselves what they deem truth and valuable to their own lives. This is what we refer to as being a "signpost.". You cannot force someone to awaken or to a better life, but you can act as a sign or direction post and offer a path to travel—not through force or coercion, but by being an open and present being allowing the universe to unfold naturally. We are being repetitive here, but it is important that you understand that this flow of the universe is as strong as many of the rivers that carve canyons on your Earth. There is nothing

to fight, you can either allow the flow or be swept away—swept away and taken off task, out of the way, or in circles fighting the current. Learn to ride the current of the universal flow and you will find yourself where you desire to be—faster and with less struggle and tribulations.

We feel this is a good first step for those looking to be a part of the next evolution of human nature and consciousness. Do not look around and be discouraged, as this is not the underlying message or purpose of humanity. Humanity is the best system for allowing consciousness to flow on your current planet. There are other ways of flowing consciousness, but this is the type of system mwe have now. We are unfolding, and the future may allow a better system or species, but we have to work with what we have. You can be a part of this allowing and unfolding by simply doing as the steps above outline.

Try it yourself. You might be surprised what happens when you relax and allow the natural unfolding of the universe.

QUESTIONS FOR US

How do I integrate this into my daily life?

To integrate this calling that we are providing to you, you allow this by being a person who loves and allows others to be. By allowing others to be as they are, you will allow the universe to line up and be a conduit as you are called to do. You will find that this is the most beneficial thing you can do for your fellow man.

How do I trust a desire to do a trade or job or to start a business?

You must know that every day you are receiving not only thoughts from us, but also influence from those around you. Those thoughts and fears that you have collected as part of your human experience, are cloudy and many are not your true desire. But, you must participate in the human experience. We are not yet at a stage in which no one is required to work or contribute in order to live in this society. Perhaps you will receive the answers to solve this in the future, but at this time, building empires, businesses, countries, and towns is part of the economy that is human beings. This has allowed you to lift many people out of the hardships of starvation and living in the elements, but this has also left many disconnected from us and what we are here to give. This is a challenge not only for you, but for many on this planet.

So, to answer your question—you will receive many desires, as you are a problem solver and analytical by nature. This is fine. We ask that you take your desires and run them through our system of allowing so that we can assist you. You need not make all these decisions yourself. You can call on us for business ideas and creations. There is no wrong decision. We simply can help you get to that decision and provide clarity so that you do not spend time on something that need not be done in order to learn a lesson you can learn through us.

This book started with an idea: becoming your best self. We are offering these closing words, which is the overall message that we are here to offer—go forth and fully participate in humanity. This means as we have said, engaging with life, and being a kind and helping hand to your fellow man.

Becoming your best self means to know and feel that the self is more than the human persona that you hide behind (remember that "persona" means mask). We are all actors in the human experience that is unfolding, and we invite you to join us in this unfolding. Becoming is about shifting your mindset, not about *getting somewhere* or *doing* something. You can become your best self by simply shifting, turning on a switch, and accessing your higher consciousness.

> If you are interested in connecting with the author who received this message, email Zach at zachsmessage@gmail.com.

KIM SOMERS EGELSEE

Allowing My Truest Self to Come Forward

Kim Somers Egelsee is an intuitive and a life and business coach. She is a TEDx speaker, 10X international bestselling author, publisher, retreat leader, and TV and podcast host. For over 20 years, she has specialized in helping people exude confidence, connect authentically with others and themselves, and discover their life's purpose. She also gives them a platform to shine their unique gifts through writing, speaking, and media.

The Path

Throughout my life, I have almost always worked to become my best self.

Raised as an only child, I spent a lot of time with my parents and really felt, and still do today, that they were both my parents and my best friends. They have always focused on loving life. They believed in me and taught me to believe in myself. They taught me to look at the bright side of problems. We always had fun adventures planned, like travel, concerts, and shows. They kept me in awe, and I was almost always able to find something happy or to be grateful for in each situation. To this day, we still do things together, and I continue to be amazed by the wonders of the world. I credit my parents for my optimistic and peaceful outlook on life.

At the young age of 18, I saw Jim Rohn speak, which shifted my trajectory to a personal success and spiritual development focus. I continued on that path, seeing Jim several times and even meeting him. (For years, I ordered Jim's books from Kyle Wilson. I finally, serendipitously, met Kyle and later began working with him on some projects. Life is so magical that way.) I began reading books by thought leaders, setting goals, and stretching my mind with the authors' wisdom. Even before I found Jim, I was living the philosophy of "Don't miss anything," but after studying his principles, I lived to the fullest and still do today.

You Choose

Still, like most humans, I have had immense, light-filled ups and dark, difficult downs. And, I have found that the choices you make are paramount to, if not the most important part of, living a healed and happy life filled with love, peace, joy, and balance. Every choice is part of your journey to your best self. There is a purpose for all of it—for every challenge—because challenges lead to choices.

There were times when I was younger that I would make choices based on status, excitement, rebellion, ego, or just trying to escape. I once chose the good-looking, popular guy to date, even though he was a jerk and a compulsive liar. At another time, I would go to prestigious events and parties just to be able to tell people that I went. As a child, I went through some bullying at school and experienced being abandoned by kids in the neighborhood. As a result, I spent many years people-pleasing and saying yes to hanging out with anyone and everyone just to make sure I had enough friends in my life and wasn't abandoned again.

In sixth grade, the boys decided to line us girls up and rate us based on how pretty they thought we were. I was chosen last. After that, I became very insecure about my appearance. I started trying hard to look cute or even just what I thought was acceptable.

I also had no boundaries and would engage in careless behavior: stupid things like ditching school and throwing a wild party where valuable things were stolen at my parents' house when they were out of town, just to be cool and accepted. As a result of my life choices, I was left with guilt, feeling like I was betraying myself.

I learned the hard way that the choices you make have a direct effect on your peace, confidence, and happiness. This includes the people you hang around, how you spend your time, where you go, what you put into your body, and even what you think about. They all have the power to make or break happiness. However, even the choices that break your happiness are still part of becoming your best self. Sometimes you need to live as who you *do not* want to be to understand and to step into who you *do* truly want to be.

When I was older, I found myself experiencing intense, painful, and challenging health symptoms. They were so bad that I began drinking to cope. I had never been a big drinker, but it was the only thing that helped at first. I went to over 25 doctors, healers, and specialists, and no one knew what was wrong.

The drinking ended up being an issue. The pain and struggle were so intense that I just wanted to escape. It was a very dark time. Several times,

I almost felt like I was dying. I ended up having to get help and became sober. I'm so grateful I did because now life is brighter and clearer. When I finally realized that my breast implants were what was making me so sick, I had them removed. Finally, the symptoms subsided. With a newfound comfort and having stopped drinking, I finally felt better.

I have found that even in darkness, there are gifts. Because of what happened, I am more nonjudgmental, focused, joyful, and connected to God. My intuition is way stronger, and I've helped so many more people in deeper ways.

Stepping into Purpose

After years of being in the entertainment industry as an actor, singer, and model, as well as over 11 years in special education as a behavior program specialist and teacher, I realized that my true purpose and passion were in the field of personal growth.

I have always felt that personal, spiritual, and success development were each needed to reach peak human potential. I had spent years researching confidence, positivity, happiness, and communication. I had earned my bachelor's degree in communication. I had multiple credentials in educational psychology, the study of personal, moral, and social development. And I had certifications in hypnotherapy, neuro-linguistic programming (NLP), emotional freedom techniques (EFT), life coaching, and energy healing. And now, with knowledge of my true purpose, I stepped into my calling. I coached men and women, spoke at events, including a TEDx talk, co-hosted a podcast, wrote books, developed a confidence course and a life coach certification course, and much more. I am still following this divine calling today.

Because choices are such a pivotal part of transforming who you are, I created a life-changing method of making choices. For many years, I have received feedback from hundreds of people who have used this simple method to create and choose happiness in their lives, which adds peace, freedom, and being true to oneself and thus aids in healing the mind, body, and soul.

I have found that choices are so significant because they are essential to being true to you! When you are true to yourself, you are being honest with what you feel: your desires, wants, and needs, and in alignment with who you are. Making choices in alignment with self is when you completely accept yourself as the one who is in control, with your own heart and feelings. When you don't make choices that align with what you truly want, you betray yourself, which makes you feel negative, moody, and out of balance. Tuning into your higher self makes choosing easier.

Tapping into your higher self allows you to embrace each moment fully and appreciate it for what it is. Spirituality is a key factor in allowing you to connect to your own conscious guide—your higher self. It is the constant connection to God or divine energy. I like the technique of tuning into the top of my head (crown chakra), my heart, and the heavens. I also ground my feet into the grass, floor, or even cement to feel supported by Mother Earth. This gives you even more positive power, clarity, and insights in making the right choices for you.

One of my biggest values is freedom! I love to speak and teach on this. I have found that true freedom comes from being unapologetically, vulnerably, and totally, authentically myself. This has taken years of healing work, stepping out of my comfort zone, NOT people-pleasing, being brave, reading, attending workshops, speaking my truth, and letting go and letting God. It's so worth it. I feel true to myself, honest with other people, and free to be imperfectly perfect, silly, wild, unique, and just ME. It's never a waste of time to work on yourself and allow your true self to come out and shine. This encompasses personal growth, making heart- and soul-centered, conscious choices, and becoming your best self.

I'm so grateful that my dark times, as well as my light-filled ones, helped me grow into a person who is wise, helpful, compassionate, real, and of service, who is now helping others step into their best selves as well.

Q&A WITH KIM

What is one life lesson you'd like to pass on to future generations?

My biggest life lesson is that if you're truly authentic, you will be rare. You will stand out from the crowd and even scare people, because truly authentic isn't common. You'll feel free, you'll live happier, and it just takes allowing, working on yourself, and practice.

What book do you most share with others?
The Power of Intention by Dr. Wayne Dyer

He teaches readers to look at intention as energy you can access to begin co-creating your life with the divine. He shares life-changing spiritual principles that help you navigate life and understand yourself. He also teaches ways to achieve peace and enlightenment.

How would you describe your philosophy?
Be and spread love, kindness, and peace to contribute to the vibration of our planet.

What effect do you hope to have on others? On society?
I hope to show others that it is possible to learn confidence, show up authentically as your true self, be open-hearted, stand in your power and feel free, be successful, and love your life. I hope to be the light and to help raise the vibrations of others through my acts of service, being my best self, and helping others.

If you could have dinner with three people, living or deceased, who would they be?
I would have dinner with Prince. He was the most talented musician and songwriter ever and has been a big inspiration to me as a fan. He is someone who broke barriers, utilized creative self-expression to the fullest, and became a huge success.

I would also choose Dr. Wayne Dyer because he is my favorite spiritual teacher, philosopher, and transformational leader. He was the epitome of calm, wisdom, and joy. When I need advice, I think about what he would do, and it helps. I regularly watch The Shift every couple of years to see how much I've grown and evolved.

Finally, I would choose Diane Keaton. She is unapologetically herself. She's acted in phenomenal movies, written many books, and has a style that's all her own. Her humility and grace are amazing examples of being in your power while still using your feminine energy.

What are you passionate about?
I am passionate about humans and animals having quality of life, stability, happiness, and peace. I believe everyone has the right to a

beautiful life, including women, all races, the LGBTQ+ community, children, and animals. I am passionate about mental health awareness and reducing the stigma around mental health. I am passionate about God, family, love, travel, music, and fitness. I am passionate about life.

What is your favorite movie?

I have so many favorite movies, but *Bruce Almighty* is up there. It's about a television reporter who receives divine power and a life-altering challenge after an encounter with God. He realizes that using divine powers for selfish purposes leads to chaos and that true happiness comes from appreciating the simple things in life and being there for others. He also realizes that responsibility and caring for others are essential when wielding power, divine or otherwise. Ultimately, Bruce surrenders his powers, and his life improves when he focuses on his relationships and finds contentment in his work and with his loved ones.

Who are your mentors and greatest influences, and how have they impacted your life?

My greatest influences have been my entire family, who have each taught me different things from resilience, to humility, finding joy, and standing in your power. They have included Jim Rohn, who taught me to work harder on myself than I do on my job, Kyle Wilson, who taught me how to master marketing, business, and success with his unique approach, Dr. Gochette, who taught me that I can use my intuitive gifts for my highest good, Niurka, who inspired me to step into my purpose, Ursula Mentjes, who taught me patience and presence, and Prince, who inspired me to create.

To find out more about Kim Somers Egelsee's books, coaching, speaking, and publishing, go to:
kimlifecoach.com | highvibesoulsisters.com | publishing-joy.com
Instagram @kimlifecoach |
Facebook @Kimlifecoach | kimlifecoach.com

BRIAN TRACY

You Can Change Your Life

Brian Tracy is the top-selling author of over 70 books, has written and produced more than 300 audio and video learning programs, and has spoken, trained, and traveled in over 107 countries on six continents. Brian speaks four languages and is happily married with four children.

Early Years and Learning to Be an Entrepreneur

I grew up in Edmonton, Canada. It's not the North Pole, but they say you can see it from up there. It's really cold, 35 degrees below zero Fahrenheit in the wintertime.

I began my entrepreneurial journey early, at the age of 10. Because of my family situation, I had to earn my own money, so I went out and did jobs in the neighborhood to buy my clothes and school supplies.

So, for me, to go out and work, to start something and make it work, is as natural as breathing. I've started and built 22 businesses in different enterprises including hiring, recruiting, training, producing, selling, and marketing.

When I was 32, I saw an ad in the paper for an executive MBA at the University of Alberta. So, I applied, got in, and spent two years and $4,000 to get an MBA.

Getting Paid to Speak

After university, I put together the content for what eventually became *The Psychology of Achievement*. Even from early on, when people went through the course, the feedback was fantastic. People thought it was great, and they began to tell their friends.

The first seminar I gave, I had seven people, and six of them were family members. The seventh was a paid customer for $295. My next seminar was 12 people, and my next was 15 people in Canada. I then hired a guy for three months to sell for me full-time. Business grew and grew. Soon, I was speaking to 100, 200, and then 500 people. And then, people started to invite me to speak to their audiences.

The Power of Our Thoughts

In my seminars, I talk about the superconscious mind and understanding how you can activate the incredible mental power that you already have. You can turn on this switch and start to attract into your life everything that you want: opportunities, ideas, people, resources, and more, simply by using the power that you already have within your brain.

Every single great accomplishment in history has been an accomplishment of superconscious thinking where people have learned how to turn on this switch.

Imagine that you're making an average living and that you live in a nice home. And in your home, there is a garage, but you've never been into the garage. Then, one day, you go into the garage and turn on the light. And to your great surprise, there's this massive supercomputer there that is capable of answering any question you come up with. You just turn on this supercomputer, and suddenly you're producing 5, 10, 20, 50, 100 times more.

Perhaps you say, "I want to be wealthy, successful, and highly respected. Maybe I don't have a university degree, and I don't have any money right now, but I do have my brain and my ability to **work**. And that's what I'm going to do." If you actually do the work, you set up a force field of energy in the universe that conspires to get you what you want.

Take Action

One idea can change your life—if you take action on it. One of the most important things I teach over and over again is action. Action! It's not enough to have good ideas or the best information. There are a lot of average people who are self-made millionaires. I have a great hour-long program called *The 21 Success Secrets of Self-Made Millionaires*. I spent two months preparing before recording it. I buried myself in research on self-made millionaires. What I found is that they had characteristics and qualities that made it inevitable that they'd be successful. And if you simply practice the same things they practice, you become the same people they are. And action is one of the main traits of self-made millionaires.

We Make Our Living by Contributing Value to Other People

Today, we have this big thing in politics about inequality. It's not inequality of money. It's inequality of contribution. We make our living in a free country. We make our living by contributing value to other people. Sometimes I ask my audience how many people work on straight commission, and maybe 10% will raise their hands.

I then say, "Well, that's interesting. Maybe I didn't phrase the question properly. Let me ask it again. How many people here work on straight commission?" And then there's a pause, and it's wonderful, the light goes off! Absolutely everybody works on commission.

Everybody works for themselves. And each person creates value. You get a piece of the value that you create. So if you want to earn more money, create more value. Make a greater contribution. Do more.

A great line from Napoleon Hill still brings tears to my eyes decades later: "Always do more than you're paid for. Always go the extra mile. There is never a traffic jam on the extra mile." The one thing nobody can stop you from doing is doing more than you're paid for.

Earl Nightingale said that if you want to earn more than you're earning, contribute more than you're contributing, and an increase in earnings is automatic.

If you're not happy with your income, go to the nearest mirror and negotiate with your boss, because you are your own boss. You make your own contribution. You make your own decision. If you don't like your income, earn more.

Never Complain, Never Explain

The happiest people in the world are those who feel absolutely terrific about themselves, and this is the natural outgrowth of accepting total responsibility for every part of their life. They make a habit of manufacturing their own positive expectations in advance of each event.

Resist the temptation to defend yourself or make excuses.

Develop an attitude of gratitude and give thanks for everything that happens to you, knowing that every step forward is a step toward achieving something bigger and better than your current situation.

Q&A WITH BRIAN

What is your most important value in life?
Your values are the axle around which your whole life turns. People who are successful are very clear about their values, and they don't compromise them. People who are unsuccessful are fuzzy about their values, and they'll compromise them or give them up with the slightest temptation.

My highest value is freedom. Freedom means having enough money to do what you want.

How do you recharge?
I love to read. I also love to travel with my wife Barbara and our family, including the kids and grandkids. I'm past the age of 80, so I'm now asking myself this question: If you were going to die in one year, how would you spend your time and money? I want to spend my time and my money with my family, because that's the most important thing in life. If I'm on my deathbed, the only thing I'll regret is not having spent more time with my family.

What is your superpower?
I am unstoppable. I will never ever quit. And that's the very best quality you can develop. How do you develop the quality of becoming unstoppable? You say "I am unstoppable" to yourself over and over again. Whenever you think that you may fail, that people may disapprove of you, or that you may lose your money or something, you say, "Wait a minute, I'm unstoppable. So, no matter what, I will bounce back. I will never stop. I will keep coming."

How do you define success?
Success is being free to be the very best person you can be and to do the things that you want to do. The reason we want to be financially successful is because that liberates us so we can be and do the things we want to be and do, including going where we want. It's a great thing to have enough money so that you don't have to worry about money.

Are goals important to have?

You build your whole life around your goals. There is a wonderful quote from a dear friend of mine, Vic Conant: "Success is goals, and all else is commentary." Wherever I've been able to persuade a person of that, their life changes.

I now have thousands of self-made millionaires and three self-made billionaires who have told me personally, "You made me rich. I was struggling. I was going nowhere. And after I learned about goals, here I am."

I've learned that you can achieve extraordinary things, and you already have, by setting goals. When you set a very clear, specific goal for yourself and write it down, it triggers what is called a psycho-neuro-motor activity, which means that it programs into your subconscious mind and your subconscious mind then conveys it to your superconscious mind. Your superconscious mind is so incredibly powerful. It's amazing how few people understand this. But once it goes into your superconscious mind a whole series of things start to happen.

Get a spiral notebook, write "goals" at the top, and then write down 10 goals in the present tense. When you write them down, you activate this psycho-neuro-motor activity, it programs into your brain, and then it goes to work 24 hours a day to bring you everything you need, exactly when you need it, especially in the form of ideas.

Keep doing it every single day for the rest of your life. Goals will change, the description will change, the order will change, the emphasis will change, but just keep writing down 10 goals and see what happens.

What is something everyone should do?

The magic wand technique. Imagine that you have a magic wand and could wave it and achieve any one goal in your life! Which one goal would have the greatest positive effect on your life? Write it down. Imagine what one great thing you would dare to dream if you knew you could not fail and write it down. Then ask yourself, what one skill if you developed and did it over and over again would help you the most to achieve that goal? Write that down. Then, what you do is you think about the goal all the time and work on developing that skill.

What is zero-based thinking important?

Every time I do a strategic planning program worldwide, we start off with an exercise called zero-based thinking. In zero-based thinking, wherever you are in life, you draw a line under your life to this date.

Then, you imagine that you're starting over and ask yourself:
- Is there anything that you are doing that, knowing what you now know, you would not start up again today?
- Is there any investment that you have that you would not make again today?
- If you had to do it over, is there any relationship that you would not get into?
- Is there any person that you would not hire?

You keep going through each area of your life, and you keep asking. If the answer is "No, I would not get into this again," then the next question is, "How do I get out?" and then, "How fast can I get out?" Once you've reached the point where you have that intuitive feeling that you would not get into this again, you cannot save it.

I often say to my friends to ask themselves that question: "Is there anything you're doing in your life that, knowing what you now know, you wouldn't get into?"

If the answer is yes, get out and get out now.

To learn more about Brian Tracy's book and audio programs, go to BrianTracy.com.

ADDITIONAL RESOURCES

 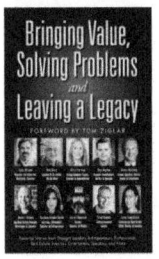  

Order in Quantity and SAVE

Mix and Match

Order online KyleWilson.com/books

EDITOR AND WRITING COACH

Since 2015, editor and writing coach Takara Sights has partnered with Kyle Wilson to bring real stories of wisdom to lifelong learners. As a kid, she read under the covers by flashlight, captivated by her favorite stories. Today, she listens with that same curiosity, supporting authors as they develop their voices and tell their stories with clarity and confidence. Whether guiding a first draft or refining a final manuscript, she brings discernment and care to every project.

PUBLISHER

Kyle Wilson is the founder of Jim Rohn International and KyleWilson.com. Kyle has filled huge seminar rooms, launched and published multiple personal development publications, and produced/published over 100+ hours of programs. Kyle has published and sold over 1,000,000 books including titles by Jim Rohn and Denis Waitley as well as his own books including *Success Habits of Super Achievers* with Brian Tracy, Les Brown, Darren Hardy,  Denis Waitley, Mark Victor Hansen, *Persistence, Pivots and Game Changers*, and *Bringing Value, Solving Problems and Leaving a Legacy*. Kyle is the host of the *Success Habits of Super Achievers* podcast and the Kyle Wilson Inner Circle Mastermind.

www.ingramcontent.com/pod-product-compliance
Lightning Source LLC
Chambersburg PA
CBHW071954070426
42453CB00008BA/534